Immaculate Contraception

Immaculate Contraception

The Extraordinary Story of Birth Control
From the First Fumblings to the Present Day

Emma Dickens

Robson Books

First published in Great Britain in 2000 by Robson Books, 10 Blenheim Court, Brewery Road, London N7 9NT

A member of the Chrysalis Group plc

British Library Cataloguing in Publication Data
A catalogue record for this title is available from the British Library

ISBN 1 86105 337 1

Printed in Great Britain by Creative Print & Design (Wales), Ebbw Vale

Contents

To Jack Hodge – for reminding us what it's *really* all about.

Acknowledgements

Thanks to Lorna Russell and Jeremy Robson for supporting such an absurd project. For their endless resources and patience, thanks to Anna, Joy and Dorothy at Sussex University's Mass Observation Archive. M-O material reproduced with permission of Curtis Brown Ltd, London, on behalf of the Trustees of the Mass-Observation Archive. Thanks to the drug companies which helped by parting with information – in particular Unipath, Pharmacia Upjohn and Roussel – to all at the British Library, Westminster Library and Cambridge University Library, and to Toni Belfield and Margaret McGovern at the FPA. For information and pictures thanks to the Wellcome Institute, and on the subject of pictures, thanks to the British Museum and Tony Kerridge at Marie Stopes International. Thanks also to Vince Graff for his unbridled enthusiasm from the outset, and to John Conway too, for his unqualified support. Thanks to Mal for his clause-consciousness and the title, and – as they say at Oscar ceremonies – to anyone else I've fogotten.

Finally thanks to Drs Anna and Peter Dickens; the latter for his tireless help with research, and both for their love and occasional flagrant disregard for any of these methods. Josh Sims – there are not the words . . .

Introduction

> Everything is harmful that hinders the occurrence of satisfaction.
> But, as we know, we possess at present no method of preventing
> conception which fulfils every legitimate requirement.
>
> Sigmund Freud, 1898[1]

The word 'contraception' is a peculiar one. It is never used apart from the context of preventing conception. Nobody thinks of it as a candidate for use in metaphors. No one has ever described censorship as creative or intellectual contraception. Nor does it represent a particular stage in the evolution of a relationship, as in, 'We're at "contraception stations" at the moment, enjoying our respective jobs and incomes. Maybe we'll start a family in a couple of years.' Or even that stage of sex where you hope the other person's got the condoms and will get them out, as in 'he's almost perfect, but just not quite contraperceptive enough.' Clearly there must be a reason for the world's failure to foster such serviceable expressions.

Perhaps we avoid using it – the word that is – because it is an ugly word. Because it is a syllable too long, or because it sounds too medical or scientific. It must have been invented by someone, it's got that manufactured feel to it – the word, that is. It doesn't flow. And it sounds like it belongs on a box, not in a chat at the pub or on the telephone. It would be like slipping the word 'neuralgia' into a conversation over a pint, or that phrase on the label of Pepto Bismol: 'darkening of the stools'.

Perhaps we avoid using the word wherever possible because we feel *guilty* about the business of contraception. But that's absurd. If we're worried about the fact that contraception stops people having babies we shouldn't be. Contraception is about having sex for fun. In fact for an impetuous split second this book was called *Gratuitous Sex*. Modern scientific theory starts off by looking as though it might even go as far as to say 'sex is mostly for fun' – although it proceeds to roll over and go to sleep just as we are starting to explode with excitement.

Sex cannot be just for procreation, the theory goes, because if we reproduced asexually it would be far more efficient, and it is in efficiency that evolution is most interested. In fact, we would be twice as prolific if we didn't need to have sex with each other, because twice as many people could have babies. The world would be full of mummies. So far, so good for the 'sex is for fun' camp. Only we actually couple because it is good for our genes to combine with different ones when we reproduce, in order for our babies to be more resistant to parasites.

Having said that, the world is not deprived of needed and wanted babies because of contraception, because in the vast majority of – Western admittedly – cases the alternative to having sex for fun is *not* having sex. Having sex for fun and producing another human being into the bargain is called a terrible mistake. The Catholic church thinks contraception is wrong. Perhaps it's that sort of guilt that makes people feel odd about using the word contraception. Aha, but you didn't take any notice of the church when you had sex out of wedlock, did you? So it can't be religion that makes us so unprepared to use the word contraception.

Hang on a minute – you're embarrassed. You are – look, you've gone all red. You're embarrassed by the fact of contraception. We shouldn't be by now, of course. We've been stumbling about in the dark, cursing inwardly, for five thousand years. But suddenly it all becomes clear. This must be why the condom has so many names (including sock, hood, bush hat, venus glove, Pariser, gummi, rubber, cocolock socks, koteka, Port Said garter and johnny). Despite all the bravado, people are constantly trying different names out for size, in the hope that eventually they won't feel embarrassed any more. And this has been happening ever since the sheath was born – ugh, 'sheath', they all make you cringe. But they probably make you cringe mainly because the sheath is a ridiculous object, and no amount of name-calling is going to change that.

Yes, that's it – we're embarrassed. After I had stopped being *really* embarrassed about raising the subject of contraception in relatively polite company, and a little before I became convinced that the subject was as fascinating as I'd at first thought, I threw that subject into a converted warehouse in Kentish Town. Converted warehouses were still trendy in 2000, you see – by now they're probably dismissed for being too cold and lacking in cosiness. As the word emerged, blinking, out of the bedroom, like an agoraphobic making his or her first tentative steps outside after a long period of reclusiveness, something strange happened. People, *British* people, started *chatting* about contraception. Not 'getting laid' or 'shagging', but *methods* of contraception. They had a plate tucked away, covered in delicate pictures of different sorts of contraception – they showed it to me. Then I tried the subject out again, in Tunbridge Wells over Sunday lunch with lots of people I hardly knew. There was a brief and uncomfortable pause – the scrape of knife on plate, the small cough behind the napkin – and then the floodgates opened. Could anyone shut the man opposite me up about 'the snip'? No, he was positively evangelical, and he was going to talk about it until everyone else had the snip too and then they, too, would see the light . . .

So many of the methods are silly, but its silliness alone is surely not enough to make whole cultures embarrassed about a concept. Why else should we be uncomfortable about that most natural of things in the world – sex, which has the most obvious and natural of consequences if we don't 'use something' to prevent us from conceiving? Initially, at least initially AD, being embarrassed was the only reasonable response to the subjects of sex and contraception. You were, in the West, a child of God, and God – according to his messengers – wanted you to get a hold of yourself; mentally rather than physically, obviously. This was so certainly before you were married and preferably while you were married too. If you were married and wanted children, sex was permissible, but not so otherwise. So to use contraception then, in the hundreds AD, was to plan to lose control, which was not what the Stoics – who really invented godliness before God was around – had in mind at all. Also, messing with the almost mystical business of the creation of human life was another huge factor, and it still is for many. The so-called 'pro-lifers' at the more contentious end of the scale – abortion – still talk about the blasphemy of 'playing God', but so too does the Catholic church, even in the context of contraception. It's that Catholic sensibility cropping up again.

Another possible reason for embarrassment is that we are all much more influenced by the media than we would care to admit. Sex, as Nick Hancock pointed out in 2000 in his BBC TV programme *Sex and Stopping*, sells everything but sex. Contraception is not a part of the films that we see. Top actors and actresses, whom we are influenced by at that impressionable pre-sex age and beyond, do not get where they are because of their dazzling condom-retrieval-from-the-bedside-drawer technique. This means that by the time we are sexually active, it is not in keeping with our cool sex/romance vocabulary. Although what a concept. A kind of safe-sex Oscar. The statue could wear a condom hat or a, well, cap, and it could be awarded to the most convincing yet stylish scene containing the use of, or explicit reference to, contraception. Or it could go to the writer or director of the most erotic safe-sex scene.

The problem is that, at the moment, stars too find contraception embarrassing and uncool. Witness Tom Cruise's comments in chapter eight. Yes indeed, stars are human too, and capable of embarrassment and – no, I insist – self-consciousness, although almost by definition many would have you believe otherwise: The god-like public profiles and paycheques bit they can handle. The god-like sense of responsibility towards their public does not necessarily come so readily – *Mission Irresponsible*, anyone?

And when contraception does figure in the movies, it is to provide a Comedy Moment – see the remarks in chapter seven on the film *The Ice Storm*. Imagine a clown, after years of playing for laughs, trying a straight role. It is not easy to achieve and writers/directors/human beings don't like to make life difficult for themselves. But if Jim Carrey could manage it by playing a universally acclaimed straight role in the film *The Truman Show*, after years of playing the fool in films such as *Ace Ventura: Pet Detective*, surely Cousin Condom and Dr Diaphragm could do the same.

It is getting more and more difficult to claim that having sex without producing children is wrong, too. If people do not believe in God, you can't appeal to them from that frame of reference. If they have contraception, you can't threaten them with children and being tied down or becoming even more poor than they were before. You can advise them against promiscuity on the grounds that they might catch diseases, but a condom provides pretty good protection against most diseases. Or you can tell them what the wise philosopher Bertrand Russell said, which is that 'civilised people cannot fully satisfy their sexual instinct without love'.

And at least contraception's better than war as a means of keeping down a population, as B. Liber, MD pointed out in the first issue of birth control pioneer Margaret Sanger's magazine *The Woman Rebel*, in 1914. 'Some might say that war, like disease and poverty, is a blessing and not a curse as we have called it erroneously,' says Liber, before dismissing these as 'stupid conclusions'. A little bizarrely to today's mind, the piece goes on to imply that if there had been birth control in Germany there might not have been a First World War. 'With a much lower population, the Kaiser would have thought it over longer, before he would have challenged all Europe. Women can easily see what a force they can oppose against war simply by a conscious, reasonable limitation of offspring!' What a different world that was.

If we decide to be old-fashioned and assume that sex is best with the one you love, why not do it as often as possible? In 1887 Charles Baudelaire said that 'sex is the lyricism of the masses,' only he said it in French. If the *Thesaurus of Quotations* is to be believed, the idea of sex as art is a common one. 'The sexual embrace can only be compared with music and with prayer,' said Havelock Ellis, of whom more later. 'Sex is the great amateur art,' said David Cort, adding that 'the professional, male or female, is frowned on; he or she misses the whole point and spoils the show'. Yet, to be pedantic, prostitution is famously among the oldest professions in the world, and there is no real reason to suppose that it will cease to flourish way into the future, so there has always been a place for the professional. Without wishing to crush the joyful sentiment of Cort, perhaps he should have said that the professional is '*officially* frowned on'. At any rate, sex is democratic, anyone can do it. You don't even need a pencil and paper to master this art. You already possess the instruments necessary for this particular brand of lyricism, and in Britain you can get contraception free too. All you need is another person. Preferably one you love. What are you waiting for? Put the book down. Get to it.

Oh, so you haven't got a partner. This book will rub your nose in the lives of those, throughout history, who did have partners, just so you know what you're missing.

A history of contraception should not *just* be an excuse to laugh unsportingly at the practices of long-dead people, although this is a lot of it, obviously. There are two reasons for not exclusively scoffing: one is that it is still not clear that, in particular, many herbal methods do not work. We have a lot to learn about the properties of plants – many are much more potent than we might imagine. The Western world's current fascination with plants such as 'Nature's Prozac', St John's wort, demonstrates that we are starting to rouse this body of knowledge which has been sleeping soundly for so many centuries. The other reason not to scoff is that many of the methods are still being used by pre-industrial societies today with varying degrees of success. Although there are obviously hardships associated with, say, living in tribal Africa which are unimaginable to the Western mind, what these societies have over ours is that, in the main, they still control their own birth control. Just as with Western societies until the early twentieth century, the medical profession in such societies is not the ultimate authority, mainly because these people do not really have a medical profession.

Such considerations should not be wholly at the expense of unsporting laughter. We have a *duty* to laugh at Casanova's placing of gold balls into many of his lovers, or the eighteenth century practice of spreading a mule skin over one's bed on the assumption that the animal's sterility will be caught by the lovers within it. We should also laugh long and hard at the behaviour of medieval French priests, whose first priority was to have sex with as many female parishioners as possible and then adapt God's laws to fit around that behaviour. More recently we should be filled with mirth about the practice of using Diet Coke as a spermicide. 'It is a soft drink,' pointed out the company when asked about its contraceptive properties by over-excited media. And Femidoms just are intrinsically funny things.

Without wishing to sound too high-minded, more than anything this book is about the human condition. A history of contraception was never going to be anything but. Pages and pages filled with human endeavour follow. Necessity is indeed the mother, as it were, of invention, and there is nothing that people have felt it more necessary to be inventive over than sex, and their ability to have it without fear of consequence. This invention takes several forms. There is the most literal kind, which results in those devices which have been invented and then used, broadly, with success. Then there are the useless devices. They too have involved effort, sometimes of this literal kind, but sometimes using a different kind of ingenuity – the kind that creates a ruse. Did the French priest in chapter two, Pierre Clergue, really believe that his magic talisman worked, or care, when the very fact of it enabled him to have sex with as many women as he wanted to? Was Casanova really convinced of the efficacy of those golden balls? Sure, you could come up with an answer to these questions based on the track record of these characters. But perhaps they meant well. Perhaps, in the face of all the inevitable unwanted pregnancies, we should really have asked their internal gene-reproducing machines. Perhaps if they could talk, those would have said, with a shrug, 'Just doing my job, guv.'

One final point. However light the course you try to run in the writing of a book, if your research throws up enough people saying Something Must Be Done it is going to rub off. And the population of the world now exceeds six billion. Most of the book is, as promised to the publisher, a romp through the history of contraception, with special emphasis placed on the absurdity of the methods and often the people who used them. The final chapter starts to get a little more Something Must Be Done. In common with most of the other commentators who have been roundly abused in this book, I don't really know *how* my suggestions are going to be carried out. If, by then, you feel saturated by the views of random characters who think they have something to say about contraception, please ignore it.

1

Romantic Love and Going Greek

People are neither heterosexual nor homosexual; they are merely sexual.

Quentin Crisp[1]

For the Ancient Greeks, the Persian proverb 'A boy for pleasure; a woman for children' was about the size of it. A man had his needs and they should, and would, be serviced – preferably by a boy. Greek philosopher Aristotle (384–322 BC), who was the student of Plato and the teacher of Alexander the Great (when he was little), tells us that homosexuality was an official population control device[2]. Gay and straight are now seen, by gay and straight alike, as mutually exclusive. You are either one thing or the other, the thinking goes, and if you are gay, matters of encouraging or preventing conception are not an issue. It was not ever thus. An ancient Greek woman was mainly a functional thing and should be seeded and not heard.

And it's no wonder. If we are to believe the great granddaddy of Greek gods, Zeus, the creation of woman was man's punishment for stealing fire. She was given crafty speech, thievish habits and a licentious mind. Before taking Zeus's word for anything, though, it should be borne in mind that he was also a homosexual rapist, having turned himself into an eagle and snatched Trojan prince Ganymede from his friends after being overwhelmed by the mortal's beauty.

Perhaps it was worth it for Ganymede. He was made immortal and became cupbearer to the gods.

In fact Ganymede was clearly quite a guy, since he had still not been forgotten by around 1120. A medieval poet without a name referred to him in a poem which put homosexuality forward as the only truly noble move for sexuality. No-Name's argument was that because humans had reason, they should not be like birds or pigs, which left only one viable option: 'Peasants, who may as well be called pigs/These are the only men who should resort to women'.[3] Gay – the choice of the gods.

Gay was the choice of some Romans, although they were more subtle. There is a wonderfully understated scene in Stanley Kubrick's *Spartacus*, which was originally cut from the film. In it Crassus (played by Laurence Olivier) shyly introduces his new slave boy, Antoninus, both to his own sexuality and to the fact that he finds the younger man attractive. As Antoninus washes his master, Crassus asks the new slave a number of questions – 'Do you steal?', 'Do you lie?' and so on – to establish that he is a morally upright young man and by implication that he, the master, is a solid citizen. Crassus then asks if the boy prefers 'snails or oysters', to which the boy answers, 'Oysters.' Crassus says, 'My taste includes both snails and oysters,' adding, 'Taste is not the same thing as appetite and therefore not a question of morals.'[4] This taste/appetite distinction is touching, if a little inaccurate when applied directly to sexuality.

Although the ancient Greeks lived in households (or *oikos*), typically with two or three children and several slaves, it is relatively safe to say that men and women lived quite separate lives in those days. This was for several reasons, one of which was their difference in age. Women were usually between fourteen and seventeen when they married, men were closer to thirty (when their fathers were either prepared to die or allow the next generation into the house).

Even then the older-man, younger-woman dynamic upset the commentators. The age gap was clearly a problem for Aristotle, who maintained that 'women who have sexual intercourse too soon are apt to be wanton, and a man's body also is stunted if he exercises the reproductive facility before the semen is full grown'.[5] He also felt that a young, and hence lusty, wife might be a bit of a handful for an older man. According to Greek biographer and essayist Plutarch (c. AD 46–120), an Athenian law existed which gave a wife the legal right to demand her husband be physically capable of fulfilling his conjugal duties at least three times a month.[6] Such laws still exist in some parts of the world, including Jordan where the figure is a slightly less civilised once every four months.[7]

Whether or not the law was adhered to, Hera, Greek goddess of marriage and childbirth and protector of married women, ensured that couples got near each other often enough and for long enough to make contraception necessary. The ideal, for the elite, was to have one son (and heir) and one daughter (to marry the son of another wealthy family). Many more children than this meant that family wealth would be split up between too many claimants, thus weakening the power of the family. In ancient times, the patter of those tiny feet was not necessarily a good thing.

Perhaps not so much has changed. The feelings of sleep-deprived parents throughout history have been the same as those of Antiphon the Sophist, who said, in around 440 BC, 'But in the very pleasure lies near at hand the pain; pleasures do not come alone, but are attended by griefs and troubles . . . Suppose children are born: then all is full of anxiety, and the youthful spring goes out of the mind . . .'[8] 'Sophistry' has come to mean being tricksy with words. Reading between the last of these lines, Antiphon is really saying, 'Watch out if you're thinking of having children. It means you'll have to grow up.'

They did things differently in the Greek city state of Sparta. The Spartans were grown-ups. There, celibacy was frowned upon and childbirth rewarded. There, a man's military duties fell away on the birth of his third son and his taxes with his fourth. It was not different just for the sake of being different, however. Sparta's priority was military, and based on producing as many potential soldiers and potential mothers of potential soldiers as possible. The principle of offering financial incentives for adding to a country's army persists to this day. In France, where national service has only recently been phased out, anyone who is pregnant is entitled to a young child allowance from when they are four months pregnant to when their child is three years old.

Outside Sparta, the combination of producing young mothers and needing heirs, but not too many, meant that births had to be controlled. Both Plato and Aristotle believed that birth control was necessary. In Plato's case this was partly because he thought too many children led to poverty and war, but mainly because he thought a lack of birth control might lead to a situation where there were not his ideal number of 5,040 households in the state. This bizarre number was just dreamt up by Plato, who clearly had too much time on his hands. Work must have been slow for philosophers in Greece that week. Aristotle also thought that a population level should be set, although he was not quite so precise about the figure.

Whilst attempting to suss out fertility, the Greeks got sidetracked into the issue of which sex should be blamed for, or credited with, procreation. Greek myth comes up with a number of ways for conception to occur. Few of them involved women. Zeus was supposed to have given birth to Athena from his head and Dionysus from his thigh. Athena was the goddess of wisdom and helper of heroes (although early on in her career she had special responsibility for arts and crafts and war). She was also famous in the UK in the 1980s for her chain of shops which sold, unsurprisingly given her origin and upbringing, pictures of men with babies. Dionysus was the wine, women and song guy. Perhaps his lack of sexual responsibility was due to the fact that a bloke gave birth to him. Perhaps he was unaware of the normal consequence of drunken mating with lots of women. At once the closest and furthest away from the beginning of life as we know it was Aphrodite's experience. She, goddess of love and beauty, was born of the foam from *castrated* Uranus's sperm. Sex was, you see, a complicated business on Mount Olympus.

Aeschylus is just one of the characters who embarrasses himself with his ham-fisted, and doubtless successful, attempts to undermine women. In his play *Eumenides*, with a feat of contrivance which comes nowhere near deserving the name 'sophistry', he decides that women are not really anything to do with the process of creating life, they are merely 'seed-beds' for the precious seeds planted by men. The woman is 'not her offspring's parent'. No, 'the male . . . who mounts . . . begets'. You couldn't move, in ancient Greece, without falling over a theory of procreation. Yet do we remember the name of Alcmaeon of Croton who, at the beginning of the fifth century BC, examined birds' eggs and believed human offspring too developed from female ova?[9] No, we remember crowd-pleasing chauvinist Aristotle, the man who thought the testes served as a counterweight to the penis.[10]

Galen, Greek physician and one of the founders of modern medicine, had an interesting theory about men's and women's parts too, which he discussed in *On The Usefulness of Parts of the Body* and managed to make 'proof' that 'the female is more imperfect than the male':

> Think first, please, of the man's sexual parts turned in and extending inward between the rectum and the bladder. If this should happen, the scrotum would necessary take the place of the uteri, with the testes lying outside, next to it on either side. The penis of the male would become the neck of the cavity that had been formed; and the skin at the end of the penis, now called prepuce, would become the female pudendum itself. In fact, you could not find a single large male part left over that had not simply changed its position; for the parts that are inside in woman are outside in man . . .

Not everybody sought to crush women. Hippocrates, the other Greek behind medicine and the person after whom the doctor's 'Hippocratic oath' is named, was the first to suggest that sexual pleasure had to be experienced by a woman for her to conceive, bless him. But then, two and a half thousand years before the days of Ally McBeal and Bridget Jones, doctors were also claiming that the woman who remained unmarried would suffer from hysteria. How far we've come . . .

Plato had a theory that not only the woman but her womb too would cause trouble if not used for its proper purpose (of generating babies). More specifically, it would become restless and wander all over the body. In fact, it 'stops the passages of the spirits and the respiration and occasions the most extreme anxiety and all sorts of diseases'.[11] The worst cases were virgins, whose wombs were the lightest, which made them travel most freely. This 'wandering womb' idea persisted in England right up until the 1600s. Aretaeus was a great physician almost one and a half thousand years before this, though, and he thought the womb was like a kind of fidgety animal:

> In the middle of the flanks of a woman lies the womb, a female viscus, closely resembling an animal – for it is moved of itself hither and thither in the flanks. It also moves upwards in a direct line to below the cartilage of the thorax, and obliquely to the right or to the left, either to the liver or spleen. Likewise it is subject to prolapsus downwards, and, in a word, is altogether erratic.[12]

If you rubbed the genitals of your woman and agitated her womb, again according to the Hippocratic texts, this would produce 'a sort of tickling sensation, and the rest of the body derives pleasure and warmth from it',[13] again suggesting that some men thought it was okay for women to enjoy sex then, and that foreplay was an option.

There was also a widely held view that the womb had the power to determine the sex of the child, according to the physical conditions within it. If the environment of that womb was, broadly, dry and hot it would probably produce a boy, they thought. If, however it was wet and cold, a girl would be the most likely result. Perhaps they were confusing human beings with alligators, which if hatched from warm eggs are born male. Crocodiles and turtles, on the other hand, are born female if the eggs are warm.[14]

If this seems far-fetched, theories on how to determine the sex of your child still abound today. In 1999, the *Daily Mirror* claimed that 'frequent sex is more likely to result in a boy', and 'having sex close to ovulation generally produces a boy'. If it's a daughter you're after, according to the paper, the man should 'engage in stressful activity before intercourse', or – which probably amounts to the same thing – be a diver, a test-pilot or a clergyman.[15]

It was not just the womb that was problematic to prehistoric man.

In *Sex, Sin and Sanctity* (1954), John Langdon-Davies gives the following account of the Ba–Ila people of Rhodesia (now Zimbabwe), which suggests that they were equally puzzled (and awed) by the male part as the female:

> They believed that the sexual organs were animals, or at least the dwelling places of animals, called *bapuka*, which controlled them and were responsible for the process of reproduction. It is a *mupuka* in the male that secretes the semen, and impotence is caused by its ceasing to function. It is thought that hen's eggs, fat and a dish of ground-nuts will prevent the *mupuka* from working or, by becoming fixed in the loins, will block the passage.
>
> In a woman there are said to be two of these *bapuka*, one male, the other female. The male is the inert creature, but upon the female depend all the generative functions. The name given to this female *mupuka* is *Chibumba*, the moulder. It is so named because it forms the child in the womb. It lies within the uterus, with its head in the orifice. When in coitus, the semen reaches it, the Chibumba catches it in its mouth. Having secured the semen, it licks and rolls it over and over and this way forms it into a foetus.[16]

Back in more misanthropic Greece and Rome withdrawal or 'coitus interruptus' was almost certainly used to a certain extent as it always has been, but, as has often been the case, there is little documentary evidence. In his scholarly tome *A History of Contraception*, Angus McLaren found what appears to be a rare example of this method from Archilochus of Paros, seventh-century BC mercenary and poet, who spoke in one of his poems about the seduction of his fiancée's younger sister:

> I took the girl into the flowers in bloom and laid her down, protecting her with my soft cloak, her neck held in my arms. Though like a fawn she hindered, I encouraged her and her breasts with my hands gently grasped. She, then and there, herself showed young flesh – the onset of her prime – and all her

lovely body fondling, I also let go with my force, just touching, though, her tawny down.[17]

Apart from coitus interruptus and homosexuality (or anal sex with one's wife, which was legal according to both the Koran and the Talmud, spiritual rule books for the Muslim and Jewish communities respectively), birth control was mainly the woman's business. This might explain why it is so poorly documented. Not because it wasn't going on, but because it was so commonplace and so much a part of life.

A weird and wonderful array of potions for drinking were concocted to prevent conception or induce abortion, including the leaves or bark of hawthorn, ivy, willow and poplar. These were not merely old wives' tales. Hawthorn is known to help menstrual problems and may well induce abortion. Ivy is known to have contraceptive and abortive properties. Willow acts as a contraceptive, traditionally consumed after sex, with honey, because it is bitter. Poplar is related to willow and although there is no documentary evidence to prove it, it is likely that it shares properties with its cousin. Some methods avoided the problem of sex altogether. It was believed, for instance, that dry cabbage would dampen the libido. Drop it in goat's milk and the opposite effect was achieved.[18]

Juniper berries too figured largely, as they continued to throughout history (sometimes under the name of 'savin'). If they were applied to the penis or inside the vulva they were supposed to produce temporary sterility. If you were not keen on effectively putting jam on your parts (and many are) there was always 'misy', which is thought to be copper sulphate. This, one Hippocratic doctor advised, if dissolved in water and drunk by the woman, would stave off pregnancy for a year. Thus he started a metal-as-contraceptive trend which was to persist until the early 1900s. At first the water from the fire-buckets of blacksmiths was drunk by the ancients, an idea which was adopted by the Europeans, as author Shirley Green noted, 'with their knack of sifting the chaff from the wheat'. In 1886 east Austrian women continued to carry out this practice, and some women near Birmingham were 'drinking the water in which copper coins had been boiled' as recently as 1914, according to the National Birth Rate Commission.[19]

Physician Dioscorides introduced the Greeks to the idea of anointing genitals with cedar gum and applying alum to the uterus. Knowing what we do today, it is unlikely that either of these methods would have been hugely successful. Ancient Greek thinking on the subject was that by combining oily substances, the womb should be made smooth and thus inhospitable to semen. Dioscorides also recommended the use of a peppermint and honey suppository before sex and a peppery pessary after, the idea being not to provide a barrier but to dry out the uterus. Honey has recently made a comeback, but at a price – and not just that of a jar of honey or a couple of bee stings. No, the 'sting' is of a more substantial financial kind.

In 1980 Dr Edward Stim first published information on the 'honey cup' or 'honey cap'. This was a one-size fits-all diaphragm which was to be soaked in a particular type of honey for a week. Although it is still available from one Harley Street doctor, it does not have Family Planning Association approval. This is because there have not been any studies to prove that honey has spermicidal properties, and the FPA does not endorse the distribution of one size of diaphragm for all women. The FPA's view is that it may have been used by Stim to mask odours and, historically, to bind spermicidal elements together. It is also likely that honey would serve as a kind of mechanical form of contraception by slowing sperm down.

More reliable than Dioscorides was Soranus, who at least pre-scribed contraceptives which were effective. As effective, in fact, as those of medical science in the mid-nineteenth century. This was due in large part to the fact that, incredibly, a fair amount of medicine was then still based on the Hippocratic texts.

Yet the Greek and Romans do not win the first-ever-writers-of-contraceptive-prescriptions prize. They are merely bronze or silver medal winners. The country which started the whole sordid business was Egypt and it did so with the Petri and Ebers papyri. The Ebers papyrus was found in 1874 by Georg Ebers, a German Egyptologist. It is a medical papyrus containing around 700 medical and magical formulae and has been dated at around 1550 BC. It is also our main source of information about early Egyptians behaving badly, and shows that they too used tampons or pessaries infused, again, with a huge array of substances. Some of these were designed to speed up labour or regulate periods. Others, including combinations of dates, onions and acanthus crushed in honey, were supposed to initiate abortion. In fact, combinations of almost anything that can be imagined were used as, or with, pessaries either to aid or prevent conception in ancient times. Some we are familiar with (honey), some are more obscure (boy cabbage). Some worked (vinegar), some would have the opposite of the desired effect.

If pessaries, suppositories, coitus interruptus and alternative sexual practices were not to be trusted, there was always magic. Protective amulets or talismans were employed at this time and continued to be worn well into the Middle Ages. Combinations such as mule's kidney and eunuch's urine were thought by some to do the trick. Aetius thought one should have sex equipped with the liver of a cat or weasel, 'or else wear part of the womb of a lioness in a tube of ivory'.[20] Less messy but more involved was Greek writer and scientist Pliny's suggestion of attaching a spider's egg containing two worms to the body.[21] Together with a deer skin. Before sunrise. All this effort would be rewarded, though. It would prevent conception for a year. However, in his mighty work *Natural History*, Pliny said he would prefer it if people did not have sex at all. Soranus made it clear to the Greeks and the Romans (he was a kind of freelancer who went where the demand was) that he was dismissive of amulets and talismans altogether.

During that free-for-all which was Graeco-Roman antiquity, there was really only one dissenting voice and that belonged to Musonius Rufus, a Roman Stoic of the first century who created the modern marriage ideal. According to Emiel Eyben, 'From this humane philosopher come the most beautiful words on matrimony antiquity has bequeathed to us.'[22] Praise indeed. Christianity liked the words so much that it adopted them as its own.

To paraphrase those words, Musonius's idea was that marriage should be a communion of souls with a view to producing children. With his strict ethical doctrine came a then rare sexual equality, with neither partner being allowed to have sex outside wedlock or before marriage. Moreover, and for the first time, sex was only to be 'indulged in for the sake of begetting children' and not for fun. He does not have different rules for the poor and rich. Both should be marrying and having large families, although he saves a special ticking off for the rich 'to me most monstrous of all, some who do not even have poverty as an excuse'. At any rate, it was to be a while before these ideas were adopted.

Apart from Soranus, the ancients did not really make a moral distinction between contraception and abortion or infanticide. A variety of methods intended to induce abortion are recorded in ancient Greece. Although philosophers were worried as we are today about exactly when human life started – at conception? X weeks into the growth of the foetus? At birth? – most agreed that it was after birth (and sooner for men than women, naturally). Aristotle for one was torn. He said on one occasion that both semen and menstrual fluid had souls.

It is relatively safe to say that, for the Romans too, abortion and contraception were not as separate as they were to become in later cultures. An array of herbal methods were used in an attempt to bring about an abortion, including 'squirting cucumber' – a cousin of the non-squirting kind we now make genteel sandwiches with – which does indeed have contraceptive properties.

The Greeks also introduce us to the 'take whatever you advise women *not* to do when they're pregnant and advise them to do the opposite' school of birth control/miscarriage induction: excessive jumping, carrying heavy loads, constricting the body and loud sneezing were all possibilities. A Greek woman in a bodice, with an odd gait, flu and a hod of ancient bricks clearly had a bun in the oven. Soranus says that Hippocrates in his book 'employs leaping with the heels to the buttocks for the sake of expulsion', although Hippocrates prohibits abortives. If these methods seem primitive, practices like these were still going on in Europe in the 1800s.

Abortion went on, although it was controversial because it had associations for the Greeks with not recognising your husband's authority and right to children. In fact in AD 536 it was seen as grounds for divorce. Obviously it had the added disadvantage of being a very primitive business then, whether it involved jumping around or ingesting poison. The Greeks and Romans were nothing if not practical. In the context of preventing contraception or inducing miscarriage or abortion, lotions and potions were banned, but not for ethical reasons so much as because, along with love-potions and sterility drugs, they were thought to endanger the life of the woman who used them. This would never do. Without women there was no future either for Greece or Rome.

As for infanticide and exposure, they were both sad facts about ancient Graeco-Roman life. Some people would strangle their children at birth, but more often they would leave them to the elements or, perhaps, in the lap of the gods, who were not always merciful, as we've seen. Indeed it was the practice of exposure which led to the founding of Rome, if the story of Romulus and Remus is to be believed. Romulus and Remus were left on the banks of the River Tiber, and were found by wolves. These wolves then took them to the Lupercal cave on the Palatine Hill – one of what are now known as the seven hills of Rome – and nursed them. When the two were fully grown, they returned to the spot where the wolves had found them and built Rome there. Romulus was so affected by the experience that he went on to insist that fathers kept all their sons and, Lord luv 'im, at least one daughter. The fact that the practice of exposure is relatively well documented does not mean that it was the most common. It may well just be the most noteworthy response to having unwanted children, be they deformed, extra girls, or born out of wedlock.

Distasteful as they are to today's mind, these methods also made sense over abortion and contraception in that there was no physical danger to the mother and you could choose the sex of your children. Exposure was mainly the poor man's solution, because (just as in Europe in the 1800s) only the rich could afford contraceptives and abortion, and children should these fail. Epictetus (c. AD 55–135), philosopher and founder of Stoicism, said he thought it was better to expose a child at birth than kill it through a neglectful upbringing. There again, he also said a parent could not help loving a child as soon as it was born. Nought out of ten for consistent hardhearted realism there then.

Before we get smug about the barbarity of the ancients, it should be added that infanticide is still practised now. The most obvious examples are found in China and India. In China, it has been estimated that their one-child policy led to 17 per cent of girls being killed. In India they favour boys too, and when given the choice they often rid themselves of girls. One hospital reported that of pregnant women told they were carrying girls, 96 per cent aborted.[23]

Of course parents were not without feeling when they exposed their babies. It would be carried out by a slave or midwife, and often the baby would be left in a much-frequented spot, perhaps the hippo-drome (i.e. theatre) or a place of pilgrimage, in the hope that someone would find it, take pity on it and bring it up as their own or, more realistically, as a slave. There was clearly a risk here too that the child would get into the wrong hands and be raised as a beggar or prostitute.

Later, in Egypt, where the idea of exposure was taken on from the Greeks, there was risk for the potential adopter of the child too. A set of fiscal regulations from the second century AD pronounced that any Egyptian adopting an abandoned child would be penalised after death by the confiscation of one-quarter of his fortune.

Texts suggest that there was some legislation against exposure, but that this was a frequently flouted law. Although children were the whole point of matrimony, more important was the authority of the man, and this included his right to decide whether his children lived or died.

Except in Sparta. In the case of exposure this led to authority being removed from the father of the child. If the child was healthy (and thus potentially a soldier or mother) it had to be raised, if not it had to be exposed at the foot of Mount Taygetus, simple as that. Strange, then, that Agesilaus, who went on to become king of Sparta, was a deformed child who slipped through the net. Less often a child would be drowned or strangled immediately after birth (infanticide, probably along with exposure, was not banned until AD 374), although this was more common if a baby was somehow malformed. If the parents had qualms of the 'champion the underdog', 'fall in love with the runt of the litter' kind they needed only to remind themselves that the child would not only be a burden to society, but might prove to be a bad omen in itself.[24]

Along with exposure, homosexuality seems to us perhaps the most unlikely birth control approach, and yet according to Aristotle, it was employed at the very least in Crete as a way of preventing over-population. Crete also provides the earliest representation of homo-sexuality, in the form of a bronze plaque dated 650–625 BC.[25]

Although it was no inconsistency in Ancient Greece for the same person to enjoy both hetero- and homosexual sex, the above demonstrates that the precise nature of the tradition, as with all traditions, depended on where you were. In ancient times, Greece alone was made up of hundreds of city states with varying degrees of tolerance towards homosexuality for various different reasons.

There were also different ways of being homosexual, although the most clearly recorded broadly involved a younger boy granting favours to an older man. At its most base this took the form of prostitution. We know both that this kind of transaction took place and that it was legal through characters like the Athenian orphan Diophantos. When a foreigner failed to pay him four drachmas for his services he felt sufficiently confident of his rights to complain to the magistrate in charge of orphans.

There was also Timarkhos, an Athenian politician, who went on trial for having been 'fucked a bit' during his youth. Apparently one could not be both a politician and an ex-rent-boy. It was not noble enough. Girls could be prostitutes (either of the busy kind or the 'kept woman' mistress kind) because they were generally seen as by nature inferior and subordinate. To live up to their own honourable opinion of themselves, older Greek men really needed a category of relationship which justified lusting after young boys.

They soon came up with it. It was the relationship of *erastes* (older man or 'lover', usually of noble birth) with *eromenos* (younger boy, often from a poorer family). Again it was a kind of commerce, but, on the surface at least, of a subtler kind than with prostitution. The older man would dote on the younger boy whom he would have admired from afar for a while, probably in a gymnasium or wrestling school, and tell him how beautiful he was. Crucially, he would also let it be known that he was a man of influence, that he could effect an introduction to someone important to the boy, or pass on some of his socially valuable knowledge, whether it be how to throw a javelin or how to speak in public. In this sense the relationship had much in common with the more recent idea of taking on an apprentice or mentoring.

It was not quite as cynical as it sounds. Indeed, in an age when in particular male beauty was so revered, some of these older guys were far from being the dirty old men we might imagine. They were more like giddy schoolgirls. The presence of a beautiful young man made them silly. Episthenes was one of these. He saved a young boy from death because he was so overwhelmed by his beauty, beginning his rescue by trying to die in the boy's place. Often the man would hope that the boy would fall in love with him, but the boy might reject him altogether.

Obviously the big question both for contraception and for the young men concerned was how much of a part sexual favours played in all of this. Perhaps predictably, because there were as many relationships as there were dynamics to those relationships, the answer is not clear.

Plato would have it that there was none at all, hence 'platonic love', and this was certainly the ideal. He had an idea that originally human beings were a complete set of two parts and were constantly looking for their 'other half'. For some men this 'other half' was male and for others it was female. In the former case they would marry and have children 'under the compulsion of custom, without natural inclination'.

Numerous decorated vases of the time would suggest otherwise. Although it was not exactly dinner party conversation, these show endless pictures of men touching up boys (usually with other people watching, incidentally) with varying degrees of success. Some actually show anal intercourse, but more common are scenes of intercrural intercourse – or rubbing your love-javelin between the boy's thighs. These pictures would also sometimes have written captions such as 'Let me!' or 'Stop it!' accompanying them.

In both Elis and Boiotia it was customary to place erastes and eromenos next to each other in battle. It must have been assumed that both would fight harder and more fiercely because they fought in the sight of the person they most wanted to impress and next to the person they most wanted to protect.

Sparta and Crete too had that strong military/homosexual tradition. Although it is not clear if these were exploited tactically, as in Elis and Boiotia, the very fact of segregating men from women traditionally promotes homosexual behaviour (much as public schoolboys and prisoners might seek to deny it). This, added to the fact that it was not taboo, makes it likely that at the very least the system in the regions perpetuated homosexuality.

Lesbianism was more likely to have been taboo. Kenneth Dover can only find one vase with 'girl on girl action' on it (not his phrase). Apart from that, there was the passionate poetry of Sappho from Mytilene on the island of Lesbos – from which come the word 'lesbian' – who spoke of women in the same terms as men did about their male lovers, as well as mentioning the male lovers in her poetry:

> He seems to me to be equal to the gods that man who is sitting facing you and hearing your sweet voice close by, and your lovely laugh. That, I swear, set my heart fluttering in my breast. For whenever I look at you briefly, then it is no longer in my power to speak. My tongue is fixed in silence, and straightaway a subtle fire has run under my skin, and with my eyes I see nothing, and my ears hum, and cold sweat possesses me, and trembling seizes all of me, and I am paler than grass, and I seem to myself within a little of being dead. But all is to be endured.

Again it's likely that these women who were shut away together all day every day did have a mutual fiddle from time to time, but getting men to be interested in that, and hence record it for posterity, was not going to happen (just as getting a record of women's feelings about their husbands' homosexual rumpy-pumpy was not going to happen). As long as relationships between men were the ideal (i.e. the opposite of today), it would be like trying to get today's 'lad-mag'-reading man to be interested in sexual experiments between, say, George Clooney and Brad Pitt. Salma Hayek and Uma Thurman? Now you're talking . . .

The very fact that male beauty was the ideal is interesting, if even more tangential. It seems most likely that this ideal grew from the fact that, since women were both shut away and regarded as inferiors, men who wanted a close, intense relationship with a thrilling chase at the beginning of it would have to look to other men for it. Women would not run away. They weren't really allowed to, and it's difficult to chase something that's stationary. Some evidence exists to suggest that men during this time were frightened of the assumed sexual energy of women too.

Obviously it was not necessarily all plain cruising for the young boys. There was potential for them to be exploited by the older men. One particularly scary account of ritualised homosexual rape in fourth-century Crete was written by Ephoros. The lover would make his intention clear, and the family and friends of the younger man would not hide him away because it was seen as an honour for their son to be chosen in this way (immediately the words 'man', 'old', 'win' 'situation' and 'win' spring to mind).

If the erastes was not seen by the family as worthy of their son the attempts of the erastes to rape would be stopped by force. If he was seen as worthy they put up a 'good-humoured and half-hearted resistance, which ended with the erastes carrying off the eromenos to a hide-out for two months'. On their return the older man would give the younger expensive presents. Big deal.

This is particularly striking because it raises the eternal question of class, or at least prestige. As far as the friends and family of at least a few young boys in Crete were concerned (we are not sure how regularly this practice occurred there) it was worth letting your young son be raped and abducted by an older man in order to have him return *kleinos* or 'celebrated thanks' to his noble 'lover'. Weird. There was nowt so queer as some of those ancient Greek folk.

Apart from their respective degrees of openness towards the homo-sexuality issue, one of the main differences between the Greeks and the Romans was that although the latter were expected to be keen on conceiving, they were less fertile as a culture than the Greeks. What little evidence there is suggests that the Romans ended up with two or three children just as the Greeks did, but their use of birth control tactics was less zealous. Keith Hopkins suggests that 'Romans avoided

large families by being unfaithful to their wives'. This was a product
of the fact that 'there was in Rome little or no ideal of the faithful
husband'.[26] When wives did feel under pressure to marry and have
children and this made them feel worn out, Soranus's suggestion was
that they rest from sex periodically, i.e. abstain. If your woman chose
to abstain, the other way of avoiding producing heirs while continuing
to have a sex life was to have sex with prostitutes, slaves or men. The
babies of slaves were not a problem; they were raised like pets, and
prostitutes tended to 'take steps', like interrupting coitus, to prevent
pregnancy.

For those women who did not want to give up their sex lives or have
children, Soranus also mentioned an early version of the rhythm
method, by suggesting caution when having sex during periods
suitable for conception. Then there was the prolonged breastfeeding
option. As long as babies are given frequent feeds this has a contraceptive effect, and this method is still used in pre-industrial countries
like Mali in Africa. Back in the ancient world, a woman was advised to
continue feeding for around three years. It is likely that this advice was
heeded more by the Romans than the Greeks, since the latter were not
huge fans of breastfeeding. Since ancient times, powerful men have
often employed wet-nurses precisely so that their wives can start
ovulating again and thus produce more children.

The same principle occurs in the animal kingdom, with infanticide
thrown in for good measure. If a group of lions takes over a pride of
females, the first thing they do is kill any suckling young, the quicker
to speed up the passing on of their own genes.[27] Monkeys often do the
same thing. When compared to these states of affairs, practised even
by our cousins the chimps, the practice of wet-nursing, which at first
seemed so abhorrent, becomes positively civilised.

Rufus of Ephesus, a writer from one of the twelve cities which
made up Ionia, was with Soranus on the idea of abstinence, but he
suggested it for men and not so much for reasons of birth control as
for the maintenance of male health. According to him, with coitus
came indigestion, memory loss, spitting of blood and fading of sight
and hearing. Caelius Aurelianus piled in with a few additions of his
own, including pleurisy, apoplexy, madness, paralysis, nephritis and

haemorrhaging. He also rejected Asclepiades's claim that sex cured epilepsy, saying that sex itself was a minor epilepsy. In short, it produced mania.[28]

Thus you were damned (or perhaps 'maddened') if you did, by Caelius, and damned if you didn't (and were Greek and female), by the Hippocratic doctors. Celsus, first-century writer, medic and, you guessed it, philosopher, suggested a third way, however. Although it was tiring, sex should only be avoided during the day, in summer, and before work or meals.[29] It may well be that this Roman fear of excess was the reason for the country's relatively low birth rate.

The Greeks also had opinions, often conflicting, on which sexual positions were best and worst for conception. Soranus and Lucretius, the Roman poet (c. BC 99–55), thought that the man should mount the woman (i.e. do it doggy style). Artemidorus (106–48 BC), author of *The Interpretation of Dreams* and thus forerunner to Freud, said that 'only the face-to-face position was taught to them by nature'. The *Daily Mirror*, in 1999, came down on the side of Artemidorus. Under the headline 'The Facts of Life', it published a list of interesting non-old wives' tales, one of which was 'a woman is more likely to conceive if she makes love in the missionary position'.[30]

Some actions were also thought to have a contraceptive effect. A combination of sneezing, holding your breath and drinking something cold was recommended to women by Soranus. Lucretius thought the best method was if the woman 'aids the man's actions by the movement of her hips, and by the flexible writhing of her breast'.[31] Hmm. He might just as well have said, 'Be a good lay and you won't get pregnant.'

There were also thought to be specific times which encouraged and discouraged pregnancy. Paul of Aegina thought that after eating and before sleep was the best time to make babies, since 'the woman falling asleep is the more likely to retain the semen.'[32] This theory is also broadly in line with the *Mirror*. According to the feature, Dr Angelo Cagnatti of Italy's University of Modena discovered that the fertility of both men and women reaches its peak between 5 and 7pm. The paper called this not 'happy hour' (which occurs at around the same time and which is so called because drinks in bars are half price), but 'nappy hour'.

Herbs were also used, as throughout history. A popular herbal tea with contraceptive properties contained willow seed. Bryony mixed with ox urine was another possible drink, as were wine, rue, wall-flower seed, myrtle, myrrh and white pepper. Dioscorides listed nine plants with contraceptive properties. They included thyme, absinthe, bryony used as a tampon, and potions and pessaries containing hellebore. These would, on the whole, have worked.[33]

Douching occurred, using a mixture of alum and wine, or sea water or brine and vinegar. These would have had an effect, since even in the early twentieth century, vinegar and lemon juice solutions were still being recommended by birth control experts because they were acidic and hence acted as spermicides. One of these experts was Marie Stopes, who recommended alum, vinegar and brine in 1927 and was to advocate the use of olive oil, which reduces the activity of sperm, in 1931.

The Greeks and Romans were not the first to use spermicides, however; the Egyptians were, as we know from the Petri Papyrus of around 1850 BC. Contained within this are prescriptions for pessaries of crocodile dung and sour milk (a combination now held to be quite effective because it was relatively acidic) and a combination of honey and sodium carbonate, which would also have been quite effective.

Nor were the Romans without barrier methods, although again the Egyptians got there first. Some kind of brightly coloured sheath made an early appearance in Egypt at around 1350–1200 BC, although it is unlikely that these were for contraceptive purposes. They were probably worn either, incredibly, to increase the attractiveness of the wearer (in which case it's no wonder the Sphinx smirks), or to fend off insects or disease, or as a status symbol. Earlier still, a fresco in the Dordogne, France, dated 10–15,000 BC, appears to provide the first record of the sheath being used during a sexual act.[34]

For the Romans as for the Greeks, cedar gum makes an appearance as a kind of barrier, this time rubbed over 'the male part'. Pessaries of old favourites alum, honey, olive oil ('extra virgin' perhaps?) and peppermint also figure. Soranus also suggested the use of a lock of wool with the above, so that together they would clog and cool, stopping seed passing into it. The idea of blocking the path of semen is clearly a sound one, if these substances succeeded. However, Soranus thought that the cooling and subsequent shutting of the uterus was the key thing, which it is not.

According to the legend of Minos and Pasiphae, they also had condoms, but for a unique purpose. Minos had serpent- and scorpion-filled semen, which made sex difficult. Luckily for him and his wife Pasiphae, their friend Prokris introduced them to the idea of slipping a goat's bladder into Prokris and voilà, a healthy sex life ensued.[35] Intriguingly, they also went on to have four sons and four daughters but, as we saw earlier when gods were being born out of the heads and thighs of other gods, legend does not always stand up to the fine-tooth comb treatment.

Then the fun stopped, at any rate officially, when it became trendy (if not rock 'n' roll) to be a Stoic. This meant a number of things: you had to at least seem to be faithful to your wife; you had to at least seem heterosexual and not bisexual; you were not supposed to masturbate; you were only supposed to have sex to procreate; and your wife was supposed to be your friend. Similar as this sounds to Christianity, Romans began to behave this way because they became suspicious of excess and wanted to master themselves.

2

Clergymen Behaving Badly

Lord grant me chastity and continence, but not yet.

St Augustine

The Middle Ages, roughly the fifth century to the fifteenth, were not a great time of innovation as far as contraception was concerned. In fact there is not a lot of evidence for its use other than by prostitutes all the way from the third to the seventeenth century. Of course, 'lack of evidence' has never been the same thing as 'not guilty'. Despite the fact that infant survival rates were low during this time, which has led some scholars, including Norman Himes in *A Medical History of Birth Control*, to conclude that birth control was hardly practised,[1] there will always be those who are doing what they shouldn't be doing where they shouldn't be doing it with people whom they shouldn't be doing it with. And these people are not going to stop thrill-seeking, however high the orders not to come from. They will continue to find ways to avoid being found out. But more on French priests later.

As far as contraception went, the Middle Ages did have some enlightened characters. Two of the most notable came along early on. The first of these was Aetius of Amida. He was a Greek who lived between 527 and 565 BC. Many of his methods were sensible and very similar to those of Soranus, but he was as capable of contraceptive flights of fancy as the next man. Amulets were a feature of his bathroom cabinet – the most left-field had to be worn near the anus and involved either the milk tooth of a child or a marble. Other amulets used during that period in history involved the use of a bone from the right side of a black cat, the dried testicles of a weasel and the earwax of a mule. Just in case one were tempted to chuckle at the quaintness of these ideas, it should be added that, even today, something like 76 per cent of Chinese men believe that eating tiger penis will increase their virility.

This last was the idea of Abu Bakr Muhammed ibn Zakariya Al-Razi, who was Persian and who died in AD 923. Despite his long name, Al-Razi, as we will call him, was a pragmatist, at a time when those were few and far between, and those few were for the most part and unfairly for the rest of the world, clumped in Islam. In *An Illustrated History of Contraception*, William H. Robertson goes into several of Al-Razi's suggested techniques, pointing out that, as with much of medical theory in ancient times, 'the rational and the what now appears ridiculous are mingled'.[2]

Cabbage, used as a vaginal suppository, figures in his thesis, as do animal membranes and salt as a spermicide. The familiar 'woman jumps backwards' method is also suggested, but an element of numerology is introduced for variety – she should jump backwards seven times if the technique is to really take hold. He is also one of the few friends of coitus interruptus to be found during this period. Of semen he says, 'There are several ways of preventing its entrance. The first is that at the time of ejaculation the man withdraw from the woman so that the semen does not approach the os uteri.'[3] He then describes what came to be called coitus reservatus: 'the second way is to prevent ejaculation, a method practised by some'. Guilt-free, natural (if a little risky) contraception.

Enter God. The birth of Christianity was a barrier both to sex itself and to the recording of contraceptive practices. The occasional character could shed some light, though, and one such was Augustine (AD 354–430), member of the North African Roman elite and later Bishop of Hippo in Rome. He was the earliest commentator on (and formulator of) Christian attitudes towards conception and the control of conception. He was also a bit of a lad in his youth, fathering a son called Adeodatus who died at the age of eighteen. The boy's African mother was abandoned by Augustine after thirteen years, because

Augustine's mother had wanted him to have a posher wife. It was not without anguish that Augustine let her go, however:

> The woman with whom I was in the habit of sleeping was torn from my side on the ground of being an impediment to my marriage, and my heart, which clung to her, was wounded and broken and dripping blood . . . Nor was the wound healed which had been made by the cutting off of my mistress. It burned, it hurt intensely, and then it festered, and if the pain became duller, it became more desperate.

What was more, Augustine was never to marry the approved bride, because one of the first priorities for Christians was to gain mastery over the body, as the Stoics had sought to do before them. By now, though, it was thought that human beings sacrificed living in Paradise as a direct result of our weakness for sins of the flesh. It was not enough just to control ourselves, we had to feel guilty about the fact that we had not done so in the past. For some the blame for temptation lay squarely with womankind. Priests Jakob Sprenger (1436–95) and Heinrich Kramer (1430–1505) held this view and wrote a book about it called *Malleus Maleficarum*, which sought to establish that there were witches and temptresses, and that it was all their fault:

> All other wickedness is nothing compared to the wickedness of a woman. She is an enemy of friendship, an unavoidable punishment, a necessary evil, a natural temptation, a desirable calamity, an evil of nature, painted with pretty colours . . .
> She is more carnal than man, as is obvious from her many carnal abominations. It should be recalled that the first woman was defectively formed because she was made from a bent rib, the breast rib. Through this defect, she is an imperfect creature, always deceiving . . . [4]

By 1903, Otto Weininger (1880–1903) had moved the debate forward thus:

Far from being separate but equal, or having different but equally valuable functions, the sexes – in ideal and mixed form – are totally different, the male positive, the female negative. Woman is nothing but sexuality, she is sexuality itself, and falls into two classes: the maternal type and the prostitute.[5]

The virgin/whore perception of women persists to this day, perhaps most successfully exploited by the pop singer Madonna. Her name, her raunchy performances, her lyrics and song titles (at least initially – 'Like a Virgin', 'Papa Don't Preach') all rely for their success on the fact that the assumptions of characters like Otto Weininger around the turn of the century still have resonance for audiences decades later. And Otto's was the development of an idea that had been around since medieval times.

Marriage was okay in the Middle Ages, thought the church – officially, if it produced children and fidelity (and no abortion or sex just for fun). This, to begin with at least, was because procreation was thought to be a rational end. Celibacy, however, was preferable, unless you were Adam or Eve (despite the fact that it was their fault that we do not live in Paradise) in which case you had sex without a 'lustful appetite', which was allowed. For women a more practical reason also existed for celibacy then. It was the only sure way of avoiding the very real possibility of dying in childbirth.

Soon, though, the world became impatient to begin its trundle towards idealising the nuclear family. Slavery was out and fertility in. With this, in around AD 1000, came a new naturalness in matters sexual ('bawdy' is the word always used to describe the Middle Ages), and married couples were encouraged to have sex as frequently as possible and hence to have as many children as possible. This encouragement started at the wedding itself, when guests would shout obscenities at the bride and groom. Obscenities in the 'give it to her', 'don't wear him out too much tonight' sense as opposed to a 'what are you marrying her for, she's got a face like an empty rucksack?' or 'I've had him and he's crap' way.

The fact that noblewomen would sometimes have a number of

children while in their twenties and then cease to get pregnant after they were thirty suggests that births were being controlled whilst all this merry marital procreation was going on. Geoffrey Chaucer, main man of medieval literature, astrologer and alchemist, in his 'Parson's Tale' (neither the first nor last time that the religion/sex connection would be made during the Middle Ages) mentions those who had sex 'moore for delit than world to multiplye'. He has a number of suggestions for subtracting the multiplication factor, any one of which he seems to regard as manslaughter – a view shared by, and often reflected in the law of, communities all over the world at that time.

Chaucer was not opposed to the idea of women being equal to men in their enjoyment of sex, if the eponymous heroine of the 'Wife of Bath's Prologue and Tale' is anything to go by. Although the Wife of Bath is a caricature, she also unwittingly serves as an assistant to the clergy, in that she joins with them in showing how great was the gap between theory and practice in matters sexual back then. In fact, Sprenger and Kramer's *Malleus Maleficarum* with its view on the wickedness and sexuality of women might have been written with her in mind, an idea which would doubtless have flattered her greatly. She did, after all, say:

> As long as they live God has granted women
> Three things by nature: lies, and tears, and spinning.

Of Christ she says:

> He spoke of those who would live perfectly;
> And sirs, if you don't mind, that's not for me . . .

Of husbands who try to control their wives she says:

> Mister Old Fool, what good is it to spy?
> If you begged Argus with his hundred eyes
> To be my body guard – what better choice?
> There's little he would see unless I let him,
> For if it killed me, yet somehow I'd fool him!

Of her fourth husband being a libertine, she says:

> But certainly I carried on with folk
> Until I made him stew in his own juice,
> With fury and with purest jealousy.
> By God! On earth I was his purgatory . . .[6]

All this, and then a story which concludes by saying that a marriage will only ever be happy if the husband obeys his wife's orders to the letter.

Although Christianity has never really subscribed to the 'much information' school of birth control discussion, it had a lot to say on coitus interruptus initially, in its own sweet metaphor-laden way. Clement of Alexandria, the third Bishop of Rome, was quick to remind people of Moses' biblical teaching: 'Do not sow seeds on rocks and stones, on which they will never take root'. Actually Clement, Moses lifted this straight from Plato, but we get your gist. Interestingly, this idea of waste has re-emerged very recently in the Western world as we look to the East for our spiritual guidance. Buddhism holds that to ejaculate without proper purpose is to waste valuable spiritual energy.

The ancient Chinese had a similar reverence for sperm and energy conservation, their logical method of preventing waste being to practise coitus reservatus. This practice was explained by American physician Alice Bunker Stockham, MD in her book *Marriage of Reform* (published in 1896), as follows:

> Manifestations of tenderness are indulged in without physical or mental fatigue; the caresses lead up to the connection and the sexes unite quietly and closely. Once the necessary control has been acquired, the two beings are fused and reach sublime spiritual joy. This union can be accompanied by slow controlled motions, so that voluptuous thrills do not overbalance the desire for soft sensations. If there is no wish to procreate, the storm violence of the orgasm will thus be avoided. If love is mutual, and if the 'Carezza' is sufficiently prolonged, it affords complete

satisfaction, without emission or orgasm. After an hour the bodies relax, spiritual delight is increased, and new horizons are revealed with the renewal of strength . . .

It was still important to sleep with as many women as you could, because the woman's yin energy (i.e. vaginal juices), strengthened the man's yang (semen). This meant not only that when you did eventually climax, with your main woman, you would make stronger babies, but also that you would be stronger and would live to a ripe old age, shagging hundreds of thousands of extra women along the way.

Celsus, the Roman physician whom we met previously, held the opposite view about frequency of sex and its effect on the body. 'Sexual intercourse neither should be avidly desired, nor should it be feared very much,' he said. 'Rarely performed, it revives the body. Performed frequently, it weakens.'[7]

Another Chinese technique based on willpower was employed by those who had a beautiful wife but didn't want too many children. Just as young hormone-filled teenagers desperately try to conjure up visions of their grannies or recite football league tables to themselves to try and prevent premature ejaculation, a Ming Dynasty text of 1598 suggested that 'every time [the man with a beautiful wife] copulates with her he should force himself to think of her as ugly and hateful'[8] in order to avoid ejaculation altogether. Which could, of course, be said to defeat the purpose of having a beautiful wife in the first place. So much for Eastern philosophy having all the answers.

Alternatively, according to the Ming text, you could 'Place a small measure of quicksilver into a bowl and to this add 16 fresh tadpoles. Fry the tadpoles until darkened and store carefully. The mixture [is] to be taken by the woman immediately after coition has occurred.' Thus, while avoiding morning sickness, almost certainly guaranteeing for the woman the middle-of-the-night variety.

Even less well known than coitus reservatus is coitus obstructus, which apparently does work and which is still practised by some today, although it is not without danger for the man. The book *The Classic of the Immortals*, which dates from just before the first millennium, describes the process as follows:

When, during the sexual act, the man feels he is about to ejaculate, he must quickly and firmly press with fore and middle finger on the left hand the spot betwen scrotum and anus, simultaneously inhaling deeply and gnashing his teeth scores of times, without holding his breath. Then the semen will be activated but not yet be emitted . . .'

This account goes on to say that the semen goes into the brain instead of the woman. In fact, and incredibly, it goes to the bladder, according to author Shirley Green, 'and passes out quite harmlessly the next time the man urinates'.[9] The same thing can be done in order to delay the man's ejaculation, but it must be done with more care than tooth-gnashing.

Despite the promiscuity of Chinese men (all in the interest of strengthening the sperm, you understand), they were probably not having *all* the fun. The ancient Chinese divination book, *I Ching*, contains a wonderful description of the sexual differences between men and women, comparing them with fire and water respectively. 'Fire easily flares up, but is easily extinguished by water; water takes a long time to heat over the fire, but cools down very slowly.'

Christianity, however, was still far from taking an interest in the finer points of human sexuality; it was far too busy misreading the Bible. The real problem with coitus interruptus was a story in Genesis 38:8–10, that went thus:

And Judah said unto Onan, 'Go in unto thy brother's wife, and marry her, and raise up seed to thy brother.' And Onan knew that the seed should not be his; and it came to pass, when he went in unto his brother's wife, that he spilled it on the ground, lest that he should give seed to his brother. And the thing which he did displeased the Lord: wherefore he slew him also.'

On this basis, what became known as 'onanism' was condemned by Christians for hundreds of years. However, the popular view now is that 'the thing which he did [that] displeased the Lord' was not the spilling of his seed on the ground but his failure to produce heirs for his brother as instructed.

Apart from 'onanism' or 'withdrawal' this method was subsequently given a number of more delicate names which were neither too condemnatory nor too scientific. Keith Hopkins of the London School of Economics discovered the manuscript of one writer in the Place Collection (which, er, places it in the 1800s) in the British Museum, who initialled his work I.C.H. and who wrote of what appears to be coitus interruptus: 'It now remains to suggest a more simple method; it is little known to the English, who are full of the coarsest and most vulgar prejudices on these subjects ... This expedient is sometimes called la Chamade, the Retreat, but most commonly by the softer name of la Prudence, or la Discrétion'.[10] In the Western world in 1375, coitus interruptus was still firmly in the file marked 'naughty', however. *The Book of Vices and Virtues*, published in that year, described it as a sin 'agens kynde and agens the ordre of wedloke'.

So withdrawal was out, officially at any rate. Fortunately there were some fairly wised-up rabbis on hand at an early stage, with suggestions of their own. The sponge makes an early appearance in an ancient rabbinical text, *The Tosephta* (AD 230). Here, three different sorts of women are advised to 'co-habit' with one another to prevent pregnancy. They are the minor (to avoid getting pregnant and dying), the pregnant woman (to avoid getting pregnant again and 'flattening' her existing child) and the nursing mother (to avoid getting pregnant and spoiling her milk).

Extended breastfeeding was certainly practised then too. Although the scholar's line is that it is not clear if they knew that this was having a contraceptive effect, it would surely be difficult to avoid working it out over the hundreds of years that were the Middle Ages. Couples often abstained from sex while breastfeeding anyway, or rather the woman did and the man did not have sex with his wife.

An alternative which was as obvious to the medieval mind as it is extraordinary to ours, was to use parts of sterile animals to produce sterility in themselves. Somehow, they thought, the sterility would sort of 'rub off' on them. According to an unknown writer, 'it has been proved' that conception will not occur for a month if a woman puts the hoof of a mule on burning coals and allows the smoke to enter her vulva.

It will, he claimed, also stop her from menstruating. By the (clearly more coy) eighteenth century it was believed that all you needed to do was drape mule hide over the marital bed. Sanitation was also big news by this time, and this approach seemed altogether more hygienic.

Back in the Middle-Aged old days, contraception/abortion was a Bad Thing. Nevertheless, ingesting food or drink that supposedly calmed folks' libido was a Good Thing. Willow was thought to be one of these drugs and beans were supposed to cause barrenness. In 1933 a man who went by the magnificent name of Boleslaw Skarzynski told the Polish Academy of Sciences that willow contained a substance called trihydroxyoestrin which resembled a female hormone. Tests in 1974 and 1985 showed that this substance affects both ovulation and implantation of the fertilised egg on to the side of the womb. So, whether he knew it or not, the unknown writer was not just telling people how to be less lusty.

To start with, Christians, like the Greeks and Romans, made no real distinction between birth control and abortion. For men and women of the time this attitude was probably both formed and reinforced by the fact that the potions used as contraceptives were also employed to bring on abortion. The one dissenting voice was that of Avicenna, the Arabic writer who thought that contraception and abortion were very different things and whose *Canon of Medicine*, written in the eleventh century, was to become one of the most important medical texts in the West.

The Canon suggests a range of contraceptives, many of them plants. Cedar is both contraceptive and abortifacient, because it 'corrupts the seed, and when the penis is oiled by it before coitus it prevents impregnation' but it also 'kills the fetus'.[11] For mint a little more forethought is required: it must be 'placed as a suppository before the hour of coitus' to prevent conception. Again, recent experiments have shown that members of the mint family do actually reduce implantation of the fertilised egg within the womb.[12] Perhaps this is how the rumours started in the 1980s that a very well known brand of peppermint, if eaten too much, would cause sterility. Perhaps it was true.

Less effective was hanging something around one's neck for the same purpose, in this case something called sowbread. Alternatively, the rennet of the wood-hare could be drunk three days after menstruation to prohibit impregnation. Some methods he describes in more sceptical tones. One of these is the menstrual blood suppository, which 'according to what some think', says Avicenna, works as a contraceptive.

Many other methods suggested by Avicenna were variations on the themes of Hippocrates, Soranus, Dioscorides and Aristotle. However, the idea of using suppositories of elephant dung after coitus is all his own. He also has an array of original methods for dampening down ardour and 'diminishing the seed', including the use of melons with lead, 'and henbane placed on the testicles and anus'. The chaste tree seems to have the whole thing sewn up. According to Avicenna, not only does it dry up seed, but it prevents pollution and impedes erection, and in women it takes away desire. He may well have got the idea from the ancients (Galen among others mentioned it), since a bough of the chaste tree was used by women as a part of ancient Greek festivals,[13] like a bizarre great badge saying 'Hooray, rave on. Look, this badge stops me enjoying sex!' More recently, in 1989, a study claimed that it disrupts sperm production in dogs, so it may well have been effective when used on people.

Early Hebrews had a different approach. It seems that men would have two wives then, one to be attractive and one to bear children[14] (nice work if you can get it, and you're a man . . .). The attractive one would drink the 'cup of roots', which sterilised her and meant there were not too many children about. By the time the Jews got hold of it, however, the system had started to break down. Sometimes, though, the wrong wife would get hold of the cup of roots, as Rabbi Hiyya found in AD 200 to his disappointment: 'I wish you had given me one birth more,' he said to the wife that had tired of being the ugly childbearing one. But it was too late.

Albertus Magnus or Albert the Great (1200–80) was known as the 'universal doctor' and was responsible for introducing the medieval world to Greek and Arabic science. His suggestion for taking away desire was to burn the penis, eyelids and beard of a wolf 'and then make the woman drink the results without her knowing anything about it'. Either that or use a red bull – not the canned energy-giving drink, you understand, but the animal. Again it was the animal's penis he was interested in, served up as part of a stew. But why all the secrecy, or indeed the actual consumption? Why not just tell the woman what you were trying to get her to ingest? That would be enough to put her off sex for life, surely. For the majority of people, the same could be said of Albert's 'drink a man's urine' theory.

According to Augustine, prostitutes were still 'taking steps' as they always had done (in Japan and China using Misugami or discs of oiled paper made from bamboo tissue as a barrier method), but now *any* wife who used contraceptive practices automatically made herself into a harlot and any man who did so became an adulterer. With his wife. A whole new spirit of conspiracy seemed to creep into – in particular Christian – men's judgements about women and their birth control methods during this time. Even the language changed. Among others, John Chrysostom mentions 'plottings without number, and invocations of devils, and necromanciers', and Clement of Alexandria refers to women who 'keep up old wives' whisperings, learning charms and incantations from soothsayers'.[15] Guibert of Nojent (1053–1124) in his *Memoirs* lays the blame for unconsummated marriages squarely at the door of the sterilising spell. It does not take a huge leap of imagination to realise that women who knew about contraception and abortion during this time would often be branded witches and, for some, their knowledge would be the death of them. Only the French gave the midwife the respect she deserved, calling her 'sage-femme' or 'wise woman'.

Prostitutes were, for the elite, a part of life, and brothels were seen as supportive of the institution of marriage and a way of preventing adultery, homosexuality and unwanted pregnancies, at least of the official kind. After all, the thinking went, a man needs an outlet for his libido. The same defence of prostitution is still used by some today. Prostitutes had few children, a fact which some put down to sexual excess. William of Clonches was one of these. He claimed that prostitutes 'have their wombs clogged with dirt', and 'the villosities in which the semen should be retained are covered over'.[16] Others said that prostitutes, in Venice at any rate, used herbal potions.

According to *Montaillou: The Portrait of Life in a Medieval Village* by Emmanuel Le Roy Ladurie,[17] prostitutes were not much found in villages, but tended to be something you combined with visiting the town, perhaps on market day. One of the characters in the book, Pierre Vidal, has a particularly interesting pick 'n' mix morality when it comes to sex. For him sex remains 'innocent' if it involves the man paying the woman and both parties are 'pleased'. He seems to be happy to share these views with anyone who'll listen, including priests.

Holy men were not, incidentally, being any more holy two hundred years later. Thomas Sanchez (1550–1610), man of the cloth and author of *De Sancto Matrimonio*, had a theory that 'if, when engaged in sex with a whore, a man withdraws before ejaculation, he is considered to have repented and not sinned against God's laws . . .'.[18]

If Ladurie is to be believed, priests were about the most consistently lusty sector of the community in medieval times. And the priest who spread the wildest oats widest and with the least discrimination was Pierre Clergue. Early on in his love life he was admired for his sensitivity towards women and was described as gentle, kind and 'comparatively cultivated'. As he grew older, and perhaps less attractive, however, he would get people into bed by mentioning his influence with the feared Inquisition (who made attacks on the area, sometimes taking prisoners).

Many of his lovers nevertheless spoke of him with fondness. One was Grazides Rives, whose mother, Fabrisse, had been another lover of Clergue's and had effectively offered the virginity of her daughter to the priest. Grazides was willing. It seemed rude not to. The seduction scene that late summer's day in 1313 went as follows:

Clergue: 'Allow me to know you carnally.'
Grazides: 'All right.'

Soon Grazides had a husband, Pierre Lizier, who sometimes asked whether the priest had 'done it' with her, to which she replied with characteristic directness, 'Yes'. Lizier maintained that as long as it was only with the priest that was acceptable. Although Grazides at least showed some consideration for God, her justification for sleeping with the priest was not on the grounds that he was a priest. She said: 'With Pierre Clergue, I liked it. And so it could not displease God. It was not a sin.' Similarly, when she and the priest stopped fancying each other, after about seven years, she told her friend Jacques (the only man in the region, you'll note, not called Pierre) that any carnal act with Clergue would be committed coldly and would, therefore, be a sin.

Like Pierre Vidal's, Clergue's morality was elastic to say the least. When questioned on the morality of sleeping with a (different) married woman, he maintained that since everything was a sin, no one act was any worse than another.

Clergue, unsurprisingly, also had the contraception issue sussed. When asked by yet another new lover, Béatrice de Planissoles, what she should do if she became pregnant by him, he said: 'I have a certain herb.' This turned out to be wrapped in a piece of linen and hung around her neck whilst they made love. It hung between her breasts 'as far as the opening of my stomach'. This last makes it sound like a sort of pessary, but Albert the Great gave a contraceptive recipe (consisting of honey and ass's milk) which he said was to be worn around the neck and over the navel. Perhaps the opening of the stomach was in fact the belly button and this was simply a magic amulet of some kind.

Either way it was effective enough to cause rows. Béatrice once pleaded with Clergue to leave the herb. Clergue refused, saying, probably quite rightly, that she would use it to prevent getting pregnant by other men. Béatrice thought he was just jealous because she had slept with his cousin before Clergue was on the scene. Not an early advocate of the women's liberation movement, Clergue thought that this birth control method should tie this woman (and others) to him. History does not relate whether or not he had different herb devices for different women. One would hope so, since it is not nice to think of the same old piece of linen and herb hanging around the openings of most of the female population of the Montaillou region.

On the subject of hygiene, everyone had lice in the Middle Ages. Delousing was such a frequent ritual that it became a kind of bonding time in its own right, much as it still is with chimpanzees. The thumb was known as the 'lice killer' ('tue-poux' in French) and only women did the killing. Pierre Clergue was deloused by several of his mistresses, including Béatrice and Raymonde Guilhou. When women deloused each other they gossiped. When men were deloused by women they would give their delouser the benefit of their views on subjects from politics to contraception. This was, you understand, pre-football.

Chaucer mentions a woman 'drynkynge venenouse herbes thrugh which she may nat concevve', and those two other themes common to Montaillou – lusty young wives and cuckolded husbands. He also refers to the old favourite 'unnatural intercourse' (or anal sex). The other option was, as far as he was concerned, putting 'certeine material thynges in hire secree places to slee the child'. If only he had been more specific about the nature of those thynges.

Perhaps because the idea of the family unit was stronger than in Greek and Roman times, despite the attitudes of all these Pierres, not so many were glad to be gay. Or if they were they were not, on the whole, singing about it. In Montaillou and the surrounding area it was seen as something done by the sons of good families who went to towns (homosexuality was almost unheard of in villages), to attend 'the schools'. Here, priests would initiate boys into what was known as 'homophilia'.

One of these was Arnaud de Verniolles of Pamier, who had, in turn, been initiated, reluctantly at first, by fellow student and future priest Arnaud Auriol. He was between ten and twelve at the time. He later tried to like women by having sex with a prostitute, but his face swelled up and he was put off once and for all. It is interesting to note that smart boys' private schools with a religious tradition still have a reputation for being hotbeds of homosexuality today.

'Going Greek' was not seen as a population control measure in the Middle Ages, and you could get into big trouble with the church for anal sex. In the fourteenth century, the reaction of archbishop and theologian Peter Palude to a woman who asked him what to do about her husband's desire for anal intercourse was 'to let herself be killed, or let her husband commit adultery, or shame himself with a mule'[19] rather than agree to it. It's a shame for the man that they were not around to buy *De Sancto Matrimonio*. Its author, Thomas Sanchez, a moral theologian, thought that it was 'permissible under God's law to commence love-making with anal entry provided that the act is concluded with vaginal sex'.[20]

Another angle, if you will, on contraception was that particular sexual positions could aid or frustrate conception, an idea the Romans too held. Albertus Magnus maintained that conception could be prevented if the woman was on top during the act or urinated immediately after intercourse. She should *not* jump backwards, though, said Edward II's doctor, because God did not approve of coitus interruptus.[21] Despite this, Yves of Chartres thought that coitus interruptus was okay when, say, you'd had sex with your bride's mother, since it was only really sex if sperm had mingled.[22] Oh, and according to Giovanni Sinibaldi in 1642, 'a sad or weeping woman cannot conceive'.[23] Sinibaldi was obviously the type to capitalise on his reputation of being a 'shoulder to cry on'.

Particular rules were made about the positions in which one might have sex while wearing the 'chemise cagoule' in the Middle Ages. Since the book seems convinced of its existence, it's over to *The Encyclopedia of Unusual Sexual Practices*[24] for more details:

> A chemise cagoule was a heavy nightshirt used by Catholic men during the Middle Ages. It ensured that they would not derive any unnecessary tactile pleasure while impregnating their wife [sic]. The chemise had a hole cut in the front to allow the erect penis access to the vagina.

And finally, the chastity belt, that bizarre contraption that will forever be associated with the Middle Ages. This is a device, according – again – to the *The Encyclopedia of Unusual Sexual Practices*, 'similar to a jock strap that is worn around the waist to prevent a person from having intercourse'. That person may be male or female and the intercourse prevented may, according to the belt, be vaginal or anal or both.

The first mention of anything resembling a chastity belt in history is found in Homer's *Odyssey*, where Hephaestus constructs a device made out of chains to stop the affair between his wife Aphrodite and his brother, although according to some translations this was more like a net which trapped the two of them when they were about to make love.

In medieval times, according to popular myth, we are told that knights fitted them on their ladies when they went off on Crusades. The Crusades began in 1095 and ended somewhere between 1270 and 1798, the exact date depending on which historian you choose to believe. How widespread this practice actually was is the subject of some controversy. For one thing, as anyone who has ever worn a chastity belt could tell you (and a quick surf of the internet confirms that many will), they are difficult to disguise. They were also very heavy and uncomfortable in those days, which would make even everyday functioning very difficult. Perhaps, one might think, the average man did not care too much about the comfort of his woman, but he might care if it was discovered by others that he thought she was likely to be unfaithful. It didn't make her look like a very good bet as a wife or make him look like a man worth waiting for, or respecting.

Most stories involving chastity belts are about jealous old men with lusty young wives, like the miller in Chaucer's 'Miller's Tale', and his young wife. This could not get much further from the stereotype of the dashing knight. Presumably the dashing knight himself would like to have kept his distance from the stereotype too. Poor women, if they did all wear chastity belts. Of the hundreds of thousands of men who went off on Crusades, a combination of war and the plague saw to it that only a fraction returned. Locksmiths, presumably, turned a profit which allowed them to move to the medieval equivalent of the Bahamas, probably Salisbury or somewhere.

Having said that, we do know that belts were owned by noblemen, including Francesco II di Carrara, for use on his wife; Henry II for use on his wife, Caterina de Medici; and Luis XIII for use on his wife, Anne.

That is not to say that the chastity belt has gone away. In the nineteenth century, 'day belts' were fitted on to young unchaperoned girls by their mothers, to ensure that nothing untoward happened while their heads were turned. A husband might also use one on his wife when she was travelling through dangerous lands, or when soldiers were expected to invade their (geographical) area.

There were also chastity belts for men made around that time. One of these, according to De'ath in *French Letters and English Overcoats*, was patented by Michael McCormick of San Francisco in 1897. Then, according to De'ath, San Francisco was still a part of the Wild West, where 'men were men and women . . . were in short supply'. McCormick's device was designed to stop cowboys masturbating, having wet dreams and 'to control waking thoughts'. It worked using 'pricking points' which caused the wearer pain 'when from any cause, expansion of the organ begins'. This obviously puts John Wayne's lopsided gait into a whole new light. The explanation continues as follows:

> If the person be asleep or otherwise inattentive, he will be awakened or recalled to his senses in time to prevent further expansion. If he be asleep, an involuntary emission will be prevented by his awakening; or, if conscious, to divert his thoughts from lascivious channels. Voluntary self-abuse will be checked as the wearer will not take the trouble to relieve himself of the appliance and cannot continue his practice without removing it. An irresponsible wearer may have it permanently attached.[25]

By 1910 Dr R. F. Sturgis, who was worried enough about masturbation to write a whole book on it, called *Treatment of Masturbation*, was providing further advice to the chastity belt wearer who was having problems during the night:

> If the penis erects while the wearer is asleep and he is awakened by the jab of metal on flesh, he should first remove the device. Next, soak the organ in cold water until it has subsided, and once again affix the apparatus to the genitals. The wearer can then return to his innocent sleep, assured that a moral as well as a material victory has been gained![26]

If this seems extreme, according to a news report from Associated Press as recently as 1999, 'Safety Underwear' was available in Bangkok, Thailand for US$40 a throw. This anti-rape device consisted of leather pants hiding a thin layer of steel, which is fixed by a three digit combination lock. According to the manufacturer, without the magic number you would need a hacksaw to get through them.

There are a weird or wonderful (depending on your outlook) variety of chastity belts available on the internet at the time of writing – far too many to list. These are for use as part of sex play. Suffice it to say that a stainless steel belt will set you back somewhere between US$300 and $600, depending on the make. Be patient, though; not only will you need it once you've got the belt, but it often takes weeks if not months for the thing to arrive.

3

The Condom Conundrum

There is only one way to achieve happiness on this terrestrial ball,
And that is to have either a clear conscience, or none at all.

Ogden Nash[1]

After the ribaldry (that's the other word apart from 'bawdy' that's always used to describe the Middle Ages – the *Collins Dictionary* describes bawdy as 'vulgar indecent talk' and ribald as 'irreverent, scurrilous') came a strange in-between time, at least in the Western world. Typically marriage had been the ideal, but women had been seen more or less as skivvies rather than partners. Now, in the 1500s, women (at least married women) were not all quite so badly treated. The offspring of those who were married were not so brutally treated as they had been either. After all, Michelangelo (1475–1564) was starting to work his creative magic in Italy, and Galileo (1564–1642) was about to do the same in the fields of astronomy and physics. The West was starting to be cultivated. Marriage was not yet seen as the team effort that it was to become from the late eighteenth century, though, as a result of new-found Protestant values.

The having of children was still the objective of marriage, and there was still a great deal of emphasis on getting the sex of your child right. If you were a young woman who wanted to choose the sex of your child, you took the advice of a little poem given to you on your wedding day by your mother:

A boy you wish? A Beauteous boy behold,
With lips a cherry red, and locks of gold;
Like him for whom Alexis sighed of old.
If female fruit you rather covet, view
A heavenly venus such as Titian drew.

Gabriel Fallopio, the man after whom the 'fallopian tubes' were named, had further advice for those who gave birth to sons about how to make their son's member big enough; along with dealing with the syphilis epidemic, he saw this as a priority. 'I urge you to take every pain in infancy to enlarge the privy member of boys by massaging, and the application of stimulants,' he said in his book *De Decoratione*. 'Since a well-grown specimen never comes amiss . . .'[2] So even then, long before there were car adverts featuring slinky women with French accents saying 'size matters', there was a perceived pressure on men to be well endowed. And what's the betting the creator of the advertisement was a man, like Gabriel Fallopio, in just the same way that it was a woman (the wife of a picture editor) that spotted the cellulite on a paparazzi photograph of Princess Diana at her health club. You can't help thinking that if everyone just calmed down a bit, there would be a lot less paranoia in the world.

Only two per cent of children were born out of wedlock, which is a fairly small proportion. In the UK in 1999 the figure was just under 39 per cent. A quarter of weddings were 'shotgun weddings',[3] which is to say that the woman was already pregnant when the ceremony took place. If you wanted to be sure that your wife-to-be was a virgin you could do the famous 'Bee Test' which first appeared in *Libellus de Mirabilibus Naturae Aracanis* by Albertus Parvellus:

It is a well-known fact that even the most irritable of bees become gentle when they are approached by a pure virgin and will not sting her. But should she go near a hive immediately after the loss of her innocence, then she will be attacked at once and her secret revealed for all to see. The reason for this remarkable proof is that bees are of but one sex and they abhor all lewdness and libertinism . . .[4]

These men must have just sat in their studies and thought these things up. Or perhaps they sat in their taverns, serving wench on knee, brainstorming with their mates. "Ere, I've got a good one. Why don't you put it about that if you're a girl and you don't stay a virgin before you get married bees will sting you?' 'Yeah, good one, mate, I like it.' There was also a medieval theory that getting your woman to eat some bees after sex would stave off pregnancy.

On the subject of wives, and for that matter on the subject of conforming to a physical ideal like Fallopio's, social historians are always telling us that the admired body shape of women has changed throughout history from large, to hourglass shaped, to waif-like and back to hourglass again. Yet in *Aristotle's Masterpiece*, a work which originated, it is thought, in the Middle Ages but was still being read right up until the nineteenth century, it says, spookily:

> It is advisable that a man look carefully at a prospective wife for signs of infertility. Remember that little women are more likely to conceive than gross women, slender more than fat, and a woman with swelling breasts much more so than a woman who is flat-chested.[5]

In 1624 an English law was put in place which meant that if a child died either in the womb or at birth, the mother would have to prove that it was of natural causes. In those 'eye for an eye' witch-hunting times, the penalty was execution, and the result was, initially, an awful lot of executions. Actually the craze for witch-hunting had taken off in a big way from about 1500 and it had taken off throughout Europe, probably not helped by the fact that, by then, 20 per cent of women stayed single for life. According to author John Riddle, one man announced that 1,800,000 witches threatened Europe, and according to existing records in Switzerland and south-west Germany, around 80 per cent of those burned were women. Of course the Catholics blamed the Protestants for witches and the Protestants the Catholics, although the Catholics, never doing things by halves, burned twice as many witches as did the Protestants. An interesting slant that some have put on all this picking on witches is that the clergy, in particular, did it out of sexual frustration, but that's another story, told by Silvia Bovenschen.[6]

For the occasional satirical writer, François Rabelais for one, this extraordinary fear of women and their wombs (which still wandered, according to many) was worthy of only one thing – ridicule:

> Nature hath posited a privy, secret place of their bodies, a sort of member (by some not impertinently termed an animal) which is not to be found in men. Therein sometimes are engendered certain humours so saltish, brackish, clammy, sharp, nipping, tearing, prickling and most eagerly tickling, that by their stinging acrimony, rending nitrosity, figging itch, wriggling mordicancy and smarting salsitude (for the said member is of a most quick and lively feeling), their whole body is shaken and ebrangled [?], their senses totally ravished and transported, the operations of their judgement and understanding utterly confounded, and all disordinate passions and perturbations of the mind thoroughly and absolutely allowed, admitted and approved of, because this terrible animal is knit into, and hath union with, all the chief and most principal parts of the body . . .[7]

By the 1800s the number of abortions and subsequent hangings was starting to go down. Between the sixteenth and eighteenth centuries the average age at which people married increased by several years. Male English peers could expect to be married at around thirty, women at twenty-three. In the rest of northern Europe, women would be twenty-five or twenty-six.[8]

The church still played a role but loosened its rein slightly. Catholicism no longer enjoyed the power it once had, and found itself having to be a little more 'market orientated' and sympathetic. There had been huge epidemics in Europe in the 1300s, but now the population had recovered and was booming a little too much, which gave the church another reason to be more sympathetic to those families that wanted to control their numbers. Confessors, although not exactly throwing key parties, were not so quick to condemn a married couple who had sex during the woman's period or before communion.[9] But having sex for fun was still viewed with suspicion, and contraception was still unacceptable to the church.

The entrance of science did not at first make things clearer. While men of science like Leeuwenhoek and Stensen (in 1667–8) started using words like 'spermatozoa' and 'ovaries', it didn't mean much to the man and woman on the street. Actually the concept of sperm didn't mean much to Leeuwenhoek, until his student told him about it and he decided to pass the idea off as his own.[10] The microscope under which sperm were first seen in 1674? That *was* his idea. Less helpfully, scientists were discovering (or substantiating their own prejudices, depending on your way of seeing) that women did not need an orgasm to conceive and were concluding that the woman could – and with time that came to mean 'should' – remain passive in sex. Out, for scientists, went the medieval idea of women as lusty equals in sexual congress, and in came a limited and boring role for women. This was not a world of which Chaucer's Wife of Bath would have wanted to be a part at all.

William Harvey, another biologist, did some useful work, establishing that the female egg was central to the process of reproduction,[11] he was the first to challenge Aristotle by not contriving a theory which left the woman as a kind of carrier bag for the creativity of men. Before that, scientists like Jacob Ryff and Thomas Fienus had been putting forward theories which involved semen and menstrual blood, but nobody really listened to them. In fact the hoi polloi didn't really listen to any of the scientists at all, remaining blissful in one of those ignorances that turns out to be a kind of intelligence.

Intelligence – kind of. They were still reading the text called *Aristotle's Masterpiece*, the precise origins of which are not known. All that is known is that it was nothing to do with Aristotle and that the first reported edition was in Latin. As to whether it was a masterpiece, its test for conception is as follows:

If the urine of the woman be put in a glass three days and she has conceived, certain live things will appear to stir in it.

If a bright needle be put in a whole night and she has conceived, divers little red Specks will be thereon, but if not it will be blackish or rusty.[12]

The woman had not only to concentrate after the event but, if she didn't want to give birth to a monster, during the act. Special attention was needed if she was an adulteress:

> If women allow their fancies to drift during coition, they may produce a deformity or even a hybrid man-beast.
>
> And, if in the act of copulation, the woman earnestly looks on the man, and fixes her mind on him, the child will resemble his father. Nay, if a woman, even in unlawful copulation, fix her mind upon her husband, the child will resemble him though he did not beget it.

This was precisely what the Roman soldier Albius Tibullus had said about women and masturbation back in the first century AD. It's okay to do it as long as you think of your husband, or rather 'they may excite the process manually, provided that they refer the act to the absent husband'. Of course, it was not at all okay for anyone to masturbate now under any circumstances, one and a half thousand years later.

Doctors could shed no light, because they were essentially still practising from the Hippocratic texts. Medicine had not advanced. Within a discussion on contraception in the Roman Empire, where he is looking at the way the Romans probably confused abortion and contraception, academic Keith Hopkins notes that, 'the same confusion has been found in Japan and India recently, in English professional medical writings at the end of the 19th century and in French literary writings of the 16th and 17th centuries'.[13] Soranus knew the difference, several hundred years BC, but the lofty English medics of the 1800s did not.

If the experience of Dr Olivier of Saint-Tropez is anything to go by, French doctors were still not particularly clued up in 1760 either. A patient came to him who had been carrying a baby for six months. She said she could no longer feel it moving. He observed that the baby was dead, but he did not know what to do. Shrugging, doubtless, he consulted Aetius – or rather his texts, since he had been dead for 2,325 years – who advised using a fern. This he gave the woman, and she aborted the same day, recovering from the ordeal quickly. In his book on herbal methods of birth control throughout history, *Eve's Herbs*, John Riddle says that the fern which Olivier thought he had redis-covered was in use in German folk medicine until the beginning of the twentieth century. One doctor, Aigremont, who observed its use in 1908, described it as a witch's drug and a prostitute's drug.

When the printing press was invented, in 1450, it became easier for druggists and pharmacists to circulate information, whether it be accurate or inaccurate, about such things as herbal potions and lotions that allegedly prevented conception or induced miscarriage. Of course an array of euphemisms were used to gloss over the fact of the last, because the climate was hostile to it. Marketing-savvy distributors would call them 'menstrual promoters' or plants to 'cure women's obstructions'. Oxford graduate John Peachey wrote a 'Herbal' in 1694, and listed in it a number of herbs which could be used for these purposes. According to Riddle, 'native plants that "provoke the courses" were calamint, cypress, agrimony, horehound, juniper, parsley, pennyroyal, rue and sage'.

Obviously Britain did not see all the action. Riddle cites two examples from Cologne. In the first part of the seventeenth century, legal records show that a woman described as having an 'unchaste lifestyle' was given savin (juniper) to terminate her pregnancy. Also in Cologne, in 1624, a pregnant woman was told by her friend to go to an apothecary for a drug, but not to be direct in her request for an abortive because some apothecaries would not sell them.[14]

By the 1700s, people had been stung by quacks and were ceasing to believe that any such methods worked. In fact the use of herbs, though still a part of birth control, had been on the decline since the Middle Ages. Even without the complication of cowboys on the make there was confusion. If even legendary herbalist Nicholas Culpeper – who translated the *London Dispensary* from the Latin and corrected it where necessary – was inconsistent, who could be believed? Riddle points out that he advised that the aromatic herb tansy was both an aid to pregnancy and a menstrual stimulator. Perhaps apothecaries were less willing to stock these drugs by now. After all, once the 1624 law was brought in they risked being accessories to murder.

Something was going on in France, though. They were making real progress. And they didn't care who knew it. Their magazines had been carrying advertisements for restoratives of the menstrual cycle all this time. Although herbs cannot be held fully responsible, between 1750 and 1800 the birth rate in France had dropped substantially – a hundred years before the rest of Europe – and continued to decline until well into the nineteenth century. Although a birth rate drop can occur for a number of reasons – in the nineteenth century the Crimean War would have had quite an effect – the general consensus is that the French were using contraception. The author of 1778's *Recherches et considerations sur la population de la France* was a part of this consensus:

> Rich women, for whom pleasure is the chief interest and sole occupation, are not the only ones who regard the propagation of the species as a deception of bygone times; already these pernicious secrets, unknown to all animals save man, have found their way into the countryside; they are cheating nature even in the villages. If these licentious practices, these homicidal tastes, continue to spread, they will be no less deadly to the State than the plagues which used to ravage it; it is time to halt this secret and terrible cause of the depopulation which is imperceptibly undermining the nation . . .'

Stop the French having sex? Was the man serious? The French were also in the process of rejecting religion at the time, and while they were at it, they thought they would reject any other lofty concepts which reckoned on governing their lives. 'If the church was a lie,' suggests expert John Noonan, 'then it was each man for himself.'[15] He has an answer as to why, in that case, Italy's birth rate did not drop at the same time. The Italians knew it all already. And Italy was closer to the church, literally, which made that church more difficult to ignore. This makes it ironic, if not surprising, that town councils in that country encouraged prostitution in order to attract the attention of young men, especially foreign ones, away from their single women.

As the faith of the French decreased, the number of Gauloises-fuelled café-conversations about coitus interruptus began to increase. According to the writer Brantôme, mistresses would make their lovers swear not to 'sprinkle a thing inside, not a single drop'.[16] As is the case throughout history, from ancient Egyptian times until now, we will probably never know the extent to which the married used coitus interruptus. Nor will we know who was the instigator, or withdrawer, during the act. Some commentators of the time implied it was the woman, women being more interested in 'forbidden positions' than men, and others that it was the man, who was worried about protecting his wife and his wallet – in that order, we are assured.

What we do know is that sponges and tampons had been used consistently since the Middle Ages, because Chaucer mentions both and sponges are clearly referred to by many, including the Marquis de Sade. Both sponges and tampons came to be associated with extramarital affairs, but, since Jeremy Bentham recommends them in 'Situation and Relief of the Poor' in the 1800s, it looks as if they were being more generally accepted by then. Another fan of the sponge, and a friend of Bentham's, Francis Place, described the sponge as 'large as a green walnut, or small apple', and assured the readers of the handbills which he distributed that it would not 'diminish the enjoyment of either party' and should be used 'rather damp, and when convenient a little warm'.

The sponge has not, however, found fans wherever it goes. Much more recently, in the 1950s, Dr Yoshia Koya did some research into contraception in three sorts of Japanese community (fishermen, rice-growers and mountain farmers) in response to the baby boom. He took with him diaphragms and jelly, condoms, foam tablets, information about the rhythm method and a sponge containing salt solution. Although the trial itself was successful, the sponge idea was not. Only 22 per cent of the people involved tried it and almost all of those gave it up after a short time.[17] In its defence, these people were probably more turned off by the salt than the sponge.

The sponge would often be accompanied by douching. As well as inventing the word, the French, perhaps taking sex more seriously than other nations, had the perfect apparatus for it, the bidet. To this day it has never really caught on in any other country. Before that, in around 1600, no French prostitute's kit was complete without at least one syringe for the purpose of douching. Perhaps a hundred years after that, the syringe made its way over to the UK, and after yet another hundred years the method was cropping up in the US. Charles Knowlton, author of the US publication *Fruits of Philosophy*, appeared to think he had invented the device. 'Any publication, great or small, mentioning the syringe ...whatever liquid may be recommended – is a violation of my copyright,' he said.

While bashing the poor for producing too many children and for, well, being poor, was yet to reach its nineteenth/early twentieth-century climax, satirist Jonathan Swift was sufficiently worried about it in 1729 to produce a savage essay called 'A Modest Proposal: For Preventing the Children of Poor People from Being a Burden to their Parents'. Here is some of it:

> It is true a child *just dropped from its dam* may be supported by her milk for a solar year with little other nourishment, at most not above the value of two shillings, which the mother may certainly get, or the value in scraps, by her lawful occupation of *begging*. And it is at exactly one year old that I propose to provide for them in such a manner as, instead of being a charge upon their *parents*, or the *parish*, or *wanting food and raiment* for the rest of their lives they shall, on the contrary, contribute to the feeding and partly to the clothing of many thousands.

The solution was as follows:

> I have been assured by a very knowing American of my acquaintance in London, that a young healthy child, well nursed, is at a year old a most delicious, nourishing, and wholesome food, whether *stewed*, *roasted*, *baked* or *boiled*, and I make no doubt that it will equally serve in a *fricassée*, or a *ragoût*.

He goes on to estimate that around a hundred thousand a year could be sold for consumption, 'always advising the mother to let them suck plentifully of the last month, so as to render them plump and fat for a good table'. 'A child will make two dishes at an entertainment for friends,' he continues, 'and when the family dines alone the fore or hindquarter will make a reasonable dish, and seasoned with a little pepper or salt will be very good boiled on the fourth day, especially in winter.' He keeps a special 'dig' for landlords: 'I grant this food will be somewhat dear, and therefore very *proper for landlords*, who, as they have already devoured most of the parents, seem to have the best title to the children.' Also 'those who are more thrifty may flay the carcass; the skin of which, artificially dressed, will make admirable *gloves for ladies* and *summer boots for fine gentlemen*'.

He signs off with another dig, this time at the high-minded social commentators who neither know nor really care of which they speak, but feel the need to speak in any case:

> I profess in the sincerity of my heart that I have not the least personal interest in endeavouring to promote this necessary work, having no other motive than the *public good of my country, by advancing our trade, providing for infants, relieving the poor, and giving some pleasure to the rich*. I have no children, by which I can propose to get a single penny; the youngest being nine years old, and my wife being past child-bearing.

We've all known the type he is mocking.

Sheaths had been around since thousands of years BC, but it was not until the sixteenth and seventeenth centuries that people started writing about them. In 1564, Gabriel Fallopio, the tubes bloke, was waging war against syphilis, which, in true playground-bickering tradition, the English called the French disease and the French the English disease ('He started it,' 'No, he started it'). His account is as follows:

> As often as a man has intercourse, he should (if possible) wash the genitals, or wipe them with a cloth; afterwards he should use

a small linen cloth made to fit the glans, and draw forward the prepuce over the glans; if he can do so, it is as well to moisten it with saliva or with a lotion; however, it does not matter. If you fear lest carries [syphilis] be produced in the canal, take the sheath of this linen cloth and place it in the canal; I tried the experiment on eleven hundred men, and I call immortal God to witness that not one of them was infected.

In fact, around a hundred years after this, Royalist officers fighting in the English Civil War had used sheaths too, probably to guard against disease rather than to prevent conception. We know about this because, in 1986, the remains of some examples of them made out of animal gut were found in what was effectively the toilet of Dudley Castle in the West Midlands.[18]

So far so successful. But there was a problem. Contrary to the letter of well-known eighteenth-century rake Lord Hervey to his friend Henry Fox which accompanied a (then standard) pack of twelve, calling the things 'preservatives from Claps and impediments to procreation'[19] was not a serious option. It was never going to catch on. A man might well be in a hurry when, say, fitting in a trip to Piccadilly (central London's red light district before – and beside – Soho) between business meetings. Anyway, prostitutes didn't know what words like 'impediments' and 'procreation' meant. It was clearly time to give the things a name.

Opinions on how the name 'condom' came about are divided. Some claim that he was a person, some that it was named after the town in France of the same name. Others maintain that the name is simply from the Latin 'condus', meaning 'receptacle', or 'condere', meaning 'to hide'. Yet others say that Dr Condom/Conton/Colkborn was a physician in the court of Charles II in the seventeenth century. Before this time, contraception had witnessed a recurring 'small loosely woven cloth as deterrent for millions of impossibly small and determined cells' theme. The defenders of the royal doctor theory go on to say that he discovered the contraceptive properties of sheep gut, and introduced the King to them in order to protect him against the many claims of his illegitimate children. The story goes that Charles was so delighted that he knighted the doctor, who went on to change his name because he had become associated with such a scandalous device. It has, however, been pointed out that the Charles II/Dr Condom/ton etc. theory is, at best, sketchy, since the illegitimate offspring already existed and the laws of succession were so strict that such claims would be fruitless. Also, if this version of events is true, it is probably the 'introduced the King to them' part that is most significant. After all, Gabriel and the Royalist soldiers had known about sheaths long before, so if he existed, Condom/ton was just one of those people in the right place at the right time.

Yet another suggestion is that he might have been a colonel during Charles's reign who was written about in an anonymous poem called *The Machine: or, Love's Preservative* in 1744.[20] One Rev. White Kennet also wrote of this perhaps fictitious man in 1723, heaping his praise on the sheath for protecting men from VD – known by some as 'Venus fire' – rather than pregnancy. Thus a man could now wage 'am'rous Fight', and be 'Fearless, secure; nor Thought of future Pains/Resembling Pricks of Pin and Needle's Point', although Kennet had previously praised the condom for protecting women from 'big Belly, and the squawling Brat'.

Whoever he was, despite being 'observ'd by the Surgeons with much envy; for he has invented an Engine for the Prevention of Harms by Love Adventures', according to *Tatler* magazine in 1709, it was still 'an Immodesty to name his name'. So the true origins of the device may well be flushed down the toilet of history for good.

Meanwhile in early eighteenth-century England, condoms found many fans, including pornographer John Marten and poet Joseph Gay.[21] In France the Marquis de Sade claimed to know of three forms of contraception: 'the sheath, the sponge and anal intercourse'.[22] He preferred the third, describing it as 'la plus délicieuse sans doute'.

Casanova, soldier-adventurer and bedhopper's bedhopper, was ambivalent about the sheath. In the middle of the eighteenth century he said, a little cryptically, 'I will never do myself up in dead animal skin to prove that I'm alive.' By 1758, several years and doubtless more than a couple of sexual conquests later, he had changed his mind about what he called the 'Redingote Anglaise', or English Riding

Coat: 'Ten years ago I would have called this an invention of the devil,' he said. 'But now I believe that its inventor must have been a good man.'[23]

It is difficult to understand the appeal of a man who was not only capable of such extreme changes of heart but who also swore by the use of three gold balls, each of 18 mm diameter and weighing 60 grams, to be inserted in the woman's vagina. These he bought from a Genoese goldsmith for around $100. He also, more usefully, recommended as a contraceptive the capping of the cervix with half a lemon from which the juice had been removed; this would have worked well as a diaphragm and is still used by women in parts of Russia to this day.

Proof, if it were needed, that Casanova was really just a rugby player in a frilly blouse, can be found in the form of a picture of him blowing up condoms – the official line is 'to test them' – in front of a lairy audience of four. The following is an account of a fitting which he had in a Marseilles brothel:

> The girl came back with the packet. I put myself in the right position, and ordered her to choose me one that fitted well. Sulkily, she began examining and measuring. 'This one doesn't fit well,' I told her. 'Try another.' Another and another; and suddenly I splashed her well and truly.[24]

Meanwhile in Russia, Catherine the Great was going about her very own brand of business. What was unique about the woman was not that she was the French writer Voltaire's penpal or that she'd revolted against her husband (this phenomenon has been known before and since), nor even that she used a squeezed half lemon as contraception – because we don't know that she did, we only know that about her fellow countrywomen. No, the most notable thing about Catherine the Great is that she reckoned on having sex *six times a day*.[25] This should obviously have got her slaps on the back all round, and any subsequent woman with an, er, healthy sex drive should have been called a Catherine, as opposed to a Casanova. But an exceptionally lusty woman has never really been thought a cause for celebration, unless she has been in a story in a porn magazine. And, it has to be said, Catherine is not as good a name as Casanova.

Dr Johnson's biographer and friend James Boswell made a number of allusions to his sexual adventures in his *London Journal* of 1763 which give us further insight into the use of condoms at that time. He was, we learn, infected, presumably with VD, by a woman whom he had assumed to be virtuous, which made him determine to be more careful in the future. His first outing after this was to St James's Park in late March, where he 'picked up a whore. For the first time did I engage in armour, which I found but a dull satisfaction.' Still, he stuck with it, and five days later 'strolled into the park and took the first whore I met, whom I without many words copulated with free from danger, being safely sheathed. She was ugly and lean and her breath smelt of spirits. When it was done, she slunk off. I had a low opinion of this practice and resolved to do it no more.'

Westminster Bridge, 10 May: 'in armour complete . . . The whim of doing it there with the Thames rolling below us amused me much.' A week later he had cast his 'armour' aside with a 'fresh, agreeable girl' called Alice Gibbs. The following morning he was racked with guilt, or rather worry about becoming infected again, and so it went on.

By the end of the eighteenth century, condoms were available at brothels in London, Paris, Berlin and St Petersburg. They were not much used by married couples, however (at least not with each other), the scholar's reason being their expense and association with disease. Their association with brothels must have had an effect too, and the extent to which, again, the French and English were in denial about our now latex mate is perfectly epitomised by the fact that the former called them *la capote anglaise* and the latter the French letter.

Despite the appeal of the condom to adulterers and prostitutes the world over, in the words of Nancy from *Oliver*, 'it ain't all jolly old pleasure at Inns' and the condom had its detractors. One such was the eighteenth century's version of Mary Whitehouse, moralist Joseph Cam. Earlier, in 1671, Madame de Sévigné too had written to her daughter with criticisms, but not, this time, of the moral kind. She described them as 'armour against enjoyment and a spider web against danger'.[26]

Parisian (and grown up) Astruc took a more serious and perhaps realistic stance. The skins which, he said, the English use (called, this time, *condus*) were, he believed, an unfortunate necessity. Unfortunate even before they were available in different flavours and colours from pub vending machines. Back then you bought them from waiters in taverns. They were not wrapped in fiddly little packets in those days, and marketing people did not claim they could 'enhance your love play'. They, if you will, had it pretty easy then.

Inevitably, profit was being made from all of this, in mid-eighteenth-century London principally by two women called Mrs Phillips and Mrs Perkins, who waged a kind of handbill war (think Virgin versus British Airways or Coke versus Pepsi) against each other in their efforts to gain the condom monopoly. Mrs Phillips opened her warehouse in Half Moon Street opposite the New Exchange in the Strand. After a successful few years of business, selling to 'apothecaries, chymists, druggists etc.' and supplying 'ambassadors, foreigners, gentlemen and captains of ships, etc. going abroad',[27] Mrs Phillips sold out to Mrs Perkins, although she was to return ten years later to resume trading, complete with advertising jingle:

To guard yourself from shame or fear,
Votaries to Venus, hasten here;
None of our wares e'er found a flaw
Self preservation's nature's law.

'She defies anyone in *England* to equal her goods, and hath lately had several large orders from *France*, *Spain*, *Portugal*, *Italy*, and other foreign places,' her handbill challenged. It was war once more.

Back in England, Gray's *Pharmacopoeia* of 1828 gives an account of the complex and messy process of condom manufacture in the UK at that time and slightly later. It involved:

The intestina caeca of sheep soaked for some hours in water, turned inside out, macerated again in weak alkaline ley changed every twelve hours, scraped carefully to abstract the mucous membrane, leaving the peritoneal and muscular coats: then exposed to the vapour of burning brimstone . . .[28]

And so on. Then as now there were also 'fine' versions, and even 'superfines doubles' which involved sandwiching two of the fine models together. As early as the late eighteenth century, condoms came in three sizes, although Boswell's secret to make the things stay on was to dip his 'machine' into the lake in St James's Park, which, though he said it himself, enabled him to perform 'most manfully'. However, the manufacturing and fitting processes were clearly a bit of a palaver.

Always advanced when it came to technology, one particular foreign place kept well away from the intestines of animals, and that was Japan. The Japanese lover of the 1820s could choose from a 'helmet' of tortoiseshell (called *kabutogata*) and a sheath of thin leather (or *kawagata*).[29]

Then, in 1843, rubber trader Mr Goodyear, most famous for his tyre-making expertise, invented the vulcanisation process. What George Bernard Shaw hailed 'the greatest invention of the nineteenth century' was to be developed the following year by Mr Hancock, in England. It was the rubber johnny, and it may have been the first but it was certainly not the last time in history that the car/sex connection was to be made.

Initially, rubber condoms were of two sorts. There was the standard condom, which was a clumsier version of the one we know today, in that it was thicker and had a seam running down it, and there was the tip condom. Tip condoms, which, as the name suggests, only cover the end of the penis, are now known as 'American tips' and are hardly used today. This is due largely to the fact that they involve a fitting, to ensure that the thing will not slip off. For the real connoisseur, animal membrane condoms are still available (apparently they afford a degree of sensitivity that man-made condoms have not yet been able to achieve), but they are very expensive. In the old days standard rubber condoms came in three sizes in the UK: small, medium and large. Men in the US were clearly more uniform in shape. They were given only one size.

In 2000 it was revealed that the standard-sized condom was too large for the average German man. As a topic of conversation at the bierkellen this was obviously never going to compete with their discussions about their big fast cars.

4

Science is Golden

William Alcott, Catharine Beecher, and other 'household divinities' laid most of the burden for perfecting the world squarely on the shoulders of wives.

James Reed, *From Private Vice to Public Virtue*

It was the mid-1800s and change was afoot. This was due in large part, to the fact that in 1859, Charles Darwin published a book called *On The Origin of Species*, which was one of the first clear signs that the human race was going to have to apply itself a little more to the question of its ancestry. It was no longer enough to say, with an airy wave of the hand, 'It all started with a guy and a girl wearing a couple of leaves and living in a really nice garden.'

As for contraception, six years after Goodyear and Hancock had invented the vulcanisation of rubber, cheap rubber condoms were available in the United States for around $5 a dozen, while the French continued to buy intestines from the butcher's. Before 'rubbers' were to be given any official seal of approval in Britain, though, a shift in attitude would have to occur. Several of the main policy makers, and the self-appointed social reformers of the sort that Swift had so roundly mocked over a hundred years earlier in 'A Modest Proposal', were at least as suspicious of and humourless about sex as the church had become.

This seriousness was partly due to the fact that the scale of poverty in Britain was now a problem, and poverty brings with it many unsavoury things, including crime. To the rich this meant that the number of poor children had to decrease. However, contraception was not, to everybody, the most obvious answer. Since the middle and upper classes had fewer children, it was thought that the working classes needed to learn to control themselves. In short, the toffs decided they had to teach the plebs how to be more like them. This was, in the civilisation-long scheme of things, a relatively new problem, which is why the commentators got so excited about it. From Roman times until now, high-status families had always produced many children, as an expression of their potency and wealth, and the lowlier had produced fewer because they could not afford them and when they did have them they would often die young. The order was starting to be reversed, and this makes human beings uncomfortable at the best of times.

One can only imagine how the business of taking orders about your sex life from on high went down with the poor – if, indeed, it went down at all. It is easy to get the impression that many of the people who wrote essays on such subjects were simply engaged in a kind of intellectual tennis with each other and that, at grass roots level, people were carrying on pretty much as they had always done. If they were taking advice, they were probably taking it from each other, and continuing to put money in the pockets of characters like the condom-purveyors Mrs Phillips and Mrs Perkins.

The first of this batch of essay writers was Britain's Thomas Malthus (1766–1834), who in 1798 had written 'An Essay on Population' which argued that human beings will, if left to their own devices, breed until they cannot support themselves. In fact, he said, 'Population when unchecked goes on doubling itself every twenty-five years.'[1] This raised questions about how to deal with an over-population problem. The population must be restrained, it was agreed by the theorists, it was just a matter of how. Contraception was not, as far as Malthus was concerned, an option.

Another essayist, William Godwin, suggested – in the most delicate possible way and in a kind of serious version of Swift's satire – infanticide, saying 'The Chinese do it'. His view was: 'I had rather a child should perish in the first hour of its existence than that a man should spend seventy years of life in a state of misery and vice . . .'[2] No legislation was put in place, so we can only assume that Godwin was thanked, at least by the theorists, for his ancient Greek/Roman contribution and offered his coat. Having said that, infanticide did go on, unofficially, among poor people who felt unable to cope. It is said that East End mothers would drown their baby daughters in the pond in London's Victoria Park. Boys were kept because they could work and there would not come a time when a dowry had to be raised for them.

Malthus managed to show how in touch with reality he wasn't by offering 'moral restraint'[3] (i.e. from marriage) as a solution. Obviously people weren't going to stop getting married, and even if they did they would not necessarily stop having sex, so this too was consigned by history to the dustbin. As Shirley Green put it in 1971: 'Malthus was not a working-class man, or he'd have seen the absurdity of preaching celibacy. Francis Place, on the other hand, appreciated their situation because he'd shared it.'[4]

As thinkers went, Place and his cronies John Stuart Mill (1806–73) and Jeremy Bentham (1748–1832) were indeed more forward-looking, inspired and practical than most in Britain. They followed the example of the French, who, ever the pioneers in matters sexual, had accepted since the 1700s that artificial methods of birth control should be a part of life. The first French advocate was A. N. de Condorcet, who has been described as a feminist, since his priorities were to limit population growth and harm to women. E. Pivert de Senacour took on the French mantle in the nineteenth century, insisting that 'une précaution' was necessary.

The humanitarian approach, as opposed to the 'only the fit should survive' (i.e. the middle-class) one, is well illustrated by a later novel called *Ginx's Baby* by a Mr Jenkins. It was published in 1877 and is about a child – the eldest of thirteen. At the beginning of the story, the child's father tries to drown him in the river because he thinks his family too large, and at the end the boy drowns himself in the same place. This is an extract:

Wherever he went the world seemed terribly full. If he answered an advertisement for an errand boy, there were a score kicking their heels at the rendezvous before him. Did he try to learn a useful trade, thousands of adepts were not only ready to underbid him, but to knock him on the head for an interloper. Even the thieves, to whom he gravitated, were jealous of his accession, because there were too many competitors already in their department.

Political economist Friedrich Engels (1820–95) admitted that even a communist state might be forced to employ contraception to prevent overpopulation, but he was more in favour of abstinence. Engels and his friend Karl Marx (1818–83) were vehemently opposed to what became known as 'Malthusianism' because the orders came from on high and not from the people. In this way the church and Marx and Engels came close to being bedfellows. Perhaps this was not as strange as it seemed. Perhaps since all concerned sought both to organise the masses and to hang on to the idea that human life has intrinsic value, this was the inevitable outcome.

Place thought that restraining from marriage was 'no more likely to be adopted than infanticide'.[5] Bentham had already made it known, in 1797, that he thought the population would not be controlled by a 'prohibitory act' or a 'dead letter' but by 'living body' or sponge.[6] In 1826 Richard Carlile published the first English book on birth control, called *Every Woman's Book* or *What Is Love?*, in which he too spoke of the sponge, as well as withdrawal and the possible use of a 'glove' or sheath by the man.

The father of psychoanalysis, Sigmund Freud (1895–1982), had views about methods too. He observed that many married couples used coitus interruptus and, because he made a living out of having sex on the brain at all times, he was worried by this. In common with many medics at the time and before him, he thought it had a harmful effect on the mind. In a paper on Freud and birth control, Angus McLaren points out that 'as late as 1904 [and the rest] John W. Taylor, president of the British Gynaecological Society, would still be warning his audiences that "mechanical shields" resulted in "purulent vaginitis" and "sexual onanism" in "brain fag"'. In other words, if you used mechanical methods you would get a pus-filled, tense vagina and if you used withdrawal you would wear your brain out. The possibility that one might have children was the least of withdrawal's problems as far as Freud was concerned. 'It is a question of a physical accumulation of excitement – that is an accumulation of physical tension. The accumulation is the result of discharge being prevented. Thus anxiety neurosis is a neurosis of damming up, like hysteria; hence their similarity.'[7]

The effect of birth control on Freud's work cannot, it seems, be overestimated. McLaren continues that 'coitus interruptus and its complications were presented by Freud as providing the basis of his entire psychoanalytic theory'. After having six children over nine years with his wife, Freud's own solution to the family planning dilemma was to give up having sex with her. Instead, in a not very subtle act of sublimation, he threw his energy into psychoanalysis, which concerned itself with birth control. Lest you should pity him, it should be added that he would also talk in a cavalier fashion about 'normal sex outside marriage'.

For a while, he also hoped a rhythm method might emerge from work on periodicity by a man called Wilhelm Fliess, who shared Freud's interest in masturbation (which should not be confused with sharing in Freud's masturbation, obviously). He should have saved himself the trouble, Fliess being, according to McLaren, 'a man who believed that there was a special connection between the genitals and the nose and that accordingly nosebleeds were a vicarious form of menstruation and cocaine a cause of miscarriages'. The following are some thoughts of Fliess himself:

There are particular spots in the nose which relate to abdominal disorders. Treating one nasal spot, for example, will cause irregular menstruations. This may be achieved by cauterising the part or numbing it with cocaine.

Women who masturbate are generally dysmenorrheal [have painful periods]. They can only be cured through an operation on the nose if they do not give up this bad practice. In extreme cases, it may be necessary to extract the nasal bone altogether in order for them to recover perfect health . . .'[8]

Freud also mentioned sponges, but the method he detested least was the condom. 'Coitus reservatus by means of condoms is not injurious to the woman,' he said, 'provided she is quickly excitable and the husband very potent.' However, he was not a radical, and clearly found the whole issue as full of problems as the majority of people did.

Part of the problem was the age-old one. Birth control had a bad name. It was associated with philandering husbands, Casanovas and prostitutes. To recommend birth control officially would be to recommend loose morals and everything that a decent society and church had always fought against – and that philandering husbands, Casanovas and prostitutes had always roundly ignored. Birth control needed a marketing strategy.

The word which was already on the rue in France was starting to spread in Britain. What became known as the 'diabolic handbills', written by Francis Place, with names such as 'To the Married of Both Sexes', were being circulated, and mentioned coitus interruptus and the sponge as possible methods of birth control. At only seventeen, John Stuart Mill, who went on to become a great political philosopher, spent several days in prison for being involved with the distribution of this literature. He also showed an early talent for lucidity during this time, describing contraception as no more unnatural than using an umbrella when it rains. Precocious? Put it this way, he started learning Greek at the age of three. He shouldn't be knocked, though. He was a great supporter of women's suffrage at a time when the subject was ignored by the vast majority of people, let alone seventeen-year-old boys.

In France the contraception story was, as ever, different. The number of deaths had started to exceed births, due to the Crimean War – which saw early hygiene-freak Florence Nightingale shoot to fame – and the 1853–4 outbreak of cholera. *The Times* spotted the population dip, and could not resist this opportunity subtly to knock the French – partly because the Brits had been involved in the Crimean War and partly because, well, it's traditional to argue with one's neighbours – saying that all the real men had been 'swept away, leaving only the rejected of the conscription to be the fathers of a future generation'.

The Economist blamed the women instead:[9]

> The mothers of France have had irresistible motives for not
> caring to provide more generous nourishment for their children
> when stunted bodies saved them from being the prey of
> conscription.

In other words, not only did French mothers starve their babies
(subtext: negligence) but they did so to arrest their development
(cruelty leading to more weak Frenchmen) and stop them joining the
military (no loyalty to their country or sense of duty). Social
commentators could still not admit that birth control was being
employed by the French, although they were having only one or two
children, or sometimes none.

Disturbingly, in England, miscarriages among the married were on
the increase. Exactly by how much is not clear. A Dr Whitehead
claimed at the time that one in seven pregnancies were affected, and a
Dr Granville said it was closer to one in three. Either way it looked as
if miscarriages were being induced, just as they had been in ancient
times. Gossip backed this up with stories of married women who were
pregnant taking rigorous exercise and making themselves abort. We
know, via a letter from governess Miss Weston to a Miss Chorley in
1807, of one married woman who 'took something when pregnant of
her little girl, intended to fall on the child'.[10] It sounds as though she
was unsuccessful.

The form of contraception Jane Austen suggested to her niece
Fanny Knight was less involved: Don't have sex. Of a mutual friend
she exclaimed in a letter, 'I wd recommend to her and Mr D the
simple regimen of separate beds.' Clearly, despite her powerful
insights into the nature of romance and relationships, being stuck in a
vicarage in Hampshire had a profound impact on her willingness to
allow others to enjoy what she could not.

Over the pond, the same advice was being given by one Rose
Williams to her friend Allette Mosher. In *Read This Only To Yourself:
The Private Writing of Midwestern Women* by Elizabeth Hampsten we
learn that, on 27 September 1885, Rose wrote to Allette advising her

as follows: 'You want to know of a sure prevenative. Well plague take it. The best way is for you to sleep in one bed and your Man in another & I bet you will laugh and say "You goose you think I am going to do that" for I don't see anyone that does.'[11] She goes on to say that what they all use is a 'Pessairre or female prevenative if you don't want to ask for a "pisser" just ask for a female prevenative. They cost one dollar . . . The Directions are with it.'

Dr Edward B. Foote was referring to the diaphragm that someone else was about to take the credit for, when he spoke of an India rubber 'womb veil'. Foote – middle name 'Bliss' – was a graduate of Pennsylvania Medical University and author of a book called *Medical Common Sense* which, he boasted, was written in language 'strictly mundane'. In his book he described the application of the device as 'easy and accomplished in a moment, without the aid of a light'. He also contributed to the argument, which still rages among feminists, about whether it is right that women should control birth control. Foote thought it was, saying of his womb veil, 'it places conception entirely under the control of the wife, to whom it naturally belongs; for it is for her to say at what time and under what circumstances she will become [a] mother'.[12]

If only Rose and Allette had known three years earlier, in 1882, that W. P. Mensinga was starting to tell the world about the diaphragm, a soft rubber shield inserted into the woman's vagina to block the entrance of the uterus. He was a little more specific than Foote, his intention being that it should be used to prevent unhealthy women from getting pregnant.

Although not the diaphragm, which remains a popular method to this day, the 'prevenative' still sounds more sophisticated than the method of one other Midwestern woman, Gwendoline Kinkaid, ten years later: 'Oh say I have got another now. I bet you will laugh. Tell me how much faith you have in it. Just blow on your wrist.'[13] Gwendoline had three more children over the next few years, until she stopped conceiving having found 'a liquid tablet'. Someone called George Willard had a 'receipt', some kind of concoction that they came to rely on, but we are not told what it was. John Riddle, for one, is convinced that drugs were the 'primary means of birth control'[14] during this time.

As a result of the campaigning of Anthony Comstock, secretary of the very strict-sounding (and acting) Society for the Suppression of Vice, contraceptives had actually been forbidden in the US since 1873, but you would never have guessed it from the above. Using one of those strange legal loopholes, the Midwestern women could have bought condoms legitimately, had they wanted to. Condoms slipped through the net because they were seen as preventors of infection. For a hundred years, in fact, condoms had to carry the label 'for disease prevention only' on the packet. In the US they were known as 'questionable rubber goods', and indeed they were questionable in that competition became so fierce between manufacturers that they were often cheaply made. Even as recently as 1938, Norman Himes was suggesting that they be blown up to test them before use.[15]

Back in Britain, God, or rather his messengers, still had some say in the matter of birth control. Some thought that if one had many children it was God's will and therefore he would provide for them. Scholar J. A. Banks says that for the lower classes, reading this sort of thing in magazines would probably 'inhibit the free expression of the contrary point of view amongst them'.[16] In other words, reading that God was in favour of people having lots of children would have put those people off at best discussing and at worst using contraception.

Nor was the British medical profession as a whole at its most progressive as regards birth control. It was still, in 1869, far from condoning what, in the *British Medical Journal*, T. E. Beatty called 'filthy expedients for the prevention of conception'. This was not helped by the fact that, after years of discussion, scientists had decided that an embryo became a person at the point of conception. There had been an idea that soul was contained within each sperm, but this was rejected on the grounds that too many were killed off in a day for this to be plausible.

Lord Amberly, father of the British philosopher Bertrand Russell, started the medics off by writing in a paper that he supported protest over 'the utterly foolish delicacy which prevails over these most important subjects'[17] of family size and population (go, Bertie senior). He thought that family size should be limited, but he literally did not want anyone to get hurt.

To start with, no one listened to, or perhaps heard, the debates of the medics and Amberly was accepted as the Liberal Party's candidate for South Devon. Then the two opposing Conservative candidates began fighting dirty – although Tories almost certainly fight in other ways sometimes – turning Amberly's views into an endorsement of infanticide. Posters represented Amberly, by now nicknamed the 'Vice-Count' by those who did not approve, as 'The Quack Doctor' selling 'depopulation mixture' according to 'the New French and American Systems'. This shows both just how far our electioneering strategies haven't come and how Britain's chosen hated nations have stayed the same.

Digressions aside, Amberly lost the election. The fact that the Tories fought, and won, on the birth control ticket demonstrated clearly that people in general were, at best, still suspicious of contraception. But the issue was now out in the open. The seed, if the metaphor is not too tasteless, had been sown.

Birth control propaganda had actually begun in the 1860s with the publication of articles in the *National Reformer* by its editor Charles Bradlaugh and George Drysdale. Despite the fact that the readership of this periodical consisted almost entirely of 'Freethinkers', the articles were also issued in pamphlet form and, according to Banks, probably reached a wider audience.

Other pamphlets with various cheery names were also circulated including 'Valuable Hints' (1866), 'The Power and Duty of Parents to Limit the Number of their Children' (1868), both published anonymously, 'Large or Small Families?' (1871) by Austin Holyoake, and 'The Marriage Problem,' published under the name 'Oedipus' but actually by a Dr Haslam. Ironic that Haslam should use the pseudonym 'Oedipus' to discuss ridding the world of excess children when the original Oedipus's concern was to keep down the numbers of excess parents. All of these leaflets aired the idea of contraception. The *Fortnightly Review* too entered the fray, introducing the idea of the rhythm method, then referred to as the 'safe' period. The real catalyst, though, came with the publication of an innocent-looking volume on contraception, called *Fruits of Philosophy*.

Fruits of Philosophy was first published in the United States in 1832;

it was written by Charles Knowlton in response to a book called *Moral Physiology* by Robert Dale Owen. *Moral Physiology* recommended coitus interruptus over the condom (too expensive and unaesthetic) and the sponge (ineffective). Knowlton's book contained advice on all sorts of methods including douching with a syringe, using acidic agents like alum, sulphates or vinegar. Spermicides were needed when douching, Knowlton decided, since semen might get 'lodged away among the folds and ridges of the vagina'.[18]

In five years Knowlton had sold 7,000 copies at $1 each, then a huge sum. This price was set in order to keep the book out of the hands of the 'immature', in other words those who needed it most. The price the author paid was three prosecutions under the Massachusetts common-law obscenity statute. On the first occasion he was fined, on the second he was imprisoned for a few days, and on the third he was made to do three months' hard labour in an East Cambridge jail. Worse punishment, though, was to come with the declaration by one of the prosecution's physicians during the trial that the book contained nothing new.

He gained a popular following, however, post publication and trial. In New York he began holding lectures for women on the subject of the male and female organs and on general anatomy. These were a roaring success with women keen to learn about their 'folds and ridges', in part due to his use of beautiful, full-sized papier mâché models of the human body and the sexual organs of men and women. His reception in Philadelphia was even more hearty. There 'upwards of four hundred ladies attended in one day'.

As ever, Britain was far behind the United States. In 1877, by which time American Thomas Edison was shouting 'Mary had a little lamb' into his phonograph and recording it, and forty-five years after the US, the British publishers of *Fruits of Philosophy*, Charles Bradlaugh and Annie Besant, were being taken to court. According to moralists, they had been 'unlawfully and wickedly devising, contriving, and intending, as much as in them lay, to vitiate and corrupt the morals as well of youth as of diverse subjects of the Queen, and to incite and encourage the said subjects to indecent, obscene, unnatural, and immoral practices . . .'

Some newspapers were nothing like as harsh in their assessment of the case. The *Reynold's News* described the book as 'far less immoral and dangerous than that which has been privately printed for the delectation of Anglican priests'.[19]

This was a reference to *The Priest In Absolution*, which gave explicit guidance to priests on how to probe into the sexual lives of women, both of the married and unmarried kind. Fitting, perhaps, to think that, around Montaillou in France in the Middle Ages, the priests would have had all this knowledge already, since they would have *been* the sexual lives of their flock. At any rate, the *News* implied that these men of the cloth were interested in women for less than holy reasons, saying that within the priests' book were 'nice sort of questions for a salacious young parson to put to a young married woman'.

Other papers were not so forgiving of *Fruits of Philosophy*. One such was *The Englishman*, which described the book as 'the most wicked work that was ever written – one which practically recommends and points out the way to an indiscriminate destruction of human life'. It was also described, a little uneconomically, as a 'dirty, filthy book'. With mischievousness that is to be applauded, the publishers called their next edition *A Dirty, Filthy Book*. Imagine that title and the former quotation on the jacket of a book today. Imagine the sales.

And, again, sell it did. According to the *Daily News*, 'a few hundred purchasers in the course of many years have been converted into more than a hundred thousand purchasers in a few weeks'. All publicity, as they say, is good publicity. The editor of *The Englishman* had already recognised the attraction of this kind of book and (slightly over-) anticipated that twenty people would read each copy – resulting in 'millions corrupted by this diabolical work'. Perhaps, then, for him only a few hundred thousand corrupted was good going.

Publishers Bradlaugh and Besant had also built up something of a fan base, just as Knowlton had before them. When they made a public address seven days after the trial, six hundred people turned up and paid between 2d. and 2s. 6d., according to *The Times*. According to *Reynold's*, a further four hundred who were unable to get in waited outside. Around a third of them were women (a large number for the time) and many of them were described as 'very young'.

An organisation called the Malthusian League, made up of 'neo-Malthusians' had been set up at the close of the trial and immediately 220 people had joined up. Clearly both the League and its members were named after Thomas Malthus, but because of his overall concern with the population problem rather than his dismissal of contraception as a possible solution to it. The League distribute three million leaflets, and of these over a million between 1876 and 1891 gave details of contraception.[20] The work of the League also had knock-on effects abroad. Aletta Jacobs, the first woman physician in The Netherlands, learned of neo-Malthusianism while staying in London and went on to set up the world's first birth control clinic in Amsterdam in 1882 ('Aletta Jacobs in "Britain More Progressive than Holland" Shock', although the Dutch were still the clinic pioneers). Another of Aletta's achievements was to popularise the cap, hence it became knwn as the 'Dutch cap'. Similar organisations to the Malthusian League were also set up in France and Spain.

British doctors still did not approve. As soon as the trial was over, the *British Medical Journal* expressed its disapproval about contraception and continued to do so at regular intervals until the end of the century. It claimed that 'conjugal onanism' (or withdrawal) in women would produce metritis, leucorrhoea (pus in the vagina again), menorrhagia and haematocele, hysteralgia and hyperaesthesia (oversensitivity) of the genital organs, galloping cancer, ovarian dropsy and ovaritis, sterility, mania leading to suicide, and nymphomania. Ancient Greek women who did not have children were supposed to go mad too, you'll remember. Men got off relatively lightly with nervous prostration, mental decay, loss of memory, intense cardiac palpitations, and mania leading to suicide.

American doctor Alexander Skene was inclined to agree, although he was particularly worried about the potential career women, or the woman with 'some fancy or ambition' who tried to 'reverse the order of her physical being'. The outlook was bleaker for your health if you were female and you tried to forge some kind of future for yourself. As far as Skene was concerned, this type of woman 'is almost sure to suffer sooner or later from disappointment and ill-health'.[21]

Banks points out that in the process of homing in on these alleged side–effects, probably because doctors had 'disproportionate familiarity with abnormal and diseased cases'[22] they saw too many dangers in contraception. Perhaps he is too kind. It is hard to imagine someone getting ill from using the withdrawal method. Pregnant, yes, but mentally ill? In fact he does go further in one respect, suggesting that the doctors may have 'shirked the issue of a true enquiry into [contraception's] physical and psychological effects'.

In the US, Knowlton aside, doctors were telling women everything about themselves except that which they wanted to know. Great strides had been made in medicine, including the invention of the stethoscope back in 1819 and the discovery of gastric ingestion even earlier in 1803. However, for birth control tips, they would have to continue to turn to books. One in particular was called *Tokology, A Book for Every Woman*, by Alice B. Stockham[23] ('Tokology' is from the Greek word for motherhood).

Stockham thought families should be planned: 'fewer and better children are desired by right-minded parents'. The best idea, she thought, was to be continent. A second bright idea was a version of the rhythm method that assumed a woman was at her most fertile during her period, and advised intercourse two weeks after this (when a woman is actually at her most fertile). She also had a not very sisterly approach to ovulation, insisting that conception 'is under the control of the woman's will; that by avoiding the least thrill of passion herself, during coition, she can prevent the ovules being displaced to meet the male germs'. This 'make sure the woman doesn't enjoy herself and there won't be any babies' method was, you may recall, also practised by the Greeks.

Less well documented is what Dr Stockham called 'sedular absorption' a variation on the coitus reservatus theme: 'in this, intercourse is had without culmination. No discharge is allowed. People practising this method claim the highest possible enjoyment, no loss of vitality, and perfect control of the fecundating power.' *Voilà*. Another relatively early advocate of Tantric sex. The church recognised this method, but could not decide whether or not to approve of it. One man, John Noyes, who called himself 'God's true representative,' certainly approved. In fact he tried to claim he had invented it. As we already know, coitus reservatus was practised by the ancient Chinese, and widely used in Japan at least into the seventeenth century, by old men who wanted to conserve their strength but get their respective ends away nevertheless.

Withdrawal was not an option as far as Stockham was concerned as it is 'incomplete and unnatural' (and intercourse without culmination isn't?) and as 'disastrous' as masturbation. It also leads to impotence in men and sterility in women as well as such a catalogue of nervous symptoms that you can't help thinking that copies of the *BMJ* had been on her bedside table for years.

In Britain, as well as disapproving of birth control from the medical angle, the enemies of contraception were, with some justification, more than a little suspicious of the practitioners, both qualified and unqualified, that it tended to attract. The *BMJ* described what these people did as 'obscene and audacious quackery'. One doctor, Henry Allbut, had his name removed from the Register because he published what, again, the *BMJ* described as 'an indecent work entitled *The Wife's Handbook*, and for having published or attached thereto advertisements of an unprofessional character, titled "Malthusian Appliances".' He is also famous for promoting the use of the soluble quinine pessary or suppository, developed by the Rendell company in England in the 1880s. Actually, the most indecent aspect of the book was, as with Stockham's *Tokology*, that the 'safe' period was miscalculated, resulting in people being advised to have sex at a particularly fertile time.

Dr Charles Drysdale, expert on syphilis, kept the birth control debate alive, but he managed to achieve this and remain a doctor by keeping that debate within the medical profession.[24] Allbut's mistake was in broadening out the discussion to include the people to whom it was most relevant. What did he expect from a profession that introduced male midwives and was soon to conclude that female anatomy was designed to fit the male midwife's fingers?

More and more advertisements for methods of contraception and abortion (the distinction was often blurred, probably deliberately) were appearing in the press. Riddle says that 'a survey of newspapers in Great Britain during one week showed 100 newspapers with advertisements for abortions thinly disguised.'[25] One such advertisement, perhaps for an abortion-inducer, perhaps for a contraceptive, was found in the *Newcastle Evening News* offering 'a secret Remedy for the Prevention of Large Families. Guaranteed infallible'. The *BMJ* continued to get into a lather about them. The *Journal* spoke in surprisingly alarmist tones of '"female pills" and other remedies, which are guaranteed to "remove obstructions" and to have "the desired effect" without pain or danger'. In actual fact, it continued, 'most of these are mere swindles' and not only did some of them 'undoubtedly contain injurious and poisonous substances', the majority were just mild laxatives, it was claimed.

A number of the potions, which were part of a tradition started by apothecaries before the 1600s, *would* have brought about abortion, as the medical profession was probably well aware. These would have included potions containing pennyroyal (a cousin of mint), savin (juniper), tansy and rue.

In the US the most famous of these potions was called Pinkham's Vegetable Compound, and its ingredients included alcohol, seeds of fenugreek (a smelly pod-bearing plant), and unicorn root. The official line was that this was a 'blood purifier' which 'dissolves and expels tumours', and its value to women in America was enormous. This can be gauged by the fact that, when the federal Food, Drug and Cosmetic Act arrived in 1938, women's groups campaigned so hard to save the mixture that they managed to keep it from being banned. In fact, according to Riddle, it is still available today.[26]

The British medics' initial case (that the potions were useless) was not strengthened by the fact that they went on to describe them as 'incitements to crime' because they were bought with the intention of producing abortion. Surely they were either a threat or they weren't.

However, as is the case today with doctors and, say, voluntary euthanasia, there was the theory and there was the practice. Although the ruling body officially takes a stance, on a day-to-day, person-by-person basis, doctors are making their own decisions about what is best for their patients all the time. By the beginning of the 1900s, doctors were starting to encourage the spacing of pregnancies.

When asked at the National Birth Rate Commission in 1914 whether it wasn't almost standard practice for doctors to advise their patients on the spacing of children, Dr J. W. Ballantyne said: 'I think there is no doubt that doctors do say that; I think so. I am very often asked.'[27] He goes on to say that he always recommends that a child be nursed for a year, which – as we know – would have a contraceptive effect if the breast-feeds were regular enough. The next question was whether this advice would have been given thirty or forty years before, to which Dr Ballantyne replied: 'When I started practice I do not think we were asked that, or ever gave that advice voluntarily'.

The alternative was seeing quacks, as the trial of the Chrimes brothers at the Old Bailey demonstrated. They attempted to blackmail 12,000 women who had ordered abortifacients from them. They were caught, but others who committed similar crimes got away scot-free.[28]

Despite the advertisements and the door-to-door selling of condoms (called 'baudruches' by Knowlton, the author of *Fruits of Philosophy*), and the astonishment of Irish doctors on visiting London and seeing 'antigestatory appliances',[29] the sudden drop in the birth rate in the 1870s was not due to a huge surge in the use of mechanical birth control methods. This we know because only around 16 per cent of married couples before 1910 used birth control, and the rate dropped in areas where devices were not readily available as well in as areas where they were.[30]

In the US there was more mechanical birth control going on and Anthony Comstock, moraliser and kingpin of the Young Men's Christian Association, was not happy about it. He was so unhappy about it, in fact, that he got a new bill passed which defined 'information on the prevention of conception' as obscene. Also in the US, the YMCA was set up to provide immigrants from rural America with somewhere to stay which was not a saloon or a bawdy house. It was certainly not supposed to be any fun at all to stay at the YMCA.

In a mild-mannered letter to the *New York Times*, one pastor took exception to Comstock's laws and proceedings 'wherein he attempts to regulate and prohibit the sale of certain things hitherto commended by prudent physicians as harmless and yet invaluable to sick and over-burdened mothers'. Comstock's reaction was to describe the pastor as 'either crazy, stupidly ignorant, a very bad man at heart' or with 'a very poor way of expressing himself so as to make people understand his meaning'. As well as not exactly moving the debate forward, this was libel.[31]

Comstock got anyone he could put away under his new law, often using decoy letters with false signatures to entrap them. Favourite pastimes of this man included paying prostitutes to walk around in front of him naked, before charging them with indecent exposure. Once Comstock ran out of birth controllers he moved on to gamblers, free-lovers and the publishers of non-Christian tracts.

The Church in England was in a quandary. Artificial prevention of childbirth was immoral, it held, but large families led to poverty. Coitus interruptus was out of the question, to the extent that, in the early 1900s Belgian bishops were still urging women to use 'prayers and blandishments' in order to dissuade their husbands. Worse than this were mechanical methods which, according to moral theologian Arthur Vermeersch (1858–1936), should be resisted by women to the same extent that they would resist rape, even if their husbands threatened to divorce them or to go elsewhere for sex.[32]

Eventually Church of England supporters agreed to recommend the use of the 'safe' period, a subject which had undergone much research, not least that carried out since 1845 by Felix Pouchet. He had been doing experiments in this area on mammals. The Church's recommendation began as a very coy, almost touching, enquiry from Antoine de Salinis, Bishop of Amiens, in 1853. He had heard, he said, of married people being informed by 'skilled doctors' that there were a number of days every month 'in which conception by a woman could not take place.'[33] Should these people be disturbed? he wanted to know. The Penitentiary's reply was as follows: 'Those about whom you ask are not to be disturbed provided they do nothing by which conception is prevented.'

Hopefully churchgoers did not take their advice about when this period was from Allbut's *The Wife's Handbook* or Stockham's

Tokology, either of which would have given pregnancy the *best* possible chance of taking hold. Certainly this – admittedly French – sector of the church had, as John Noonan points out, roundly ignored one of their founding fathers, St Augustine, who had said that sex on sterile days was itself preventing conception.

Women in the US were unwilling to give birth to the ten to thirteen children it is calculated they would have in a lifetime without precautions, and they continued to educate themselves. Threatening stuff, thought Harvard academic Edward Clarke. He thought the only solution might be to start getting in some new, stupid, wives from abroad.[34]

The Social Purity Alliance saw to it that, as regards prostitution, society no longer 'permitted it, did it, and looked the other way', as the BBC's 1949 programme *Victorian Ideas of Sex*, put it. This and its accompanying publicity led, according to Banks, to a new emphasis on chastity before marriage. It also left the church with another dilemma. Whether prostitutes were serving men who were marrying late or married men, they were keeping the birth rate down. Without prostitutes, there were going to be more children (either from earlier marriages or from more sex within wedlock). Neither the 'safe period' nor some churchy preaching of 'self-control' would sort this one out.

5

Handbags at Dawn

'Soon the only class callously and carelessly allowing themselves
to hand on bodily defect will be the morons of various grades.'

Marie Stopes[1]

From the 1910s the birth control roost was ruled by two people: Marie
Stopes (1880–1958) and Margaret Sanger (1879–1966). Apart from
the fact that they came from opposite sides of the Atlantic (Marie from
the UK, Margaret from the US), the two had a lot more than their
initials in common. They also, ultimately, failed to support each other
in the way that two egotistical individuals who want to be stars and
somehow occupy the same territory often fail.

Sanger, a bored New York housewife and ex-nurse, was responsible for replacing the unwieldy term 'neo-Malthusianism' with the
snappier and suitably euphemistic 'birth control'. Many phrases were
tried out for size first, including 'voluntary parenthood', 'conscious
generation', 'preventception', 'family control', 'race control'[2] and
birth-rate control'. Although she later traced her birth control
epiphany to a 1913 trip to where else but France, where she was not
the first to be amazed by how advanced the women there were in
matters sexual, she was in fact introduced to the concept by anarchist
Emma Goldman who was defending birth control publicly in 1910.
However Goldman was to become a rival of Sanger's, which led
Sanger to skate over the extent of her influence.

Emma Goldman and Dr Ben Reitman were the Bonnie and Clyde

of birth control and had twentieth-century contraception's First Great Love Affair. Not only did Ben share Emma's taste for subversion, but he had curly dark hair and dark eyes and was, frankly, dangerous. Both had tired of wishy-washy liberals and their lack of practical advice and decided that what the subject needed was the anarchist's touch. Both went to prison for distributing leaflets which contained far better preventception methods than any of the medical journals. If 'Birth Control' had been a boy band, Ben Reitman would have been the one that caused the band to split up due to his waywardness. Eventually the couple turned their attention to anti-war campaigning because, according to Reitman, birth control was 'getting to be terribly respectable'.[3]

Another flamboyant character called Havelock Ellis was Sanger's next BF (that is 'best friend' not 'boyfriend', she was cagey about whether they were ever intimate, making them twentieth-century contraception's Second Great Love Affair). He had written books on sexuality, but more interesting was his own sex life; he was clearly a bit of a lad. He had many, many lovers (there was time – he also had a problem with premature ejaculation until he was over sixty), he liked to watch women urinating because his mother had done it standing up in front of him when he was twelve years old, and he thought fetishism 'the supreme triumph of human idealism'.[4]

On whatever footing, Sanger was obviously hooked. When asked whether his premature ejaculation could be counted as a kind of impotence she sprang to his defence: 'Then about 65 per cent of American men could be called sexually impotent,' she barked.[5] Another lover of his, Françoise Delisle, agreed with Sanger, saying 'there are various means of achieving physical satisfaction . . . the important thing . . . is not alone the physical method, but the reverence and the spiritual oneness created through the physical contact . . . This was a subject . . . Havelock and I often discussed . . .'[6] Three words: 'hook', 'line' and 'sinker'.

Sanger's first attempt to gain the support of the masses took the form of a magazine called *The Woman Rebel* which she put together along with her Greenwich Village mates, including Havelock Ellis and Emma Goldman. The first issue came out in March 1914. It contained a piece by Goldman on 'Direct Action' which accused capitalists and kings of exploiting the uncontrolled birth rate in order to benefit from the provision of cheap labour and expendable troops to fight in wars. It also contained a 'Preamble', which began:

> The working class and the employing class have nothing in common. There can be no peace so long as hunger and want are found among millions of the working people and the few, who make up the employing class, have all the good things in life.

This 'crimson burst of anger', as the magazine was later described, advised women to 'look the whole world in the face with a go-to-hell look in the eyes; to have an ideal; to speak and to act in defiance of convention'. With the exception of leading feminist writer Germaine Greer, few women today are capable of that degree of rousing anger, which results in more and more Pamela Andersons and fewer and fewer Germaine Greers. *The Woman Rebel* also set down a bill of rights for women, many of which still have resonance today. These included:

> The Right to be lazy.
> The Right to be an unmarried mother.
> The Right to destroy.
> The Right to create.
> The Right to love.
> The Right to live.

'It is also the aim of this paper to circulate among those women who work in prostitution,' it stated. Whoever the woman rebel was, she would not be worried about where she was being it: 'The woman rebel has strong and rooted conception, but as for her dinner she has it sometimes in bed, or on the roof or in a boat. She argues from the same fundamental principles, but she does it anywhere; in bed or in a bath or in a balloon.'

The ultimate woman rebel was also, after a long search for a publisher, to publish a book called *Family Limitation* which was

A young Greek man approaches his willing mentor in that special way. A guy
with a beard looks on. (*British Museum*)

Marie Stopes – founder of the modern birth-control movement and cat person...

... and at her marriage to Lieutenant Humphrey Roe, the dashing aviator who financed her first book.

Geri Halliwell – U N Goodwill Ambassador for reproductive health and ex-Spice Girl. She is seen here at the Capital FM party in the Park 1999.

From left to right/clockwise: Hypericum (St John's Wort), Asplenium ruta-muraria (fern), Mentha Pulegium (pennyroyal) and Juniperus communis (juniper). All of these have been used as contraceptives... (*Royal Horticultural Society, Linley Library*)

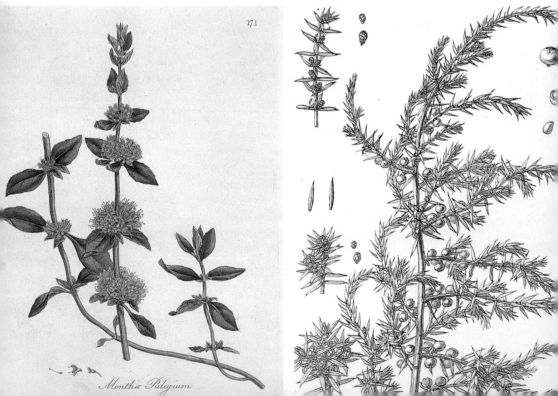

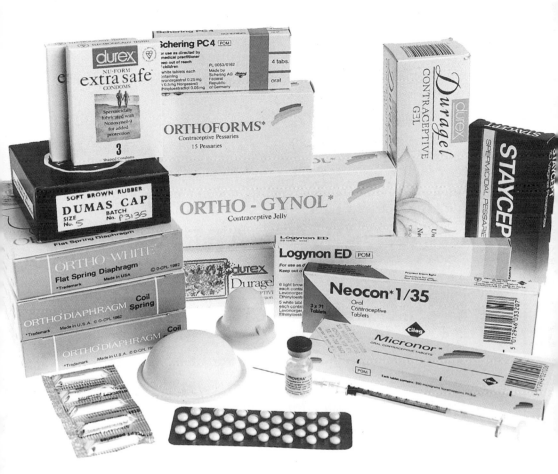

… as have all of these.

3 TEA TIME TALKS

AT

CLARIDGES (BROOK STREET)

BY

Marie C. Stopes, D.Sc., Ph.D., F.L.S., etc.

(Author of *Married Love, Enduring Passion,* etc.)

ON

DIFFICULT PROBLEMS IN MODERN MARRIAGE

To LADIES ONLY

Questions on relevant personal sex problems from any of the audience will be answered as fully as time permits, and may be asked at the time or sent in in writing

on 3 Thursdays

February 28th.   Chair: Dr. Evelyn Fisher, M.D., D.P.H.
March   7th.   Chair: Mrs. Laura Henderson
March   14th.   Chair: Mrs. Stanley Wrench

Lecture and Questions 5—6.30   Tea served at 4.45

TICKETS :—For the Course of 3 Lectures . £5 5 0
              Single tickets for any one Lecture £2 2 0

To be obtained only from the Lecture Secretary,
108, Whitfield Street, W.1

An advertisement for Marie Stopes' lecture series on 'Difficult Problems in Modern Marriage' held at Claridges Hotel, London. (*Wellcome Library, London*)

MIL-SAN
The Scientific Contraceptive

12 SINGLE APPLICATION TUBES

BRITISH PATENT Nº 407610.

MIL-SAN is the outcome of medical research into all methods of contraception.

Its principle is in closest harmony with the biology of the vagina. It does not depend upon the action of toxic or corrosive chemicals but prevents conception by means which occasion no functional disturbance. It is independent of time, temperature, moisture or foaming. It is immediately effective.

The method of application ensures the quantity, is hygienic and "fool-proof."

Specimen tubes for examination and literature stating the principle, the tests and ingredients are sent on request to members of the Medical Profession.

Sole Distributors for the British Empire
MENOSINE LIMITED
24, MAPLE STREET, LONDON, W.1
'Phone: Museum 6760

A Mil-San advert from the BMJ, 20 July 1935. At least Menosine Ltd had the sense to put the words 'fool-proof' in inverted commas. (*Wellcome Library, London*)

Rendell's 'Wife's Friend' gels. According to the packet these are 'as recommended in *The Wife's Handbook*'. (*Wellcome Library, London*)

W. J. Rendell's "Wife's Friend" Soluble Gels.

In active principle these Gels are identical to Rendell's Pessaries as recommended in "The Wife's Handbook," page 50.

Be sure and look for autograph Trade Mark on the labels to prevent disappointment.   W. J. RENDELL, Hitchin, Herts.

REGISTERED TRADE MARK   *W. J. Rendell*

Margaret Sanger (left) with Professor W C Nixon and Margaret Pyke at a party held in the former's honour on July 1957, in London. (*Wellcome Library, London*)

intended to interest the working class in using douches, condoms and pessaries. The attitude of people like Sanger is now rightly questioned, due to its eugenic undertones. At the time, though, eugenics was a respectable and widely discussed liberal intellectual theory and in some countries, including Sweden, an accepted practice.

The second issue of *The Woman Rebel* articulates the feeling that was around that magazine at least, in a way which suggests compassion rather than Nazism, although it appeared under the headline 'The Unfit':

> Women and men of the working class are so drained and exhausted in health and energy by their work, poor food and bad housing, that it is impossible for them to give birth to healthy offspring, thus making them unfit.

Sanger was on a mission not to purify the human race but to improve its lot, and her book, the first phase of that mission, landed her a prosecution by the federal government.

After visiting the UK and meeting Marie Stopes, to whom she afterwards wrote, addressing her as 'lovely one' and not only declaring that 'the evening with you was a delight' but praising her 'abundance of strong characteristics', she returned to the United States riding high on the wave of publicity which had surrounded the court case. The charges were dropped. A lecture tour followed, during which in those heady early days she turned her cause into a free speech issue. She also established a birth control clinic in Brooklyn, New York, which quickly won her an arrest and a short spell in jail.

It was not for nothing. During Sanger's trial, one of her clients at the birth control clinic took the stand for questioning and gave testimony of a sort that had an effect on many of the middle class people present during the trial. Never before had they been able to relate in a direct and personal way to this 'population problem' they had heard so much about. Several questions were put to the woman, but the most powerful were saved until last.

'How many children have you?' she was asked.

'Eight children and three didn't live,' she answered.

'What does your husband earn?' asked one of the judges.

'Eighteen a week when he works,' she said.

In 1949 the first national survey of the sexual attitudes and sexual behaviour of British people was carried out by a body called Mass-Observation (M-O), which had been founded in 1937 in order to find out about all aspects of ordinary people's lives. The sexual survey took place in response to Kinsey's study of male sexuality in the US, which had been published in 1948. Years on, it was decided that another survey of the sort carried out by M-O should be done. Respondents to the Mass-Observation Archive's survey of 1990 also had heart-wrenching stories to tell of their combined naïveté and poverty; these relate to a time slightly after that of the woman quoted above. One was from a woman who was born in 1908:

> After the birth of my second child I started to use Rendell's pessaries as an aid to fertility control but they cost 2/6 for a packet of 12, so when my husband was out of work I could not afford to buy them and became pregnant with my son in 1936.[7]

Meanwhile, as Sanger ploughed her furrow, Marie Stopes, product of a progressive upper-crust family and the first English female paleobotany PhD, was realising she had been naive and was resolving to do something about it. In 1912, having been married a year, she started to sense that something was amiss. That something was that her husband, a Canadian botanist called Reginald Ruggles Gates, couldn't get it up, and hence, she now realised, the marriage had not been consummated. In 1914 she began annulment proceedings and an urgent study into sexuality, which took place in what was known as 'the cupboard' of the British Library – the section containing the most scandalous books – where her 'eyes were opened to a new and fascinating world'. The outcome was the infamous book *Married Love*, and its main message was that married women had as much right to sexual satisfaction as men did.

At first it was rejected by many publishers. Then salvation came, in the form of dashing aviator Lieutenant Humphrey Roe. Not only did he put up the money for the publication of Stopes's book, he married her into the bargain. The book was an instant success, selling 2,000 copies within the first fortnight, and going on to be reprinted seven times. It sold over a million copies in all.

The marriage started well too. It seemed that her 'search for the body beautiful' (which is what she believed every human being was involved in) was at last over. Not only did she tell her friend Mr Aylma Maude ('Maudy'), who carried a great big rampant torch for her, that 'he seems utterly made for me' (Maud confessed to having mixed feelings), but she not very kindly let him know, in a letter written just after her wedding, when she had first had sex with her husband. Perhaps Maudy found some solace in the addition 'but naturally I haven't had it at its best yet'. Whether he would like to have been her 'tiger' and to call her his 'wood nymph' as Humphrey and Marie did, we will never know. They were certainly one of twentieth-century contraception's Great Love Affairs.

Many qualities of Marie Stopes contributed to her being declared Woman of the Millennium by *Guardian* readers in a poll conducted by the newspaper. One of them was not her ability to write poetry. The following was composed on the occasion of her separation from Humphrey:

> To have loved, to have kissed,
> And – oh, God! – to have missed
> The completion of love!
> A more pitiful thing
> Than the broken wing
> Of a bird that has soared,
> Is one driven by fate
> To return with hate
> Where she once adored.[8]

She also wrote a short play which received some critical acclaim, although not from her playwright friend George Bernard Shaw, who thought it was rubbish. Actually, although she had many distinguished friends, including the novelists H.G. Wells and Arnold

Bennett and classicist Sir Gilbert Murray (all men were called things like Arnold, Humphrey and Gilbert then), only Maudy, green-eyed monster and biographer of Tolstoy, liked it. He read what he called her 'playlet', and pronounced it 'a work of genius'. It should be borne in mind that he also wanted to sleep with her.

Stopes's writing about how to obtain the ideal in marriage, where both parties were 'young, happy and physically well conditioned', is part jargon-filled computer manual/sociology textbook and part evangelical reverie. One minute, mutual orgasm is being described as 'the coordinated function', the next, the unlocking of passion leads the marriage from its 'brutalised and hopeless and sodden' state to a place where it is 'rapturous, spiritual and vital'.

Her first marriage had been anything but rapturous, and ended with Ruggles accusing Marie of being a 'dominating maneater who thinks of nothing but sex sex sex', and Marie taunting him for his impotence. He, in turn, slapped her for her bitchiness. Very soon a doctor was declaring of Ruggles's condition, 'such incapacity is incurable', and thus both the man and the marriage were annulled. At this point she decided she was not alone in her feelings: 'The young man who marries is generally too ignorant to give his wife all her nature requires.' This leads, on the woman's part, to a 'series of disappointments' and a 'longing for fresh adventure'. She now had a mission: 'I believe it is my destiny,' she declared 'to tell [young married couples] how to make love successfully.' She was now 'at the service of humanity'.

With that success came ever-increasing self-confidence (although, she said, 'I have, for a long time, felt like I am a priest and prophet mixed') and an enormous amount of mail. Thousands of those letters still exist today, and around 40 per cent of them are from men. For some, her book just provided a titillating read – containing, as it did, such topics as the function of the clitoris – but others wanted to share with her their experiences of discovering the female orgasm. One husband described how, on having read the book, he brought his wife to orgasm for the first time. 'I was frightened,' he confessed, 'and thought it was some sort of fit.' Many people seemed to be saying something else. All this sex was all very well, but the problem was that it produced babies. Too many babies. Stopes had not thought much about birth control before this (let's face it, she hadn't really needed to), but she took note, and then took notes which she made into another book called *Wise Parenthood*, which came out in 1918. This she filled conscientiously with diagrams of the reproductive organs and descriptions of contraceptives.

Tragically and ironically, this was around the time that her first child was stillborn. She was heartbroken, having wanted a child since being with Ruggles and aware that, now aged thirty-eight, the clock was ticking. She roundly blamed the doctors for not letting her kneel or squat in what she saw to be the most natural position.

Although *Wise Parenthood* was another hit with the educated classes, the poor, who were the target audience, could not afford books and anyway needed more than words to help them on their way. They needed cheap contraception, and the doctors and chemists were not prepared to flog it to them. Many of the former still saw it as too immoral; the latter would have said, 'What do you think we are, a charity?', 'We've got a business to run.' So, in 1921 (and five years after Sanger's Brooklyn offering: one-nil to Margaret), Stopes opened a 'Mother's Clinic' between a sweet shop and a grocer's in London's Holloway Road (but she wasn't arrested for it: one-all), as a kind of model to show how the system could work. From there nurses dispensed rubber caps designed by Marie herself. She did not encourage the use of chemical methods such as spermicide, saying 'never put anything in your vagina that you would not put in your mouth.'

Expansion followed in 1925, which involved Stopes moving to larger premises in Whitfield Street, London. During the Second World War strict instructions came from Marie to ignore any air raids and go on fitting contraceptives. In fact, the notice on the wall said: 'Only when the sound of gunfire or bombs is very near is danger point considered to have been reached.' Twice the sound of bombs was very near indeed, when the clinic itself was hit.

Sanger and Stopes were striving both to get contraception to those who had been excluded previously and to get it generally accepted. Both also wanted their government's help. The best way to get support was to exploit the then current, and approving, fascination with eugenics. The argument would have gone as follows: Only the fittest should survive. The poor are not the fittest either physically or mentally. This leads to them having unfit babies, which does nothing for the strength of the human race. Therefore the poor should not survive – at least in large numbers.

Certainly Marie Stopes saw the poor as intrinsically inferior people, although the British Library archivist who now looks after her work insists that her concern with eugenics is not prominent within the literature and huge number of letters.[9] She says that Marie's main concern was the – not unusual – penniless family with eighteen or twenty children, adding that this would have been a particular problem because (nightmare of nightmares) the working classes were not free to serve the middle classes. Both Stopes and Sanger believed that working-class births should be controlled in more of a hurry than middle-class ones.

So, thanks in large part to Marie Stopes, female sexuality was no longer as taboo as it had been. But the pressure was not off yet. It was not downhill with your legs stretched out beside your handlebars, all the way into the twenty-first century. According to marriage texts such as *Ideal Marriage*, by Theodore van de Velde, which was available in translation in 1926, women were no longer simply *allowed* to have orgasms, it was *expected* of them. In fact, if they did not they were threatening family stability and thus society. And they were probably frigid. Or lesbians. Welcome, presumably, to the wonderful new world of the faked orgasm.

Working-class women, though, had neither the time ('oh oh oh oh oh oh oh yes yes yes yes . . .' etc) or the energy (all that clawing of your husband's back and so on) to do what was being prescribed for them by the authors. Wives just wanted careful husbands and a kind of anti-Viagra pill to take away any ardour that those husbands might have. Stopes, amazed that they did not want passion, let it be known, sulkily, that no such pill was available.

She – and Sanger – then proceeded to turn against almost all of the methods of contraception they used. Continence was out – the single bed was the 'enemy of marriage,' said Stopes – extended nursing weakened mothers and coitus interruptus was not only extremely unreliable, according to Stopes, but physically and psychologically dangerous. Yes, the 'psychologically dangerous' myth still persisted. Withdrawal was also undesirable because, along with countless teenage boys, Stopes was a firm believer that contact with semen was beneficial to women. According to her, any method which prevented this, while not actually giving women acne, would be detrimental to them in some way.

Condoms were unacceptable for the same reason, and because they were unromantic and unaesthetic. So what was left? Stopes advocated the use of the cap and Sanger the diaphragm (well, they couldn't just agree could they?). There was a clear shared belief that women should be responsible for birth control. This was, according to Sanger, because other methods 'placed the burden of responsibility solely upon the husband – a burden which he seldom assumed'. This attitude is still widely held by many women and men today and has almost certainly slowed down the development of the male Pill. Can men be trusted to take the pill when they are not the ones to get pregnant? That, rather than 'to be or not to be', is the question.

One thing was for sure, Stopes was not in danger of being branded a witch, having been suspicious from the start of the sorts of drugs that housewives bought from apothecaries. Perhaps she had always come at birth control from more of a medical angle than she cared to admit.

Although nineteenth-century German-Hungarian women are said to have made their own caps from melted beeswax, the problem with the kind that Stopes distributed (and with diaphragms for that matter), even if they could be made affordable, was that they necessarily involved a visit to a clinic for a fitting. Clinics were medical places, when you were used to leaning over your garden fence for contraceptive advice. Fittings were often conducted by men, although Stopes made a point of hiring women to work in her clinics. This, combined with the reluctance of the medics themselves to come forward, made progress slow on both sides of the Atlantic. And the more medical the clinics were made in an attempt to attract doctors, the more repelled the punters were.

The problem of the attitude of doctors carried on both in the US and the UK into the 1920s, and not just because they were square. Medical students were ill-informed on the subject of contraception because it was not taught, and it was not taught because the survival of the institutions was dependent on wealthy philanthropists or the church, and *they* were square. However, with the Depression, at the very end of the 1920s, the better (and non-Catholic) schools felt that they could no longer avoid the issue of poverty, and began to teach their students about contraception.

In fact, the thin ends of wedges were being driven in all over the place. The Vatican sanctioned the rhythm method in 1930.[10] The Anglican Church and British Medical Association approved birth control if further pregnancy was judged to be potentially detrimental to the mother's health. The Canadian courts said distribution of birth control information for the public good should be allowed. And finally, and crucially, arch-square Comstock's law of 1873 (which prevented the mailing of contraceptives or advice about them) was overruled.

A particularly poignant example of Comstock's censorship was found in *Call*. The editor of this newspaper's women's page was Anita Block, and she asked Margaret Sanger to rework some of her lectures into a series of articles. Comstockery determined that one Sunday this column took the form of a headline, 'What Every Girl Should Know', with the word 'Nothing' written vertically below it, and below that, 'By Order Of The Post Office Department'. Sanger's crime had been to mention syphilis and gonorrhoea in previous articles and Comstock had managed to take time out from raiding art galleries which displayed paintings of nudes to notice this.

Although in the UK the main form of contraception in the early 1900s was still coitus interruptus (despite the best efforts of Stopes), the use of mechanical methods rose from 9 to 40 per cent for the middle classes between 1910 and 1930 and from 1 to 28 per cent for the working classes.[11] The top four methods were, in reverse order, pessaries, safe period, sheath – which was now available in the more comfortable and skin-tight latex, a material which got its first proper airing when distributed among troops in the Second World War – and withdrawal.

Ever since the time of Soranus, weird and wonderful variations on the barrier method theme have been and usually gone. One of the 1920s' very own was the block pessary, which can be seen in the Museum of Contraception in Toronto. It is a kind of cube with an indentation in each of its six sides. The idea was that, when put inside a woman, one of these sides would cover the cervix.

More than this, contraception was going global. 1930 saw the first international clinic on contraception in Zurich.[12] There had already been congresses held in Paris in 1900, in Liège, Belgium, in 1905, in The Hague in 1910 and in Dresden, Germany, in 1911, in London in 1922 and in New York in 1925 (two–one to Marie). In 1921 Sanger took the birth control message to Japan, and in 1936 to India. Societies were formed in both Czechoslovakia and Poland by 1931.

The 'female methods' favoured by Stopes and Sanger were not yet the method of choice for most people. When they did start to catch on in a bigger way it was in the US (two–all). Apart from women, the other group in the US that was starting to get wise to birth control was big business. It entered the fray armed with a huge array of spermicides with names like Rendell's, Norform and Zonitor. By 1935, two hundred types of so-called mechanical contraceptive – either condoms or pessaries – were available to the Western world.

People from the Mass-Observation Archive can remember them all right. 'The condom was available long before I was sexually active,' said one man who was born in 1922. 'I can well recall the coded question being asked by barbers when an adult client was paying his bill: "Was there anything else, Sir?" Which puzzled me because I was never asked the same question, as a boy.'[13] Another respondent, a woman, remembers the spermicidal pessary:

I used a tablet which had to be inserted before intercourse. It had to be in place a certain time before, as it was only effective over a given number of minutes. Even so it wasn't reliable and I felt most grievously let down when I found myself pregnant because the tablet hadn't been in long enough to be activated.[14]

Others wanted children but inadvertently guarded against

conception. One woman was overheard gossiping about a couple she knew, the male half of which had been serving abroad and had used quinine, presumably to guard against malaria:

> I'm sure it's because he's simply soaked in quinine. I know several cases like that. Men who have been in the East for some years and now want children and can't have them. I'm quite sure quinine has a sterile effect.[15]

Gossip or not, she was in line with the scientific thinking of the day. In fact, Rendell's pessaries were officially 'soluble quinine pessaries'.

A different woman was aware of the alternatives but opted, ultimately, for onanism, thus producing that rare thing in history – the document to show that it goes on: 'When we first married we used condoms, but neither of us liked them,' she said. 'Next came the Dutch cap, which was a performance, so we decided that for us withdrawal was the answer.'[16]

Publications were still advising against withdrawal for the same reasons which had been cited for hundreds of years – that it would make you mad. Nurse M. R. Hooper, MRCN of the Birth Control Advisory Bureau in Holloway, London, printed a booklet called 'The Voice of Experience' in 1938. She said of withdrawal that it was 'bad from a health point of view', being 'a great strain on the nerves, and if practised for a period of years [it] can cause severe mental illness'. Just how innocent the voice of experience could afford to be in 1938 is also shown by the beginning of the booklet: 'Many people imagine that birth control is practised only by those who don't like children. This is not so.' Moreover, when discussing caps, she demonstrates just how pre-PC she is. 'In cases of very fat women we find it is necessary to get an extra strong spring cap made.' No nonsense about 'larger ladies' then.

Relatively innocent letters were still being sent to the Marie Stopes Clinic in 1944. A typical one read: 'Dear nurse in charge. I have just had another baby and do not wish to have another baby for about two years, so could you please give me advice on the best methods of birth control. Thanking you very much . . .'

Another form that the innocence took, to today's businesslike eye, was the apparently pointless, and thus quite touching, chattiness of them. A 'young soldier's wife' with two children writes: 'I would not like another [baby] while the war is on as I think two enough to keep on army pay.' Another woman explains that she lives in only two rooms and would like advice on birth control because she is 'afraid a baby would mean us finding elsewhere to live and houses are very hard to get'.

Men still wrote too. One was a corporal with a premature ejaculation problem who was convinced that this meant he could not have a child. He does not say as much in his letter, but it is implied that he thinks his wife must climax in order to become pregnant, because he points to how very quickly he becomes 'excited' and how long it takes her to.

It should be noted that the interest in contraception was not due to an overall rise in the birth rate, as it was before and has been since. Between 1880 and 1930, the birth rate in Britain had actually declined by 50 per cent. So some of the enemies of birth control were just worried about the population declining. This led to comments like: 'Well, if nobody has children it shows that people are losing heart, I should say.' And indeed, some were losing heart and it was due to the First World War. Said one man:

'For many years I nursed the conviction that the only way to avoid wars and disputes between people is to reduce the population of the world to something like 2 million. There would then be so much for everyone to do that there would be no time to go to war. If it takes two to make a quarrel, how many quarrels may be engendered by the present population of the world? So I approve strongly of the decline in the birth rate. People are not being silly when they say, '"I'm not going to have children to grow up to become cannon fodder"'. They have every excuse for disquiet and cynicism.[17]

The 'cannon fodder' worry crops up again and again in the comments of those interviewed in the mid-1940s.

In a report by the Mass-Observation Unit called *Britain and Her Birth Rate* by John Murray, it was spotted that there was a kind of fatalistic attitude towards pregnancy, which seemed to have a lot to do with people's level of education. Of those with secondary education only 16 per cent said that the number of children a family had should be left to chance. Of those with only elementary education the figure was 40 per cent. Typical comments by the latter category included, 'Well, I didn't want the three I've got. I suppose I'll have to have all I get.'

Never fear, though, the moral guardians were still there too. One man was a company assistant executive:

> People have begun to dissociate the idea of sexual intercourse from that of conception, and the implications of this one change in ideas are enormous. For they imply far-reaching changes in other ideas, religious, social and moral.
>
> Obviously I have been discussing the more intelligent, who have thought their way to the position or rationalised it. But the curious thing is that 'the general' have also gone the same way. I have no doubt that even the most abandoned would still protest vigorously against any imputation with regard to their ideas of God, but they manage quite successfully to keep water-tight compartments for their loose morals and their respectability.[18]

An extension of this view which was popular and which was, again, isolated by the Mass-Observation report was that not having children was selfish. If the non-parents were questioned, the report said that 'we find, as we do with most of the reasons people give for having few children, that they look to *them* like common sense'. One woman who 'doesn't want children "for a long time anyway"' illustrated this by saying:

> Well, as soon as my hubby comes back, we want to catch up on some of the good times we've missed in the last few years. Babies tie you; you and your hubby can never get together or anything. It's just staying at home washing nappies.[19]

This 'selfishness' view is still around today. Not so popular today is the view that children with unmarried parents are somehow lesser than those whose parents are married. Another 'moral guardian' type then was a shop assistant. She thought 'illegitimate' children should be given a hard time for having unmarried parents:

> One result of the changed viewpoint is that the children are not penalised as formerly, and made to feel different. I know a girl of a very decent family who had a baby from a soldier who went abroad before they could marry. Far from being a disgrace, the child is the joy of the family, and his likeness to his father openly spoken of . . .[20]

Thankfully so. We may presume from her comments that not all children in his situation had such enlightened families.

As far as attitudes during this time go, occasionally the comments of the M-O observers are at least as revealing as those of the people they are observing. In 1943, one young girl is interviewed and says that she realises she would have to give up all thoughts of a career if she married and had a family, and she really wants to be an archaeologist. 'Good for her,' say we. 'Still at Bedales: more intelligent than attractive,' says the interviewer.

Meanwhile, in the 'overheard' section of the archive, a man from Chelsea has a wry slant on the whole shooting match:

> It makes me laugh, all this stuff in the papers. They can talk and talk in Parliament, but they don't know the first thing about what people really feel. I don't say there's anybody else wearing just my pair of shoes. But you get all this stuff about the birth-rate, and I got a wife at home that won't let me come near her, and that's life I say.[21]

Marie Stopes was not the first to think of separating sex from procreation. Robert Dickinson (1861–1950),[22] a liberal-minded doctor, had thought of it in 1908. One of his (professional) passions was female anatomy, and he became famous for his beautifully illustrated articles on the subject. He was also one of the first to note that the breaking of the hymen was not a reliable gauge of virginity, since hymens may stretch for all sorts of reasons, allowing a woman to be penetrated for the first time without pain.

Overall, he was insistent that medicine should maintain a human face, and his own humanity was evident in almost everything he did. In the 1890s he began to worry that corsets were damaging women, as indeed they later proved to be. By 1895, during the great 'does cycling encourage masturbation?' debate, while describing masturbation as a 'horrible habit' he added that it was common and people should not become hysterical about it. Whether willingly or not, this led him to be considered the authority on masturbation.

He thought sex should be enjoyed equally by men and women, and that children should be planned and their births spaced out by parents. He also thought abstinence was bad for both husbands and wives. He was therefore a great believer in contraception and felt that research needed to be done, because not enough was known about it. His passion for the subject was such that, according to his friends, it took him ten minutes to turn any conversation into one about birth control.

With sophistry not seen since Plato invented platonic love as a justification for the dirty old men of ancient Greece to do as they pleased (Plato, incidentally, was as into eugenics as Stopes and Sanger), Dickinson convinced an arch-enemy of birth control, George W. Komak, not only to form but also to serve on a committee which was to study contraception. He convinced him by saying, more or less, 'You're right about these long-haired radicals getting involved with birth control. What the world needs is a proper serious examination of birth control, an examination which would be best headed up by people like you and me.'

Meanwhile a survey among college women in the United States had shown that 74 per cent were using contraception.[23] Hospital trials in 1924 showed that the most popular form of contraception was clearly going to be the diaphragm, which had been used in the UK and Holland for some time, but was still not available in the States. At one stage diaphragms had even been on their way into the country, but most had been turned away by customs. Six hundred of them. What's more, the four hundred that did get through were only in the smallest and largest sizes. You couldn't, as they say, make it up.

Dickinson had until now studiously avoided Sanger because he saw her as 'promiscuous' and too keen on self-promotion. Little by little, though, he started to realise that his mission was closer to hers than to anyone else's. Not only that – she had a stash of diaphragms. Meanwhile Sanger had started to realise that there were some useful things about medicine and its approach. Very soon they were working together, at first to the disgust of most of Dickinson's colleagues.

Clarence Gamble (1894–1966) – as in Procter and Gamble, now a giant pharmaceuticals company – had made a big slippery pile out of soap, but was first heard to show an interest in birth control in 1925 when he was engaged in other kinds of biological research, and his wife was heavily pregnant. On that first occasion, he was chatting about birth control with some students in his cluttered lab, when one joked that he ought to be able to find a better method than the diaphragm in amongst all his stuff.[24]

Being a rich scientist with a social conscience, the next thing he knew was that it was 1933 and he was president of the Pennsylvania Birth Control Federation. The central tenet of this organisation was that 'human life is too fine and too sacred a thing to be brought into the world except by the voluntary act of responsible persons'.

Gamble was also one of those who thought that the poor were inferior and those of 'good stock' should be encouraged to have the most children, a popular and defensible view at the time. However, he had sufficient sympathy for the poor to realise that they hated all things medical, and he was soon desperate to find a form of contraception which did not involve clinics and doctors or nurses. His solution to this was to develop a 'Standards Programme' which tested contraceptive products already on the market for reliability, the end result being that the quacks would be exposed and cheap, reliable contraception would be available to all.

There was still a level of dismissiveness and arrogance from parts of the medical establishment which was reminiscent of the 1800s. One

Scientific American article described the only methods available ('the pastes and creams and jellies') as 'messy little gadgets' and made it clear that these were offensive to 'the scientific mind'. Despite this, work on the effectiveness of spermicides had already begun in Britain. In Edinburgh, not before time, Cecil Voge, an animal geneticist, had begun to test substances long assumed to have spermicidal properties to see if they actually worked. It was lucky he did. Among the results were that quinine, which had long since been used as a contraceptive, was not effective, whereas coconut oil soap, which sounded like an old wives' tale if ever there was one, did the trick. Meanwhile scientist John R. Baker was testing chemical spermicides in Oxford.

The quality of condoms was to improve too, as the side-effect of a new concern about syphilis. When a huge cargo of them was tested and it was established that they were faulty, the whole lot was destroyed, ushering in a new era of safety – if not a new reputation – for the condom. Far from being our friend, it was still seen as Astruc's 'unfortunate necessity'.

Although he was a snob, Gamble continued to be modern in his outlook. He even suggested that a birth control aspect should be added to the fiction found in popular magazines. At the same time, he kept the doctors happy by keeping them informed about developments in contraceptive research. The culmination of all this fine activity, and the sign to the world that a whole new phase had begun, was an article by Robert Dickinson in 1943 in the *American Journal of Public Health*, giving definitive standards for contraceptives and listing the available brands that met them.

Gamble also discovered Christopher Tietze, a medical statistician who, when hired by Gamble to work on developing contraception, brought with him a new outlook.[25] He saw the population question not as one of 'good stock' being taken over by 'bad stock', but as one of humanity itself being in crisis. One of the projects that Gamble got him to work on was the development of what became the Intra-Uterine Device or IUD.

The principle of putting an obstacle in a womb to prevent conception occurring had been around for a long time. North African Arabs, for instance, had for centuries been putting a stone in the womb of their female camels to stop them becoming pregnant on long desert journeys.[26] In fact, from the time of Hippocrates early versions of the method had been used on human beings. These included experiments involving wood, glass, ivory, gold, and platinum studded with diamonds. In the mid-nineteenth century too when, as James Reed points out, 'physicians first began to venture into the vagina as a matter of routine',[27] a number of pessaries were developed with varying degrees of success.

To start with, these successes would have been seen as failures, since the 'stem pessary' at least was designed to *aid* conception by easing the journey of sperm into the fallopian tubes. They also frequently caused infections of the pelvis, which enabled the moralists to rub their hands with glee and cry things like 'See? See what happens when you flout the laws of God and nature and have sex without intending to procreate?'

The difference between these devices and what Ernst Grafenberg, a German gynaecologist, was trying to do in 1909, was that his developments were completely contained by the uterus, so that nothing stuck out and provided a path along which bacteria could pass. His device evolved from one that used silk gut as its main material to one combining this with silver wire.

By 1930, at the International Birth Control Conference, Grafenberg was able to tell the world that, in trials using one thousand patients, the method had been a roaring success. There was general interest immediately after the conference, but although Ernst had stressed the need for his 'Grafenberg ring' to be inserted only into healthy uteri, many doctors ignored his advice and the method either exacerbated the condition or was held responsible for it anyway.[28]

This led most of the ever-cautious medical establishment to turn against it, with a measure of good reason. Infections of the pelvis (with whatever cause) were still highly dangerous before the medication existed to treat them. Doctors were not prepared to take the risk. Perhaps it gave them an excuse not to fit the things too, a process for which throughout history, doctors had failed to show much enthusiasm.

Some madcap maverick medics did continue to fit the IUD, and one of those was Mary Halton. As early as 1924, Halton had fitted the stem pessary (although she went on to employ the Grafenberg ring) for over a thousand women, some of them actresses and working women. She showed the results of these fittings to Dickinson, who was cheered enough by the results to suggest that there should be more formal research into the IUD. Eventually, Gamble had Tietze help Dickinson to get Halton's results published.

The publication did not go down well with the establishment, although some of the more enlightened doctors recognised that it was likely, in time, to become an important method. It was already important in a functional way, in that it did its job better than any other method ever recorded. The failure rate was 0.9 per hundred woman years, which is a roundabout way of saying that if you used a stem pessary, you were extremely unlikely to get pregnant.

Despite all this excitement, birth control was about to lose Tietze to the State Department. He had become fed up with the lack of 'institutional support' for birth control, although he maintained that it was 'one of the most urgent problems in today's world'. Eventually, when his own colleagues deemed him too radical to be invited to the Conference on Population Trends and the Family, he packed his bags.

The fortunes of the IUD were not to change until the early 1950s, after Gamble paid for a scientist, Prof. John E. Gordon, and a doctor, John B. Wyon, to do some research in Khanna in massively over-populated India. It was soon clear that the villagers involved in the study were reluctant, to say the least, to employ contraception. Although the figures were not precise, it was estimated that only around 20 per cent of them were willing to try any of the proposed methods – which were the rhythm method, withdrawal and a contraceptive paste/salt solution on a cotton pad.

After five fruitless years of research – during which time Gamble flushed over $1 million down the pan – the leaders of the village were asked why they thought the enterprise had been such a failure. The best that the researchers could come up with was that the community thought it needed the labour and loved children. The leaders thought that the main reason was that the villagers were too shy to go to a place where they had to ask for medical supplies of this sort. The researchers working in the field said this was combined with a lack of motivation on the part of the women. Brutally put, if something was to be done about the population problem in areas like this, it would have to involve a method that was long-acting and effortless to use. After spending all that money, all they had managed to conclude was that the world needed to find a radically new form of contraception.

Here was an obvious reason to resurrect the IUD, and Alan F. Guttmacher, a member of the Population Council and previously an arch-enemy of the method, was ready to listen. One of the men in his obstetrics department at Mount Sinai Hospital in New York City had the idea that the IUD could be made of plastic. That way, the argument went, the flexibility of the device would prevent damage to the womb, because the cervix would no longer have to be stretched to allow it to enter the uterus.

Hesitantly, because he had heard the scare stories about the IUD at medical school, Guttmacher allowed Dr Lazar Margulies to try out his theory. It worked. Guttmacher would not have to use penicillin, which had been discovered since the IUD was first tried out, to rid women of their pelvic inflammatory disease, or worse.

Meanwhile, Willi Oppenheimer, an Israeli who had previously done work on IUDs in Berlin with Margulies, had been invited to contribute to the *American Journal of Obstetrics and Gynecology*, by writing about his experience with the Grafenberg ring, and the resulting piece was generally applauded. This was an official enough stamp of approval for the world. By the mid-1960s, the Population Council had invested $2.5 million in the development and trial of the method, and after they established that it was highly effective for seven out of ten women, it was only a matter of time before the device was having an effect on the population growth of several developing countries, including South Korea, Taiwan and Pakistan.

Quite apart from all these mechanical goings-on, the most cutting-edge of scientists were looking to nature for the answers, setting up the circumstances for the next great discovery . . .

6

Pill Papas

If you have abandoned one faith, do not abandon all faith. There is always an alternative to the faith we lose. Or is it the same faith under another mask?

Graham Greene – The Comedians[1]

By the 1920s, US scientists had been thinking about hormones for some time. Thinking *about* hormones that is, not thinking *with* hormones, which would have produced quite different results – lots of arguing about who had the biggest test-tube or the fastest lab rat, and so on. It would also have resulted in doctors with many, many children, which would not have helped the cause at all. At any rate, it was in the 1920s that they turned their thoughts, professionally at least, to sex. This was helped by injections of cash, one in 1923 from the Bureau of Social Hygiene.

Thanks to George Corner and Willard Allen of the University of Rochester,[2] it was soon clear that progesterone was one of the key hormones required if conception was to be prevented using chemicals, in that it had an effect on ovulation. In 1930, however, scientists were held back by the cost. Pigs were used to get hold of progesterone, but a ton of animal organs was needed to produce just one gram of it.

Then an American scientist by the name of Russell Marker became convinced that synthetic and cheap hormones could be created from steroids found in the roots of many types of lily. Experiments showed that the answer could indeed be found in Mother Nature's medicine cabinet, within a particular type of wild Mexican yam (*Dioscorea mexicana*). As before with spermicides and condoms (which, incidentally, got their 'reservoir tips' in the 1950s, as well as being joined by a 'sensation deadening' condom which was supposed to prevent premature ejaculation), the race was now on between competing businesses to exploit this discovery first. The world had well and truly realised that sex sells contraception – and thus that where there was contraception there was money.

Corner then introduced the idea of using progesterone to calm periods down, simultaneously, for a time at least, calming down the media and hence the Frankenstein-fearing public. People were suspicious of scientists then as now, but the idea that chemicals were being developed for the purpose of interfering with that most sacred and magical of processes, the creation of human life, was just too much for many. Obviously if they were being used to lessen the severity of menstruation this was less sinister. It is interesting to note that women who have very heavy periods, or suffer from extreme period side-effects, still go on the Pill today for the purpose of combating these problems. And yet this result is generally regarded as a side-effect of the Pill rather than the origin of it.

The first guinea pigs able to confirm that high doses of oestrogen – the hormone controlling the female reproductive cycle – suppressed ovulation were mice and rabbits. They agreed in principle that this was an important advancement and a potential alleviator of the population problem. The rabbits particularly looked forward to a time when they could have lots of sex without the pressures that lots of children bring (crowded warrens, finding enough grass for everyone to eat and so on). However, they recognised that oestrogen was still far too expensive to be used in a widespread way. By the end of the 1940s, science was all set to discover the contraceptive Pill.

Gregory Goodwin Pincus (or 'Goody' to his friends) was born in New Jersey to a Russian Jewish family. He wanted to be a farmer, but his father disapproved because there was not enough money in it. So he decided to study genetics. Some say this was because he was colour blind, which gave him an interest in heredity. Perhaps he wanted to establish scientifically that his father was to blame for his colour blindness. At any rate, lots of plants were grown to feed the lab animals at Harvard's Bussey Institute, the place where he decided to study, so it looked a bit like a farm.

His other main passions were for precision and analysis, which led him to Prof. Crozier, a tutor at Harvard whose approach was very much the same. This attitude led the two to share a hatred of biological mysticism, a kind of conspiracy encouraged by the Church that allowed theologians, as Donald Fleming so mischievously put it in his introduction to Loeb's *The Mechanistic Conception of Life*, to 'slip a soul in while nobody was looking'. Both were agreed, in common with several philosophers but very few laymen, that there was no biological evidence for the existence of a soul. By now they could discuss it too. Although such suggestions might still raise the eyebrow of a passer-by, Pincus and Crozier were no longer at risk of being burned at the stake for raising the subject at all.

By 1931, Pincus was made assistant professor in Crozier's department, and became an expert on sexual physiology in mammals as a result of his work on the eggs of rabbits. Most controversially, he was studying the process of fertilisation and the very beginning of embryo development. This remains a touchy subject to this day, the accusation that research scientists are 'playing God' being the most common. Despite this, Crozier managed to secure financial support from research councils for his work.

The first media storm was whipped up when he succeeded in producing test-tube rabbit embryos. The *New York Times* drew the inevitable parallel with Aldous Huxley's *Brave New World*, presuming to know that Pincus's research was undertaken with a view to hatching human beings in the same way.

To begin with, Pincus enjoyed the attention in the same way as Marie Stopes had done, and stars like Bradlaugh and Besant before her. Crozier too approved, especially of the fact that Pincus had succeeded in upsetting the Spiritualists. However, the uglier aspects of the media during that time soon became evident: its anti-semitism and its misogyny. Pincus's obsession with producing test tube babies was about to render men redundant, at least as far as *Collier's* reporter

J. D. Ratcliff was concerned: 'man's value would shrink . . . the mythical world of the Amazons would then come to life'. More than this, he was doing work on *animals* and, worse still, had 'small, almost feminine hands'.

Further ammunition was provided by Alexis Carrell, surgeon and mystic, whom Ratcliff got 'on side'. Carrell helped Ratcliff capitalise on the image of Pincus as a mad professor with no social conscience, or sense either of responsibility or spirituality. This view was further supported by a snap taken by a *Collier's* photographer of a wild-haired Pincus, fag in mouth and big white fluffy rabbit in hand. He learned the press lesson and, for the moment, stopped talking to reporters.

Then, in 1937, he was both granted leave of absence to spend a year in Cambridge (the one in the UK) and informed that there would be no post for him at Harvard on his return. Pincus was convinced that the decision to remove him was political, just as he was convinced of his superiority over some of his colleagues who were able to stay. Certainly the public were suspicious of 'genetic engineers' and the kind of mud that the media slings can be the stickiest of all. He was going to have to learn to play the media game.

Rescue came in the shape of his friend Hudson Hoagland, head of the biology department at Clark University, who made Pincus Clark visiting professor of zoology. There was no salary with the post, but a fellow researcher at Cambridge, Baron Nathaniel Rothschild, gave him $2,500 with which to continue his work. He was also learning to deal with the press to the extent that one article in the *New York Times*, about 'the first fatherless rabbit', described what he was doing as providing 'valuable knowledge' which would eventually help towards 'the birth of healthier human beings, the ultimate purpose of the experiments'.

Disillusioned by academia, Pincus and Hoagland then left it, together resolving to survive on research grants and forming the Worcester Foundation for Experimental Biology. Pincus got to look after the animals – nearly farming, again – and Hoagland had friends in high places. The friend in the highest place of all was the mighty G. D. Searle and Company, a pharmaceuticals manufacturer. After a halting start with the company, Pincus went to its director of research and asked whether the company might consider backing research into a contraceptive injection or pill. Although he continued his work on steroids without the extra cash, the dressing-down he received along with the refusal of more money managed to be both short-sighted and prophetic at the same time:

> You haven't given us a thing to justify the half-million that we invested in you . . . to date your record as a contributor to the commerce of the Searle Company is a lamentable failure, replete with false leads, poor judgement, and assurances from you that were false. Yet you have the nerve to ask for more for research. You will get more only if a lucky chance gives us something originating from your group which will make us a profit . . . '

Enter Katharine Dexter McCormick, educated daughter of a big US attorney and a schoolteacher, and from a long line of distinguished people including lawyers and politicians. While at the Massachusetts Institute of Technology (MIT) in Cambridge (the American one), she fell in love with the college's golden boy, Stanley Dexter, who had at least enough credentials to join the family (he was a rich, good-looking tennis player who could succeed academically and paint a fair picture into the bargain). They were married and the future could not have looked rosier. It seemed almost too good to be true.

And it was. After two years of marriage, Stanley developed schizophrenia and was very soon so far gone that power over his estate had to be transferred to Katharine. He was clearly not much cop as a husband but failed to die until forty years later. The response of Katharine, the beautiful and intelligent wife who both did and did not have a husband, was to throw herself into causes. The first of these was women's suffrage, which by a series of events led her to give financial support to Margaret Sanger in contraceptive research and her international work.

Before Stanley's death she had also held out hope of a cure for schizophrenia, and for this reason had put money into the work that Hoagland was doing on the disease. However when her husband died, McCormick's interest in and hence funding for schizophrenia research dried up. This meant that when on one day in the early 1950s, she ran into Hoagland's office crying 'What are we going to do about it?', he assumed a change of heart had occurred, and that she was interested in schizophrenia once more.

She soon put him straight. The problem was the impending population crisis. He called Pincus into his study, just as McCormick had in fact intended, since she had already heard of his work, and the beginnings of the battle plan were drawn up. Margaret Sanger too was drafted in and there was excitement all round.

Rightly so. The upshot was that McCormick put between $150,000 and $180,000 into the campaign every year until her death in 1967. It was hardly forgotten on the event of her death, either. She was to leave research into the contraceptive Pill $1 million in her will. By 1956, a year after the world had been changed from a different quarter, when 'Rock Around The Clock' by Bill Haley and the Comets introduced the idea of youth rebellion that would go on to provide fuel for the use of the Pill, the first successes in using synthetic steroids as an oral contraceptive were being reported by *Science*.

The first person to be hired by Pincus was Min-Cheuh Chang, an eminent scientist in the field of mammalian reproduction. He was suspicious of what he saw as the rest of the research team's pandering to big business, and thought that everyone should relax a little more. Although he often received public praise from Pincus, he was never a household name and remains, sadly, something of an unsung hero of birth control. Even then, being good at your job was not necessarily enough. You had to have a talent for self-promotion in order to be recognised.

Another of the people recruited by Pincus was John Rock, a Roman Catholic gynaecologist and an old friend of Pincus's. Sanger was against the appointment at first because she thought the Catholic thing would get in the way. She was soon proven wrong, at least in the respect that it did not get in the way of their research or the success of the Pill. In fact, the only real conflict was within John Rock's head. Sanger had the dignity to backtrack to the extent that she described him as 'handsome as a god'.

He was also willing to enter the debate on birth control, thinking it 'shocking to see the big family glorified'. In one article he defended birth control on the grounds that 'whatever genetic trait may contribute to the intellectual deficiency which permits [the deluded mates] selfishly to seek more immediate comfort, is at least kept from the inheritable common pool, and in time their kind is thus bred out'. Later on, he seemed to change his view on the type that sought 'immediate comfort'. It wasn't just the intellectually deficient ones, but rather anyone who was cohabiting, he decided, insisting that a couple could not live together happily without having sex often.

Meanwhile Searle's chemists had manufactured a new kind of progesterone which did not need to be taken in huge quantities. Again there was a clash between them and Pincus, with the chief chemist, Francis Saunders, reluctant to support the development of the contraceptive pill and Rock's proposed trials for it. On this occasion, Saunders was troubled about subjecting women to high doses of a drug like this over prolonged periods. Not only was he worried that it might damage their health, he was concerned about how the idea might be received by the world. Furthermore, the trials would take time, and the women who took part in them would have to be prepared to have sore breasts and to feel sick and/or dizzy. In other words, there was a chance that life could effectively turn into one long period. Eventually a combination of two hormones which could be taken in relatively small doses was found. It had limited side-effects and almost no bleeding at the wrong time of the month. They were ready for trials to take place.

The place that they decided on was Puerto Rico, where the inhabitants were poor and uneducated. Perfect. The one hundred volunteers needed were easily found, although over the next few months thirty of those dropped out because, among other reasons, there was bad press coverage, they got sterilised, and they found themselves to be already pregnant when they signed up. One woman's husband had hanged himself because he was so poor. Even the drop-outs served a purpose, though, because it was soon clear that women who had been on the Pill were able to return to having perfectly normal, healthy babies.

By the time the team's ally who had arranged the trial for them in

Puerto Rico had left to join the World Health Organisation, she was able to hand Pincus data on 221 patients, adding that 'we have not had one single pregnancy which could be attributed to method failure'. There had been some minor problems with side-effects, but these were soon overcome. In fact, the women who had the side-effects had been so fully briefed on possible reactions to the drug that there was some question as to whether their side-effects were real or imagined, and a placebo usually did the trick.

The team decided that the revolution was almost upon them, and McCormick put up the money for Pincus and his wife to do a world tour, the purpose of which was to shout as loudly as possible about the Pill's imminent arrival. In 1958 Pincus decided to do just one more year of tests before putting the drug on the market. Some 'suits' were still sceptical, and in fact the drug was reduced in dosage after being available for a year.

One party which still needed convincing was the US government. Rock went to see the official physician in charge of scepticism and was kept waiting for half an hour, a terrible insult to a stickler such as he was. Once he did see the physician he found the man to be without any experience in the gynaecological or any related field. Rock was 'livid' and let this be known to the highest authorities he could find. The application was then approved by the Food and Drug Administration, possibly due to Rock's temper.

After two years, the Pill had caused sales of prescribed contra-ceptives to rise from $20 million to $50 million per annum globally. By 1962 the figure was $56.6 million, as more and more women became confident about seeing their doctors knowing they would not having to undergo a fitting, as with the diaphragm. The Searle company was ecstatic. And getting rich.

In 1962 there was a major scare when, tragically, some babies were born deformed as a result of their mothers taking the sedative thalidomide during pregnancy. This was expected by the world's media to have a damaging effect on the Pill and possibly to sound its death knell, because it would remind people to be afraid of science, particularly when applied to reproduction. However, the Pill was declared safe by several distinguished bodies and women largely ignored the press reports suggesting it was damaging. By 1974, ten million American women and fifty million worldwide were on the Pill. It seemed like a near-perfect method, the only real threat to its success being the fallibility of the women who took it (or forgot to). Okay, so the Catholic church was kicking up a bit of a fuss about it all, but this was the generation that had lived through the social revolution of the sixties. Everybody knew the Church wasn't very groovy, so no one cared very much about that.

Actually John Rock cared. He cared very much. He was, in fact, in the process of losing his religion. In 1964, after years in which he argued for support for the Pill from his Catholic church, the Catholic journal *America* made a statement which showed, once and for all, that he had lost his fight. The journal's editorial concluded, 'No amount of word juggling can make abstinence from sexual relations and the suppression of ovulation the same thing.'[3] Four years later the Pope himself announced that all 'artificial' methods of contraception were against the Church's teachings.

A part of what Rock had tried to do was to increase the Pill's 'naturalness', and hence its acceptability both to women and to the Church, by making it produce a twenty-eight day menstrual cycle. In the *New Yorker* in 2000, the results of fieldwork carried out in 1986 by scientist Beverly Strassmen in Mali, Africa, led journalist Malcolm Gladwell to conclude that this was a mistake on Rock's part. In Mali, one of the most 'natural' communities in the world, it was established that between the ages of twenty and thirty-four the average woman has one period a year. This can be put down to the fact that much of this time is spent being pregnant or breastfeeding. 'In other words,' says Gladwell, 'what we think of as normal – frequent menses – is in evolutionary terms abnormal.'[4]

This means to Strassmen that Western women's bodies are subjected to stresses for which they were not, in evolutionary terms, designed. Not only could Rock have helped to redress the balance for women, the idea runs, but he would have had a case in telling the Church that he was reintroducing a long since lost 'naturalness' into the bargain. Not only that, there is evidence to suggest that long-term Pill use helps prevent some sorts of cancer (especially ovarian and endometrial), contrary to popular belief. Since Pope Pius XII had approved the Pill for therapeutic purposes, argues Gladwell, it is, with hindsight, possible to spot a missed opportunity on Rock's part. 'If he had known what we know now,' says Gladwell, 'and had talked about the Pill not as a drug to prevent life but as one that would save life, the Church might well have said yes.'[5]

Instead Rock ran away to the hills of New Hampshire to read books about Darwin. A year before he died, in his last public interview (with writer Sara Davidson), having utterly renounced the idea of an afterlife he described 'all the Church stuff' as 'for the solace of the multitude'. Finally, in the *New Yorker* piece at least, came the achingly sad bit: 'I was an ardent practicing Catholic for a long time, and I really believed it all then, you see.'[6]

But this revelation followed more innocent times. Innocent in some respects at least. There was certainly naïveté among the young on matters sexual. In the UK, one 1990 Mass-Observation respondent remembered particularly clearly the time when he first had sex education at school. He was one of the lucky ones. Many more received no education either from their schools or their parents.

> The revealing of the 'facts of life' to me and my school mates, at the age of ten, contained one or two amusing little cameos. Having been accepted for the local grammar school, right at the end of the summer term we boys were herded into a little classroom and addressed by the Headmistress – angular, stern and forthright – 'Now! I shall expect you all to be irreverent,' she snapped. 'Hands up any boy who doesn't know how to be irreverent!' It is incredible that not one of us, at 10 or 11, knew the FOL. It was to be a two–lecture session. At the end of the first session, which contained the information about the mother carrying the baby – and we were *seriously* impressed – George Jenkins, a podgy and earnest lad, leaned forward and asked, in a Birmingham accent,
>   'Please, miss, wot does the father 'ave to do, then?'
>   'That, Jenkins, is what we shall discuss tomorrow.'

That lunchtime I went home on the bus, and met my father on board, as I often did –

'Well son, what did you do at school this morning?'

I, being excitable and very full of enthusiasm wanted – but some little Pinocchio-like figure stopped me just in time – to blurt out all over the bus,

'Yes! We've started learning about how I was born! And guess what, tomorrow we're going to find out what it was that you did!'

Good job I didn't, bus full of ladies with handbags and stylish hats, men all wearing trilbys and smoking grim pipes.

That afternoon I was with two friends – yes, in that traditional place, the corner of the playground – who reckoned they knew something about it. But their theories on it were in fact wildly wrong, as we found out the next morning in lecture Number 2, when the truth was revealed. And it was devastating. It's a poor comparison I know, but as a piece of truth more shattering than anything I'd expected, I can only compare it with the revelations about life in Nazi Germany after the death camps had been discovered.[7]

Later, other Mass-Observation respondents were confused about who was actually having the sex. 'This was the fifties: the era of *Scandal*, the film about the Profumo affair, involving Stephen Ward and his beautiful "girls",' said one woman. 'Sex was for the better off and the readers of the *News of the World*,' she continued.[8] Be that as it may, there were enough people around in the late 1940s who believed that the plebs were having sex too for public-access birth control to become an issue.

One of the most pioneering of these was Helen Brook, who began working at the Family Planning Association (FPA) in 1950, before being appointed director of the Marie Stopes Clinic. Very soon she started to become concerned by the fact that the FPA only catered for married women. It was when the Association began to see 'premaritals' – women who had a marriage date firmly fixed for a few weeks ahead – that her rebellious streak came to the fore: 'I'd say we can't see you unless you have a date of marriage, so you'd be wise just to give me a date. The better educated young women understood immediately,' she told the *Guardian* when she retired in 1974. 'But if they were a bit thick, I'd have to tell them to remember the date when they saw the doctor or shut up and not talk about it. Of course I kept this to myself.'[9]

Having decided with the FPA and the Marie Stopes Clinic that it was best that she should strike out on her own, Brook opened up a separate clinic in 1964 with a £500-a-year grant from the Stopes Clinic and a £15,000 gift from one of her merchant banker husband's colleagues. It was a success, opening its doors to around six hundred girls that first year. By 1968, the year after the Family Planning Act had been passed, when, according to *The Times*, 'only 25 per cent of the 204 local health authorities provide[d] a full family planning service in accordance with the Act'[10] (and that was not even to help the unmarried), the eighth Brook clinic was being opened, in Glasgow. By now it was estimated that, in London alone, 10,000 people of between sixteen and twenty-five had been given emotional and sexual advice by Brook's clinics. By the time she retired there were nineteen Brook Advisory Clinics, helping an estimated 34,000 per year.

Helen Brook's feeling about the resistance of Britain to family planning and the prevention of unwanted pregnancies was clear: 'People under 40 are generally very much in favour of what we are doing; but it is the older age group who are [sic] deeply imbedded in their own prejudices. I think it is due to a dog-in-the-manger attitude. They are envious of the new freedom which we are giving the young, largely because they didn't have it themselves.'[11]

Resistance came from the same quarters as it always had done: the Church, the media, and the medical establishment itself. In 1968 the Bishop of Portsmouth resigned from the Family Planning Association on the basis that 'the legislation making contraceptives available to all is based on the assumption that only two choices are open to young people – pregnancy or contraception. There's no sign that the third alternative – chastity – should be considered.'[12] At first sight this is fair, but it was totally out of synch with 1960s life. Family planning had become something that was to do with minimising the effect of an already very real situation where young people just *were* having sex.

The horse had, in many cases, long since bolted, because that is what horses naturally do. Family planning was not there to shut the stable door, it was there to make sure the animal did not go too far and do itself an injury in the process.

It should be added that not everybody was left with rosy memories of those early birth control clinic days, although the Brook Advisory Centre comes off relatively well in this account from a woman who was in her early twenties at the time:

> I remember in the sixties going to the Brook Aid Bureau in London and being recommended to go on the Pill, having been refused the Pill by an old toad of a doctor in Notting Hill Gate. Disgusting man.
>
> The FPA in Bristol was also a tastebud experience which put me off for life, with rows of forms, and a dreary old bag of a nurse shouting out your name and private information for the edification of all waiting.[13]

A teacher, on the other hand, thought it an essential part of the education of her pupils. 'I always made it my business that no girl should leave without knowing the basic facts of life and the address (12 East Street, on the 12A bus route) where one of the Brook Advisory Centres was,' she said.[14]

There was irony, as it emerged that Battersea, the place where the 1968 film *Up The Junction* (a gritty film in part about abortion) was set, contained by far the most single female takers for new, free, family planning services. The area's Conservative-controlled Merton Council chose not to provide such facilities to the unmarried, much to the annoyance of Labour councillor Mrs Joy Vowels who described the move as 'nineteenth century, self-righteous hypocrisy' and went on to say, 'I can't be part of drawing a line between the unmarried and married. Who are we to say married women are more moral than single girls?'

Top people's paper the *News of the World* looked set to get its knickers particularly twisted in 1966 by two fairly inoffensive-looking women called Dr Wilson and Dr Tattersall. 'They Run Sex Centre

For Youth', blared the headline. The piece began encouragingly enough: 'The green painted terraced house . . . fashionable suburb . . . red and pink roses growing, has something unusual to offer teenagers.' But that 'something' was advice, and contraceptives at the going rate, and the *NOTW* was not nearly as shocked as it at first seemed, ending the piece by rolling over and quoting the modest fee for 'little talks' (5s. each) and 'long discussions' (10s.).[15]

Genuinely startling news, at least to us today, came from the same source a month later. 'More than 50,000 doctors have been warned that they could be liable to legal prosecution if they supply certain birth control services to women without having their husband's written consent,' it began.[16] This was the doing of the Medical Defence Union, it emerged. According to that body, 'a husband has a legal right to the opportunity of having children by his wife'. More than this, should a doctor fail to let a husband know that he had offered birth control help to that husband's wife, 'the husband can sue the doctor for deliberately and directly interfering with that right'. The MDU's justification for this decision was, apparently, a case where a man complained that his wife kept from him the fact that she was on the Pill. The public, and the MDU, obviously knew nothing of the nature of this man or of his relationship with his wife. And yet he was allowed, officially, to set the scariest of precedents. A dark day indeed for civil liberties – and the Beach Boys had the gall to sing about 'Good Vibrations'.

Women were not the only victims. In America the state continued to interfere in the private lives of adults when it came to anal sex, that favourite method of the ancient Greeks. Indeed, in 1990 seventeen states still outlawed consensual anal sex, sometimes known as sodomy. Back in 1966 in Indiana, this had its advantages, at least for the odd vengeful wife. One case which gleaned more publicity than most was that of a man who was imprisoned for having anal sex with his wife.[17] He got *Playboy* magazine on his side, and one of its lawyers helped him to file an appeal attacking the constitutionality of the Indiana sodomy statute. If, as his letter to the magazine had it, 'whatever my wife and I did in bed was as much her wish as it was mine', why did she grass him up? It seems that they had been arguing and an interfering friend had encouraged her to 'put him away', whereupon she had signed an affidavit accusing him of committing 'the abominable and detestable crime against nature' with her. She changed her mind about the allegations, but it was too late by then; her husband was fighting his legal battle against the state of Indiana. The judge sentenced him to 'not less than two nor more than fourteen years'. He served three. If he saw Buzz Aldrin land on the moon in 1969, he saw it from behind bars.

Back in England, a more touching illustration of the way attitudes towards sex and, more specifically, birth control clinics had changed, if not the attitudes of some men towards women, appeared in the *Daily Mirror* in 1964.[18] Mr Watkins was the director of a London birth control clinic, and was worried about an application that had been made to open a betting shop next door. He thought there was a risk of 'a lot of men hanging around outside the doorway – perhaps with the odd wolf whistle or cat call'. The man who was applying for the betting shop licence – notably, on at least two counts, called Mr John Cash – assured everyone concerned: 'I would be willing to cooperate with the clinic.' He was not given the chance.

7

Blame it on the Boogie

> Is is too much to ask that woman be spared the daily struggle for superhuman beauty in order to offer it to the caresses of a subhumanly ugly mate?
>
> Germaine Greer – *The Female Eunuch*[1]

Key parties, wife-swapping, adultery . . . they were at it like rabbits in the seventies. At it, it should be added, not exclusively using the Pill, since the backlash had started. At last Margaret Sanger and Marie Stopes had, at least partially, got their way and people were using barrier methods, although they were not always the 'female methods' that they had favoured. In the 1998 film of Rick Moody's novel *The Ice Storm*, depicting 1970s suburban life in the US, the female half of an adulterous couple jumps out of bed at a crucial moment saying 'Birth control', before running out of the room. She doesn't return. Pretty effective barrier method, that.

Yet this was the decade when Jimmy Osmond wanted to be your 'Long-haired Lover from Liverpool' and Harry Nilsson was worrying about being 'Without You', Ziggy played guitar, 'Papa was a Rolling Stone' and there was 'Anarchy in the UK'. This last was what the grown-ups were worried about, that and (by the end of the decade) the fact that it sounded rather too much fun to stay at the YMCA. There was no doubt about it, Something Had To Be Done. In 1972, according to the *Daily Express*, family planners in Stevenage, Hertfordshire, sick of the rise in teenage pregnancies, found a solution of sorts. In the town square they put a large model of the woman who lived in a shoe and *had so many children because she didn't know what to do* – geddit? It appeared in the paper under the headline 'You Are Warned'.[2] There was a certain ingenuity at work here, although they could have been accused of setting the age of their target market a little low. All the people they were aiming for were far too busy trying to stay upright on platform soles and learn the words to Slade's 'Mama Weer all Crazee Now' to appreciate the layers of meaning in a nursery rhyme which they had probably last heard ten years before. Perhaps a better approach would have been to adapt one of the cartoons of the time, which featured a boy and a girl, each with a huge head and a tiny body, under the words 'Love is . . . '. Each cartoon would have underneath it a fairly innocuous suggestion as to what love might be. You never know, perhaps people in their early teens would have responded to 'Love is . . . risky'.

The worst offenders were those fresh out of school who went looking for fun, frolics and a few quid in seaside towns. The same year as the Stevenage woman in the shoe, birth control clinics were being opened in seaside towns for these seasonal workers. 'The pattern is well established,' Dr William Parker, Medical Officer for Brighton, Sussex, told the *News of the World*. 'Arrive at Easter, seduced by Whitsun and seeking help because of an unwanted baby by August.'[3] A gynaecologist at Torbay hospital added that these girls were 'lonely and desperate to know anyone'. He said, 'We want to make it easy for these girls to take advice about precautions. We think prevention is better than cure.' Hear, hear. Some were, doubtless, lonely victims, others were probably just a bit too drunk, aware of their freedom and happy to be away from home for the first time to think too much about what they were doing. In short, for them the blame could be placed squarely on the shoulders of the boogie.

Taboos were being broken in broadcasting as, following pilot schemes in parts of Scotland and London, approval was given by Britain's Independent Broadcasting Authority (now the Independent Television Commission) for family planning clinics to advertise on air.[4] This was in response to surveys such as that carried out by the Institute of Community Studies, which showed that almost half the mothers in England were having unwanted pregnancies, or were having children much earlier than they had planned. But it was going to be a long haul before the IBA allowed a free-for-all. At the same time as the approval was given, a list of what was not allowed to be advertised was issued. Included in that list were private detective agencies, slimming clinics and, a little confusingly, pregnancy testing services and contraceptives.

There were more definite signs that a shift in attitude was occurring. One good indication that boys and men were about to be held at least partially responsible for their actions arrived in the form of an advert brought out by advertising agency Saatchi & Saatchi for the Health Education Council of England in 1970. This showed a picture of a heavily pregnant man, and carried the tag-line, 'Would you be more careful if it was you that got pregnant?'. The image was so arresting, and the advertisement represented such a turning point, that the poster made it into the Design Museum's *Book of Twentieth Century Design*.[5] In the opinion of the book's author, Catherine McDermott, this 'touched upon the newly emerging ideas of the women's movement' but its power really lay in the effectiveness with which it used humour and surrealist imagery.

The Marie Stopes Clinic was not allowed to put its advertisements on London's Underground in 1972, because 'they might offend', it was claimed by the London Transport Board. In fact the Board had gone much further in a statement: 'Posters will not be accepted for display on undergrounds if they are thought likely to offend – either through the wording or the product advertised.' The Marie Stopes Clinic was baffled, and decided to approach MPs armed with that bafflement. 'Some of the advertisements they do accept are very suggestive,' said its secretary, Joan Windley, to the *Guardian*. 'It is not just our dirty minds.' This was too great a challenge to pass up for *Guardian* journalist Dennis Barker. Thus 'a one-man *Guardian* flowing mackintosh squad began its enquiries in Chancery Lane underground station'. The squad was not to be disappointed: 'The very first advertising poster inside the entrance showed a pair of women's legs naked to past the thigh and bore the wording: "Hundreds of women take them off for us every day . . . and quite a lot of men do too!" It turned out to be an advertisement for the Auto-Magic heel bar . . . ' And so it went on, with the journalist finding lots and lots of racy posters on the underground, leading him to conclude: 'as if all this did not put the out-cast Marie Stopes Memorial Clinic firmly in its place, London Transport also accepts advertising for pregnancy testing at three quid a time. The word "offensive" is, indeed, as long as a piece of string.'[6]

By 1978, the *Daily Mail*, at least, was very worried about schoolgirl pregnancies, if not about preschool children having babies, as the Stevenage family planners had been. Although the headline promised, 'One question: whose children *are* they?', the article concerned was actually about the pros and cons of handing out contraceptives to under-age girls.[7] It did not seem to be as interested in assigning blame as first appeared. In fact, the Doncaster Community Standards Association was thinking of the parents of the hypothetical girl who goes on the Pill and starts 'having sexual intercourse – whenever she feels like it, however unsuitable and even morally dangerous the partner might be'.

Moreover, the *Daily Mail* journalist immediately recalls a story she heard about a *real* fourteen-year-old girl, 'who had been persuaded to go to a clinic, not in Doncaster I hasten to add, by a schoolfriend who told her she didn't know what she was missing'. This girl had apparently gone on the Pill, and 'since the boys at school heard about it they had been forcing her to have sex with them'. This would, obviously, be a terrible thing to happen. It is also a little alarming to imagine a fourteen-year-old girl describing the sex she was having as something not to be missed. Show me a fourteen-year-old's sex life and I'll show you anti-climax and disappointment; that is, if they have a sex life at all. If they do, they need contraception more than most.

One clergyman's views on the Pill were far more pragmatic than might be expected, according to what he told the M-O observers in 1990:

'I always thought the Pill Happy Society would be of limited duration. I thought it would be because of the resurgence of the better known sexually transmitted diseases [rather than due to the advent of AIDS]. When I joined the RAF in 1944 we had films and lectures which made the hair curl. Prior to that one of our schoolmasters, who was a colonel, told us that the Germans were infecting prostitutes and, as they retreated, dosing them with enough antibiotics to suppress the symptoms but not cure them.[8]

Condoms would also be used by soldiers to keep their weapons and possessions dry, incidentally. One resourceful ex-sailor kept in a condom what he called a 'survival pack' (consisting of a bar of chocolate, a packet of cigarettes and a box of matches) in case the boat sank. To this day, every member of the SAS keeps one in their survival kit, not (officially at any rate) for that special kind of active duty, but for the carrying of drinking water.

On the subject of disease and condoms, the condom had a world-wide surge in popularity in the 1970s, due to an increase in venereal disease (VD). There also proved to be a direct correlation between how relaxed and open a country was prepared to be about condoms and sex in general and the spread of the disease in that country. In Sweden, they were very relaxed and proactive in launching advert-ising campaigns suggesting that people use condoms – and the VD rate halved. In Britain, the attitude was altogether more, well, British – and the rate doubled. Since then, Thailand and Japan have launched inspired campaigns to get people to accept the condom as a part of life and again it has been accepted readily.

The Pill had friends as well as enemies. In *The Curious History of Contraception*, an otherwise interesting and objective book written in 1971, Shirley Green writes her section devoted to the Pill with alarming zeal. Not only does she describe it as 'foolproof', but she adds, 'as for the disadvantages, they've been blown out of all proportion'. To be fair, she does go on to say that the long-term effects are not yet known because it is a new drug. More worryingly, though, she talks about the 'psychological barrier' the Pill can create in people, summing up with the thought that there's no point in going on the Pill 'if you're going to turn into a neurotic no one's going to want to sleep with'. And this from the woman who dedicates her book 'To Women's Lib . . . with love'. Women's Lib was one year old at the time. Inconsistency? That had been going on for a little longer.

Herein lies an interesting fact about the Pill. With hindsight, many have started to say that the sixties and seventies were more about men's liberation than women's, since the Pill meant that men were required to take even less responsibility for their actions than they had before. This was reflected in the comments of one primary school teacher from Birmingham, born in 1947, when she was asked by Mass-Observation what she thought about developments in contraception since the 1940s:

> My generation had a real choice in when to have children and felt liberated. Now I'm not so sure! Girls are liberated from fear, but pressure to say 'yes' is even harder to resist. It seems that men have benefited *again* (sorry, I'm letting my prejudices show).[9]

Even men who were there concede that things were stacked in their favour. As one wrote:

> After university I had a 'flowering' – girls on holiday in Finland and Germany, a married teacher, two young girls (16) who were in the same political movement as me, a single parent woman shop steward. No love, just sexual enjoyment – exploiting the male slant of late sixties/early seventies permissiveness, I suppose.[10]

Okay, so he was a social worker, but he's still technically a man.

Couple these men with women whose priority is to get men to want to sleep with them (which is obviously not the same thing at all as women wanting to sleep with men) and you do not have a recipe for female emancipation. Far from it. Statements by hippy chicks who, in the new millennium, feel they sold themselves far too cheaply in the 1960s and 70s have started to appear as testimony to this, although others were doubtless having a great time. As with the stories of wild fourteen-year-olds taking the Pill and getting it wherever they could, the sex 'n' drugs aspect of this and the decade before it is exaggerated.

Most baby boomers had the flares and the silly hair, but the general consensus is that unless you lived in New York or on the King's Road in London, you really only read about the rest.

On the other hand, there are those who realise that they would have been stuffed without it. One woman, a teacher who was twenty-seven in 1970, said: 'I would have had a lot more than one abortion either legally or illegally, if the Pill had not come in.' She said that she still has a friend who is Russian and who has had five abortions, 'because Russian contraception is no good'.[11]

Another woman, a radiographer by trade, who was born in 1926 in Asia and who was interviewed as a part of the same 1990 M-O survey as the teacher, did not see the advent of the Pill as a feminist issue at all, but as one of morality, pure and simple. And she thought the world, not just the King's Road, was suffering. 'The Pill changed an entire sector of social life,' she said. 'Promiscuity became rife, standards of living collapsed and moral values became laughable to the trendy young.'[12]

Some of those 'trendy young' were in the King's Road, and there hippies were superseded by punks at the end of 1975, as a result of Malcolm McLaren and Vivienne Westwood's shop Sex. According to Fred Vermorel in his book *Fashion and Perversity*, Sex peddled 'malevolence off the peg . . . and by courtesy of the Sex Pistols'.[13] Being a punk involved having spiky hair, preferably in a primary colour, and wearing a leather jacket – just in time for the long, hot summer of '76; punks were nothing if not dedicated – with accessories hanging off it (although you wouldn't tell a punk that she or he was wearing 'accessories' or you'd most likely get your head kicked in). These accessories included, most famously, safety pins and chains, but sometimes dummies were also a feature, as were the London Rubber Company's finest – condoms. As if to reaffirm just how silly the seventies were, condoms were now appearing in different colours, although almost never on the leather jackets of punks, who favoured the more traditional flesh-coloured version. Nobody was quite sure why this happened; presumably just wilful seventies silliness on the part of the manufacturers. It was tenacious silliness, though, the kind of silliness which hangs around for thirty years or more.

*

In 1990 a nursing assistant who was born in Kent in 1921 said to the M-O, on looking back to the seventies: 'I escaped from the danger of the Pill. I find all forms of contraception distasteful. I wish we had been offered sterilisation.'[14] There were many grown-ups who shared this view, according to *The Times* in 1978, which announced 'a change in attitudes to sterilisation'.[15] This conclusion was reached on the basis of a government survey. 'At the rates prevailing in 1975 either the wife or the husband in more than a quarter of couples would be sterilised by the time the wife is 35.' The Pill had introduced people to the idea of not having to fiddle around with *things* in the middle of the night, and once they had what they thought were enough children they didn't see the need for putting hormones into their body either. Another practical reason for the surge in sterilisation's popularity was the introduction of the National Health Service (Family Planning) Amendment Act in 1972, which allowed local authorities to provide vasectomies in the same way that they provided other contraceptive services.

Another reminder of how long ago the seventies are can be found within the results of a survey carried out by the British Pregnancy Advisory Service, which came out in 1979. According to the survey, 'most married women [a precise figure is not mentioned] complete their families and finish with child-bearing for good by the age of 30 or soon after'.[16] It hardly needs saying that many women now, at least in the metropolitan West, are not even thinking about children when they are thirty, let alone planning to have their last. As for being sterilised at thirty-five, the broodiest are reading about the desperate and dateless single professional female Bridget Jones and stalking dinner parties where there might be any old bachelor, and the rest are getting on with their work.

Surgical sterilisation has been possible since 1890, and the Church had been struggling with its stance on the subject since the late 1930s. At the start, the method was only used on the mentally ill. By 1903, this was becoming law in America, first in Indiana and then in twenty-two other states, on condition that the people concerned were 'feeble-minded or insane'. This kind of eugenic sterilisation did not make it to Europe, via Switzerland and then Denmark, until 1928.

If this seems shocking, in the High Court in London a mother won the right to force her 'extremely attractive' twenty-eight-year-old handicapped daughter to have a hysterectomy.[17] The year? 2000. The woman, who looks after her daughter day in, day out, still wanted to take this ultimate measure to protect her from what she thinks of as 'this cruel world'. The idea was that the girl might be taken advantage of or raped. Two charities for the disabled described this as an 'extreme measure', because the justification for it was social not medical. What was even more disorientating when it emerged during the case was that this practice has been carried out in similar circumstances a number of times before in recent history – but these cases did not make it to court, so the public has not heard about them. The only aspect of this that stops it from being quite as worrying as the eugenics of the early twentieth century is that the state did not impose it.

As ever, the Church raised its hand, stood up, gave a small cough and offered to say a few words, this time about sterilisation. The first person from the Catholic camp to imply that everyone might benefit from sterilisation was Alois de Smet, who saw it as a possible way of avoiding the sin of onanism or withdrawal. He could have argued this in a couple of ways: 'You don't have to spill your seed any more' or 'you don't have any seed to spill any more'. However, what the Church really got worked up about was whether the operation itself was sinful.

The 1920s theologian Vermeersch – with a set of morals reminiscent of Pierre Clergue in the Middle Ages and St Augustine before him – was of the opinion that if one had achieved permanent sterility, one should say sorry to God and then have intercourse guilt-free.[18] This was because coitus was not, he believed, intrinsically sinful. If the operation could be reversed, however, sex whilst sterilised was sinful; because he saw this as a kind of onanism. He never launched himself into arguing that one out logically though. Probably very wise.

There was a general feeling within the Church that the removal of one part of the body was sometimes okay if it was for the good of the rest of the body. Obviously this was problematic for any Catholic who wanted to set about defending sterilisation. Theologian Gerald Kelly found an ingenious way of making the reproductive organs the exception to this rule. These parts of a person, he maintained, were there for the good not just of the body but of mankind. If parts of the body were mutilated, the whole thing became more complicated and the rules could be flexed a little.

At least the methods used now are not so primitive. The male vasectomy under the NHS in Britain is carried out as follows:

> The doctor will make a small cut(s) in the skin of your scrotum, to reach the tubes (vas deferens). The doctor will remove a small piece of each tube, or cut the tubes and close both ends. The cuts in your scrotum will be very small and you may not need to have any stitches. If you do, dissolvable stitches or surgical tape will be used. The operation takes about 10 to 15 minutes and may be done in a clinic, hospital out-patient department or doctor's surgery.[19]

On the down side . . .

> Your scrotum may be bruised, swollen and painful. You can help this by wearing tight-fitting underpants to support your scrotum, day and night for a week. You should avoid heavy exercise for at least a week.

And avoid sex without additional contraception for two to four months, because sperm are left within your tubes for a while afterwards.

For women it is more complicated. Sometimes a general anaesthetic is used, and tubes may have a small part removed (excision), be tied (ligation), be sealed (cauterisation), or have clips or rings attached. The fallopian tubes are reached by making one tiny incision below the navel and another just below the bikini line. Women must continue to use contraception until their first period after sterilisation has finished. They can expect a little pain and bleeding and, if they had a general anaesthetic, the feeling of having been hit over the head with a sledgehammer that this brings. Periods occasionally get heavier.

Of course, the problem with sterilisation using these methods is that people change their minds. Traditionally it is women who change their minds the whole time, but when it comes to sterilisation, men are, statistically, far more likely to want the operation reversed than women. This is because, at least until recently, when women remarry they are likely to marry an older man who has children and does not want any more, whereas men (hold the front page) are likely to marry someone younger who does not necessarily have children but might want them. With someone old enough to be the children's grand-father. This should surely mean that there are lots of spare potential sugar-mummies for men, and toy boys for women, floating around. Indeed, one source predicts this is about to become a trend. Perhaps Barbara Windsor, star of the BBC's *EastEnders* and ex-star of the *Carry On* films, was starting something big by marrying toy boy Scott Harvey.

Along with the obvious convenience of 'the snip', doctors were starting to do it more quickly and cheaply. Gone were the days in the sixties, described by one woman, when you would be refused an abortion on the grounds that you didn't have enough children yet. 'I feel that sterilisation should be available on request,' she said. 'I was denied it because I had only two children and my husband didn't want me to be "done".'[20]

The first press reports of cut-price 'quickie' vasectomies started appearing in 1971, when it was announced that a clinic was to be opened in Glasgow. The doctor who was to perform the operations, who remained nameless, had already performed more than 3,000 sterilisations over eleven years. 'I'm not a philanthropist and hope that I'll make a living out of this,' he told the *Daily Mail*, in his best bedside manner. 'At the price we plan [which was £8], we shall have to rely on turnover. There will be none of the social graces. Patients will arrive, undergo the operation, and then leave the clinic the same day. If they want to they can even go to work the next day.'[21] A kind of vasectomy factory, then.

Seven years later, Anne de Courtney, a journalist for the *Evening News*, wanted to allay people's potential fears about all this haste, but in the context of sterilisation for women. She had one story about a woman who said, 'Frankly I'm terrified', at the prospect of having a hysterectomy. 'So why aren't you having a vasectomy instead?' the journalist asked the woman's husband. "It's different for men," he replied, puffing out his chest and speaking firmly and decisively. "They have a psychological block on questions of this kind." "Why don't you just tell her the truth?" hissed his wife. "That you're just too much of a COWARD."'[22] But they weren't all cowards in those days. For one man, a Surrey solicitor surveyed in 1990, the pros far outweighed the cons: 'In 1973, following the birth of my third son, I voluntarily underwent a vasectomy,' he told the Mass-Observation Unit. 'The feeling of freedom is very much a part of this type of contraception.'[23]

The operation de Courtney described, which took place at the Marie Stopes Clinic, was, at £65, pricier than the men's version in Glasgow seven years before, but it only took fifteen minutes. The women concerned were allowed to go home after an hour. The difference between these operations and the old sort, which would involve spending two nights in a clinic, was, she explained, that these were done under a local anaesthetic. The result of the operation she witnessed was a patient who was so relaxed that she was able to say to her doctor, 'You make a great cuppa.' The doctor in Glasgow wouldn't have made a cuppa. He would have carried on snipping and earned himself a couple of hundred pounds within the time it took to boil the kettle.

Perhaps inevitably, 'quickie' sterilisation for women was not treated in such a relaxed way by doctors fourteen years later. In fact Robert Winston, the consultant gynaecologist in charge of the fertility unit at Hammersmith Hospital, said to *The Times*, 'I am horrified that women can simply walk in and get this operation. It is very undesirable and I deprecate such rapid decision making.'[24] In his hospital the waiting time was six weeks, he said. 'That time in itself is therapeutic. It allows the patient the chance to make a mature decision.' The operation itself is simple and quick by its very nature. The part that should not be 'quickie' is the decision–making process.

Of course, even when the decision is not made lightly, sterilisation has never been able to solve all problems, as the moving account of a woman who was born in 1923 demonstrates:

The relationship between myself and my husband was very tense [after having had four children]. I was terrified of another increase to the family. I went to a Birth Control Clinic, but came away feeling dirty and more like stepping in front of a bus.

I had a hysterectomy in my late 30s and things were a bit better then, but a lot of damage had been done. We had never talked about our feelings for each other, or explained what was upsetting us. I once found a 'girlie' magazine under his side of the mattress. Acutely aware of my own inadequacies I imagined that when he made love to me he was wishing I was one of those girls. I replaced the magazine, had a good cry, said nothing, but 'froze' for quite a time.[25]

Of sterilisation it should be added that research into the reversible vasectomy is well advanced. It involves – of all things – the use of superglue to block the vas deferens, which can be dissolved with the injection of another chemical when the time is right. The future will also see a very cheap and easy form of female sterilisation become widely available, involving a drug called Quinacrine which, when inserted into the womb, causes inflammation of the fallopian tubes. With time this produces scar tissue which blocks the tubes. For a long time it was not made available because, in part, of scare stories about the health risks that might be associated with it, despite the fact that trials had suggested it was safe. It has to be said that, as a concept, it seems a little like self-mutilation – although in reality no more so than traditional sterilisation. The speed of its development was also hindered because it is 'off patent'. Because no single drug company in existence discovered it, none can alone profit from it. Despite this, the Food and Drug Administration in the US has passed Quinacrine. Britain has yet to follow. It is more important, though, that it should gain large-scale approval in the developing world.

By the time the seventies were drawing to a close, a number of more bizarre methods had been reported in the newspapers. A nasal spray was being developed which introduced the hormone oestrogen straight into the systems of women via their nasal membranes.[26] After rigorous research, it was established that the advantage of this was that it is a very direct route. The disadvantage was that it induced menopause in women, complete with hot flushes. Obviously this led to that particular line of enquiry being closed, but the efficiency of the route has been noted. Currently it looks set to be used as a way of administering hormone replacement therapy. The nose has a bright and shiny future.

Another innovation which did not make it very far past the drawing-board stage was developed in Cardiff at the Tenovus Cancer Research Institute. This was a *bra* which measured the woman's temperature and thus, by means of a green (or red) light, told the wearer if she was in a 'safe period' or not.[27] The Family Planning Association said: 'We view the whole thing with a good deal of scepticism. The safe period is not particularly safe.' It didn't even feel the need to say 'Go and do some real work instead like, say, finding a cure for cancer.' The Catholic Church, on the other hand, received the idea rapturously. 'We encourage birth control by natural methods,' gushed a spokesman. 'The new bra is most welcome.'

Astrologer Linda Goodman had other ideas. She said the answer lay in the stars. A report in the *Daily Mail* stated that, according to her book *Love Signs*, there are only two hours in a woman's lunar cycle when she can conceive.[28] This is when the sun and moon lie in the same relation to each other that they did when she was born (the woman concerned, that is, not Linda Goodman). The author says, 'Without exception, a woman can conceive at no other time than this approximately two-hour period', although she still recommends leaving a day or so on either side of the two hours, for safety's sake. 'Astrobiology', as Linda calls the method, only had a two per cent failure rate, and there was even an explanation for that: the women involved in the research didn't know their own birthdays.

The decade thus drew to a close with people using the Pill, although not unquestioningly, using barrier methods and getting themselves sterilised in droves – and still one in two babies was accidental. Yes, people were still having sex, and they were having it, in 1979, to the strains of Donna Summer's 'Hot Stuff', Rod Stewart's 'Do Ya Think I'm Sexy' and Michael Jackson's 'Don't Stop Till You Get Enough'. What a way to go.

8

Yuppy Love

Man is the only animal that blushes. Or needs to.

Mark Twain[1]

In the 1980s, the Village People were *still* having fun at (amongst other places) the YMCA but, due to the shattering arrival of AIDS and HIV, they were starting to equip themselves with rather more than Indian head-dresses and cowboy boots. The cartoon character Wicked Willy was everywhere, which was as good an illustration as any of the fact that Britain was starting to give up its Victorian values and enjoy a more open, if irritating, attitude towards sex. We started calling the johnny the condom, Katharine Hamnett designed boxer shorts with a condom pocket, British entrepreneur Richard Branson deemed 'safe sex' safely sexy enough to launch Mates condoms, and Jiffy launched their range of condoms with the slogan 'Come In A Jiffy'. Along with excessive eye make-up and heavily lacquered hair – and that was just the boys – the 1980s will forever be associated with the sheath.

By 1990, 144 million condoms were being sold, 30 million more than in 1980. In fact, the London Rubber Company (LRC), manufacturers of Durex condoms, then the condom kings, were doing so well that the Monopolies and Mergers Commission felt it necessary to tell them to keep an eye on their prices, due to their 90 to 95 per cent share of the British condom market. (In 1993 it was estimated that it costs manufacturers around 6p to produce a condom – it doesn't take

137

the brightest of sparks to work out that there is money to be made.) The safe sex message had clearly got through. *The Times* said that, according to an LRC report which covered the last third of the decade, the 33 per cent increase in condom sales over this time was due to 'increased awareness of AIDS and HIV, concern among young women about possible side-effects of oral contraceptives, and wider availability of condoms'.[2] The company also said that the 'snigger factor' had been overcome, which helped.

Actually the snigger factor had not been completely overcome. In Britain we were still far from being as relaxed as the Swedes. One particular class of thirteen-year-olds in around 1983 was having its first sex education class, and its teacher, Mr Borowski, had left the pupils with, as far as the source can remember, several different condoms to inspect. He departed to allow us 'five minutes' sniggering time'. We sniggered, not because of the 'johnnies' as they were then still known (we'd all seen those before on pavements and beaches), but because of the obvious embarrassment of this poor, awkward teacher. Still, he came back and, smiling bravely through, proceeded to teach us everything we already knew.

Of the men surveyed about the snigger factor, who were between sixteen and twenty years old, 76 per cent said they were not embarrassed about buying condoms.[3] But then again, 99 per cent of men of between sixteen and twenty tell lies. The research went on to say that, when men do buy condoms, they are more likely than women to do so in the supermarket where, presumably, they can hide them under the pasta where fellow shoppers can't see them. Even so, there's always that awkward bit with the person behind you at the checkout.

One elderly man interviewed by Mass-Observation in 1990 had the following wry comment to make about the revived interest in the condom:

> It seems ironic that, since the advent of AIDS, people are talking about using condoms – one of the oldest forms of contraception. It suggests to me that perhaps there has not been as much progress as we like to think.[4]

A woman in her late fifties also had views on AIDs and condoms.

'I would not have sex with a bisexual man even for love [now]. I know one can use a rubber, but some men cannot come in a rubber and I do not like the smell or appearance of these contraceptives.'[5]

There was also a new concept to be contended with – condom etiquette. Far from being a code of conduct as one might expect, it was really a phrase designed to *ask* a lot of questions about condom use. Did the arrival of AIDS make it okay to ask people about their sexual past? Could women carry condoms without seeming too sexually available? Could men carry condoms without looking like they were only 'out for one thing'? When was the right time to mention using condoms? Over dinner? At bed time? As things started hotting up? Just before climax?

Wendy Dennis, author of *Hot and Bothered: Men and Women, Sex and Love in the 90s*,[6] interviewed one man who did not see the 'who carries the condoms?' question as a real problem at all. He thought 'the guy should bring the condom' because 'girls brought the diaphragm and the Pill, didn't they?' Interesting use of the past tense for those two methods, you'll notice. Still, it was all right by him if the woman carried it too. 'Sure it's presumptuous,' the same man went on, 'but presumption in sexuality is flattering, don't you think? I mean, she brought one, it's so nice. I feel targeted.'

On the timing issue, Dennis has another tale to tell. One woman took the 'over dinner' option – the point at which the brandies were being carried out, to be precise. At that moment she reached across the table and put two condoms into the hand of her intended sexual partner. 'Not only did he find this gesture outrageously forward on a first meeting,' says Dennis, 'the fact that she handed over two inspired performance anxiety.' Perhaps she didn't want to sleep with him at all. Perhaps she hated him and wanted to intimidate him. Perhaps, in fact, everything went according to plan. Or perhaps she took her leave, deflated, unsated and embarrassed. We will never know.

Apart from speaking to people who are anti-condoms – 'Wearing a condom is like slapping down a perfectly cooked steak and then shooting your mouth full of Novocaine,' said one; another, 'Call me picky, but I happen to like the way a penis feels inside a vagina' – Dennis has a very good story about a woman who found herself *more* attracted to her partner rather than less, when a condom became involved. According to Dennis: 'While he was passionately French kissing her, one woman reported, her lover did a deep backhanded retrieval from the night-table drawer and, stopping only momentarily to unwrap the package with his teeth, resumed kissing her while applying it, one handed, to his stalwart erection. "I was utterly amazed," she said, a faraway look in her eyes. "And totally impressed".'

Condoms were also the unspoken subject of a 1983 TV ad starring actor-singer Adam Faith which targeted teenage boys. It featured two eighteen-year-olds talking in a burger bar about a friend of theirs who had got his girlfriend pregnant. Earlier on in the year a similar ad had been banned by the Independent Broadcasting Authority for containing the less than graphic, relatively inoffensive, phrase 'up the spout' to refer to getting a girl pregnant. The new, approved ad ended, 'If you're man enough to make love, you're man enough to use birth control.' The script concluded: 'Any idiot can *get a girl into trouble* [as opposed to "up the spout"], don't let it be you.'[7]

The same year, Tom Cruise starred in the raunchy teen flick *Risky Business*, which, incidentally, caused a rash of RayBan-wearing that persisted for some time – in the main by people who didn't suit the sunglasses. Later on, in 1988, when asked whether he thought Hollywood stars such as himself should be pointing out to the impressionable young just how risky the business of sex in the 1980s could be, Cruise was resolute. 'I don't think it's my job to educate people on safe sex,' he said. 'Do I have to wear a condom in my scenes on the screen? This is the eighties. There is AIDS. There is alcoholism. People should be able to figure it out for themselves.'[8] So no help there, then.

Again, perhaps, not very helpful was a 1987 condom ad, which upped the advertising industry's sophistication ante by attempting to exploit the snigger factor. It scored an own-goal with some, however, by confirming the worst fears of teenage boys. In it, a teenager goes into a chemist's and is served by the assistant, played by Gina McKee, also Hugh Grant's sister-in-law in *Notting Hill*. He is desperately trying to pluck up the courage to buy some Mates condoms (they're the cheapest and best, you see), but when he opens his mouth he finds himself asking for 'cotton wool' and then 'tissues'. Meanwhile subtitles appear, showing what each of them is thinking. From the start she thinks 'he wants some condoms', but instead of helping she archly suggests he is after 'man-size tissues'. As if this were not off-putting enough for the teenage viewer who was just about to start practising safe sex, there is the payoff. The voice-over says the line that you're supposed to remember: 'She sells hundreds of packets. She's not embarrassed. So why should you be?' But the answer is there in a flash: after our hero has finally plucked up the courage to ask for the condoms, and we think we're home and dry, the bitch shouts, 'Mr Williams. How much are these Mates condoms?' The band Madness's song 'House of Fun' dealt with the same subject, young boy in chemist's on first condom-purchasing mission.

America, or at least its government, was more reluctant to air the subject of condoms. The first advert in the US promoting condom use was aired in 1994, a full thirteen years after the first reported AIDS cases, when hundreds of thousands of people were already infected. It featured Anthony Kiedis, of the band the Red Hot Chili Peppers, taking off his clothes and putting on a condom. Evangelical and Catholic churches both claimed it would serve to promote sex rather than condoms.

Overall, British men in the 1980s were still shy about buying condoms, however many lies they told the people conducting surveys. A little surprisingly, they must have been most shy of all in Manchester (not swaggering so much now, eh boys?), because for the first time in Britain, men were given their own family planning clinic. Long before the band Oasis was even a twinkle in their manager's eye, the Gallagher brothers and their pals were free to get their johnnies (because they would have carried on calling them 'johnnies' and probably still do) in a place where no birds were allowed. Manchester Health Authority opened it because men were not attending other regular clinics in the area. Dr John Guillebaud, medical director of the Margaret Pyke Clinic in London, was suitably positive: 'It is an excellent idea,' he said. 'Men often feel intimidated in female-dominated clinics.' And although it was indeed an excellent idea, the Gallagher brothers wouldn't have gone. There'd have been no one there to cop off with. And they were twelve at the time.

These were by no means the wildest and most unconventional of family planning clinics springing up in Britain then. The *News of the World*, with its tireless tradition of investigation in the line of national duty, discovered what were called Private Alternative Birth Control Information and Education Centres.[9] These were, in fact, sex shops. In a loophole discovered by ingenious and enterprising sex industry types, it was found that, as long as the shops displayed Family Planning Association leaflets, according to the paper, 'they can go on selling porn videos, sex aids and erotic undies without having to apply for sex shop licences, because they can claim to be birth control clinics'.

Scarily, the shop staff even followed through, giving out advice on sterilisation to the paper's reporter. She was urged to 'think carefully' about the operation by a young woman in a 'medical-style' jacket who 'admitted she had no formal qualifications'. Luckily for the doubtless tiny minority of people who went into the shop wanting advice, rather than a news story or a dodgy video, dubbed by considerably less excited Germans reading the paper hundreds of miles away, the advice the assistant was handing out was sound.

Incidentally, sales of porn movies soared in the 1980s.[10] To some, this, and an increase in the amount of sex on TV and in mainstream cinema, was a reaction to the AIDS/HIV epidemic. If real sex might kill you, went the thinking, the safest way to enjoy it was vicariously, by watching other people do it, or pretend to do it, on screen.

Genuine birth control clinics continued to cause controversy, both because they were giving out advice and because they were failing to. At the end of the nineties, a clinic in Manchester which claimed to give impartial advice was shown by the *Mirror* to be run by vehement anti-abortionists.[11] Pregnant women would be given leaflets which said, 'When you have an abortion, you feel you have been raped and your baby killed.' The newspaper's reporter posed as a twenty-year-old, pregnant after a one-night stand. One of the counsellors told her she had had an abortion at seventeen and still regretted it at forty-two. The other said she didn't want to use scare tactics, but then read from a leaflet which stated that if she had an abortion she was 'likely to miscarry or go into premature labour in future pregnancies'. What the leaflet, one of their own, actually said was 'you *may* miscarry'.

By 1999, one clinic had actually made it through the gates of a school in Gateshead, Tyne and Wear.[12] In that area the number of teenage pregnancies was particularly high and the school in question was particularly isolated, so it was not always easy for pupils to get advice on health matters. For this reason the clinic was set up in the playground. Doubtless the initiators of the project got a few of the stock 'burn in hell' letters which people who set up these places have come to expect, but, overall, thought Anne Furedi of the British Pregnancy Advisory Service, they were winning. 'It's pretty clear that the minority who oppose these initiatives have lost the argument,' she said.

Of course, the fact that the spotlight was back on the condom in the 1980s allowed all the old jokes and stereotypes about men and their equipment to come to the fore. According to the *Sun*, condoms sent to Kenya as part of a Swedish aid package were returned because they were 'too small'.[13] 'The condoms measured 6 ½ inches when fully extended. But the Kenyan Government demanded bigger ones – at least 7 ¼ to 8 inches in length,' the newspaper panted. Boys, whether they are Kenyan officials or hacks from Wapping, London, will be boys.

The first condom containing spermicide appeared in 1984, to the excitement of all but the London Rubber Company, which was no longer guaranteed to get the vast majority of the £20 million a year British condom market, comprising sales of 115 million condoms. The new product, called Lifestyles Ultrasure, was made by the pharmaceuticals company Warner Lambert, and was reckoned to be 97 per cent effective. Lifestyles Ultrasure have since become such a part of life that it is difficult to believe that they have only been around for that long.

In the same year, author Bret Easton Ellis published his novel about the sex, drugs and rock 'n' roll-filled lives of a group of disillusioned American Gen Xers. It was called *Less Than Zero* and it became as essential a part of the teenage kit as the condom and hair crimpers in that teenager's drawer.[14] It also had a picture of a condom on its cover – cool! – although the characters in the book would probably have referred to condoms as 'scumbags'. So 'condom' turned out not to be the most unattractive word in the English language after all.

The late eighties and early nineties saw the increasing acceptability of condoms reflected in the design of their packaging. Before, condom packets had been discreet, low-key affairs containing contraceptives with medical-sounding names. Now Richard Branson was producing his Mates condoms in silver boxes with a huge unapologetic 'M' logo on the front of them. Catherine McDermott's *Book of Twentieth Century Design* described this as making Mates 'a kind of accessory for the young club-goer'. McDermott also notes that this was one product that did not sport the Virgin name – presumably because it would have looked silly on a condom packet.

This was not the first time that the packaging of contraceptives had reflected a change in the world into which those contraceptives had emerged, or had perhaps even changed the world itself. It had happened with the Pill in the 1960s. Again the *Book of Twentieth Century Design* notes, of one particular 1980s box it chooses to illustrate the idea, that 'the technological aspect is softened' by the use of 'almost personal diary-like abbreviations' – each pill is labelled Sun, Mon, Tues, Wed and so on – and the use of the colour pink which, as everyone knows, all girls like. For the boys, there was the Durex Arouser ribbed condom. Its packaging came complete with an image which neatly combined the 1980s 'greed is good' ethos with sexual symbolism – a red Ferrari.

The packaging of both the condom and the Pill confirmed that contraception had now become a commercial seam to be mined as deeply as any other. More than this, those who were trying to get ordinary people to choose their product over another were realising, as time passed, that the way to get them to do it was to 'demedicalise' contraception. Marie Stopes had started to recognise this fifty years before by ceasing to use male doctors; Richard Branson's condom packets were at a point a little further along that same continuum. Perhaps, by the turn of the next century, pharmaceuticals companies will not give themselves such medical-sounding and intimidating names.

One company, Chartex International, responded to the fact that the condom was, once more, the most popular guy in school by developing the female condom or Femidom. In the United States the device was called 'Reality', presumably referring to men's reluctance to use condoms. This is not to say that it was an entirely new idea, since African women had been applying the same principle using hollowed-out okra pods for centuries, with goat's bladders believed to have been used by Roman women to the same effect.

The main difference was that the Femidom was made of plastic. It was a pouch, 15 cm long, with two rings. One of these fitted over the cervix, like the ring of a diaphragm, and the other just sort of hung out of the woman's vagina, creating a rather more literal tunnel of love than any the world had thus far seen. The upshot was that the woman's vagina was lined during sex, as opposed to the penis being covered. Initially it was lubricated with spermicide. But after it was established that the most popular type of spermicide, Nonoxynol 9, might, if used on a day to day basis, cause abrasions to the vaginal wall which could make easier the transmission of HIV, it was replaced by a non-spermicidal lubricant. In line with other barrier methods, it had a failure rate of twelve to fifteen per hundred woman years – that is, of a hundred women using the method for a year, twelve or fifteen will get pregnant.

None of these facts really sank in when the Femidom was launched. Most people were so blinded by tears of laughter at the look of the thing that they could not read the leaflet inside the packet. Not only that, but the man had to thread himself into this tube and then, rumour had it, *it rustled*. Actually it doesn't exactly rustle, but the fact that someone once said it did, and that one female comedian likened it to a plastic carrier bag, was undoubtedly enough to stop some people taking the poor method seriously ever again. Sex was filled with enough self-consciousness as it was, at least for the British, without this. Young sophisticated urbanites would not take the risk. Rustling while you made love had never been a priority, and it was not about to become one now.

Yet for the unselfconscious who did, and still do, use the method (and in fact 18 million have been sold around the world since 1992, many of them destined for Africa, where women feel they have to be in charge of birth control) there were rewards. The rustling happens because it is big and baggy and it is made out of polyurethane rather than the traditional latex. This makes it many times stronger than a condom and hence less likely to break. Indeed, polyurethane condoms were also beginning to appear at around this time. The material is unaffected by all the chemicals, spermicides and lubricants that cannot be used with latex condoms, which means you can use baby oil, Vaseline and, say, butter or custard, for instance. Another advantage is that, unlike with the condom, the man does not have to be rock hard (and frankly, he's likely not to be with this method, if he's the visually stimulated type) in order to be able to penetrate the woman.

When the Femidom first came out in the UK, Fay Hutchinson of the Brook Advisory Centres said to the *Sunday Express*: 'It will become as natural as using tampons.'[15] The method never did rival the male condom, though, and people never really embraced the idea of the man and woman taking it in turns to look after birth control, which had been one hope of birth controllers. For most, the words of birth control campaigner Victoria Gillick, which echoed what people had said about the condom ten years before, were closer to the mark. 'It sounds like one huge passion damper,' she said.[16] Still, condoms recovered. Perhaps the Femidom will yet have its day.

There was also the inevitable controversy about sex education for the young. The peg for the same old media story, this time, was the Brook Advisory Centre's Contraception Teaching Pack. This contained a booklet called 'A Look At Safe Sex' (nothing too irresponsible there, then), of which the *Daily Mail* said: 'Clearly the author feels [the booklet] is aimed at an audience which has a better grasp of sex than of the English language because it continues in a prose style little more complex than you'd find in a Noddy book.'[17] Surely if its readers did know more about sex than about the English language, this would increase the urgency of educating them about *safe* sex, rather than, say, concentrating on their sentence structure.

To add insult to injury, there were 'nude pictures of a man and a woman' in it, 'with their sexual characteristics arrowed and defined, both in the language of the gutter and the more genteel Latin of the medical dictionary'. The last being a momentary lapse in tastelessness by the author, presumably. James Pawsey, then Tory MP for Rugby, was wheeled on, doubtless due to his reputation for careful deliberation and balance in all things. 'It contains some of the most pornographic material I have ever seen,' he said. 'There is very little left to the imagination and even less left to prayer.'

'Some of the people who complain about our being too explicit should come into our waiting rooms for a day and get the flavour of what young people are all about,' countered Suzie Hayman of Brook Advisory. 'Our material is explicit because that is what some children, especially those in inner cities, need.' On the subject of 'language of the gutter' and 'genteel Latin', she continued, 'I don't believe there should be two sets of knowledge, one right and correct and the other dirty and wrong. These are words people use. You don't go home to your husband and say: "Let's have sexual intercourse tonight", do you?' Perhaps you do if you're a *Daily Mail* reader.

Many of the older people questioned by the Mass-Observation Archive had strong views on sex education. Most believed that the young should be educated, although there was concern that children were being taught too early. Where there was opposition to sex education, it sometimes came from the most unlikely of quarters:

I have worked as a family planning nurse for 22 years in September [1990] and I hold an unpopular view, in that I do not believe in sex education. It is started far too early, should be done by parents, is taught badly in school, still goes totally over the heads of 50 per cent of children, and leads to the practice of sexual intercourse as something to do when the television is rotten, with no, or very little, emotional involvement.[18]

What if sex education isn't given by the parents, though? This was the experience of another man (a pensions adviser, born in 1921) involved in the same survey:

> I wish I had had some sex education – it would have saved a lot of worry and unhappiness. My father was too shy to talk about it (my mother said once that he would 'one day' but he never did). When I did find out, from an older boy at school, I said 'I didn't know my dad was dirty'.[19]

The family planning nurse also said: 'Personally I would never ever take the Pill or use a coil. The risks are too great. Barrier methods are much safer all round.' By which, presumably, she means safer for the health of the user rather than as modes of contraception. She also had an interesting and, we must give it to her, honest response to being asked what she would do if approached by a pregnant young girl or a young gay person asking for advice: 'In both these cases I would maintain a totally detached professional image and advise as the case demanded,' she said. However, 'if they were my children I would explode'. But it got better. At the end of her document it said, 'PS I have handed in my resignation for my job.' After twenty-two years. Perhaps it was something about seeing her double standards written down . . .

And there was the old, 'Girls Aged 13 Given the Pill' story, which ended up with outraged parents demanding a meeting with Northampton Health Authority officials.[20] The chief of that year's disgraced clinic remained defiant, saying, perhaps a little provocatively, 'I'm not paid to be a moralist.' Again, without wishing to be too girls-are-great-and-men-are-rubbish, it should be noted that Dr Alanah Houston of the clinic had also figured out that she was not paid to be a moralist, but didn't see that as a reason to be without morals. She said, 'I don't approve of young girls having sex, but if I didn't help them there would be a much more serious situation to deal with.'

By 1983, a *Which?* report was indicating that, after the Pill and the sheath, the most popular method of contraception was withdrawal. In an article in the *Sunday Mirror*,[21] Penny Kane of the Planned Parenthood Federation was keen to allay the unbelievably still-lingering age-old fears that there were 'psychological consequences' in using the method and that 'the abrupt end to sex led to tension and frustration'. She said, 'While the abrupt ending may be a factor in how acceptable you find the method, there is no evidence that it causes any psychological damage.'

Another ancient 'natural' method was unearthed at the beginning of the eighties – breastfeeding.[22] Professor Short of the Medical Research Council's reproductive unit in Edinburgh studied Kung bushmen of the Kalahari, in Botswana. There he discovered that they produce from four to seven babies, with a four-year space between each birth. The suckling, which must be done often in order to work, triggers a reflex in the brain; this releases the hormone prolactin which in turn suppresses ovulation. He recognised, though, that 'Western women want to get back to work quickly.' It was the 1980s, after all. They were having far too much fun putting on *Dynasty* power suits – from 1981 at least, when the programme began – and breaking men's balls in the workplace to have time for such frequent feeds.

Another 'lost' natural method, which has been used by Australian and African tribes for thousands of years, was rediscovered by a couple of surfers – well, Australian doctors – called Evelyn Billings and Ann Westmore.[23] It was a variation on the rhythm method theme and involved the studying of cervical mucus. This changes its consistency in response to hormonal changes in the woman's body; these can be learned by a woman and applied to birth control. According to Szarewski and Guillebaud in *Contraception: a User's Handbook*, 'a lot of teaching and practice are involved' and 'many things can interfere with cervical mucus'. Moreover, the first child born to a contemporary of the author's was a product of the Billings method. She was, and remains, as delightful as she was accidental. The Mass-Observation Archive threw up one example of its use by a carer: 'I have only benefited from knowing the Billings method,' she said. 'The Pill, loop, vasectomy and cap are all questionable.'[24] If pressed, she could recommend one mechanical method: 'I feel the main benefits recently have been through the use of condoms.' The doctors wrote a book on the Billings method, called *The Billings Method, Controlling Fertility Without Drugs or Devices*, for the fast-learning or foolish, depending on your point of view. Hippies.

Up there in the risky business stakes is reliance on the temperature of the hands, fingers and toes of your woman, which, according to King's College Hospital in the mid-eighties, is an indication of fertility – a woman's extremities are colder when she is fertile.[25] This is ironic if you also listen to Italian Giovanni Sinibaldi who, in 1642, described cold feet as 'a powerful hindrance to coition'. There was hope, though. You could still have had a baby. Sinibaldi's solution was not to abstain but rather to 'wear soft, noiseless slippers'. Two Femidoms ought to do the trick.

The sponge made something of a comeback, British women first hearing about a new version of this ancient principle when they were invited by the *Daily Mail* to be involved in trials in 1981[26]. The sponge which they were being asked to test for the Mary Pyke Centre in Soho, London, was made from polyurethane foam which was impregnated with spermicide. There was great excitement when the method first arrived, and further trials in 1985, but it is not yet on our shelves.

Then there was the 'supercap', which came about, according to the *Sunday Times* in 1983, when gynaecologist Uwe Freese told dentist Robert Goepp about the problems inherent in the use of the conventional cap[27]. The main problem was that the device only came in standard sizes which were easily dislodged and, not very erotic this, 'may cause bad odours'. The dentist told him of a technique used by dentists to make false teeth, which must be custom-made. This enabled an impression of the individual's cervix to be taken which could, in turn, be made into a cap which would stay put due to surface tension.

There was also an advance in temporary female sterilisation in the United States. The method involved pumping liquid silicone into the patient's fallopian tubes; this hardened within five minutes.[28] These were kept in place by plugs of silicone at each end, with the result that eggs could not travel down the tubes to the uterus to be fertilised. The process took half an hour, a bit longer than conventional female sterilisation, and could be carried out under a local anaesthetic. Its main advantage, however, was that, if a reversal was called for, the plugs could simply be removed.

Towards the end of the decade there was renewed interest in sterilisation, due in large part to further scare stories about the Pill. Women thought both that they needed to take breaks from the Pill – which was no longer the case according to contraception expert Guillebaud – and that they should not take it if they were over thirty-five. Actually, said Guillebaud, as long as women did not smoke they could continue to take the Pill until they were forty-five or over.[29] Predictably, the conclusion of the Pill company, Schering, was that the Pill was both the way forward and the British nation's favourite method of contraception, just as the London Rubber Company was to claim that their method was the title holder over that same period.

The 'morning-after pill' was certainly making a difference, according to the Brook Advisory Centre, which defended itself, not for the first time this decade, to the *Daily Mail*.[30] This time it was explaining that it gave out the morning-after pill to girls 'as young as 14' because they 'would rather give a girl the morning-after pill than see her six weeks later deeply distressed by an unwanted pregnancy'. The number of abortions carried out on under-age girls fell between 1984 and 1986, from 4,158 to 3,894. This was just after the oestrogen/progestogen combined morning-after pill was released in 1983. So doctors and family planning clinics were obviously doing something right – or teenagers were, which seems less likely. Before this, high doses of oestrogen alone had been used as emergency contraception.

There were also reports, such as the one in the *Evening News* of August 1987, that 'men could be taking the Pill within the next five years'.[31] How soon it was to become available was apparently to be determined by trials on twenty men in Edinburgh. Whether these men were particularly virile, or unreliable, and hence the trials never led to a Pill being made available, we will never know. What we do know from the paper is that no loss of libido was to be suffered: 'Doctors have promised worried wives and girlfriends that the human guinea pigs won't lose their longing for a bonk.' Did they, though? Did doctors really say that word?

Potential new ways of putting hormones inside people were also being researched all the time. The idea of doing this via injection was one of these ways, and one of these injectables, Depo-Provera, became licensed for long-term use in Britain in 1984. It was not to be approved by the US Food and Drug Administration until 1992. The drug's life actually began a lot earlier, however, in 1958, when Upjohn began trialling it. Its first trials as a human contraceptive began in 1963. Depo-Provera is a three-monthly injection of the hormone progestogen. It was found to be particularly effective – 0 to 1 failure per 100 woman years, or one failure per hundred users per year – and was approved by many distinguished expert bodies, including the International Planned Parenthood Federation and the World Health Organisation.

Controversy hit in 1988. Newspapers like *Today* began to report that the drug had been given to Asian women without warning them of its side-effects.[32] These side-effects included, at worst, heavy bleeding and depression. The World Health Organisation also warned that women taking Depo-Provera for five years were twice as likely to suffer from cervical cancer. Although there are still unanswered questions about its relationship to breast cancer, the drug is not now thought to encourage ovarian or cervical cancer, which was the original fear. Although the drug was tested on beagles, it was concluded by the medical profession that this bore no relation to the effects the drug would have on humans. Obviously the fact that it was being tested on animals at all did not go down well with animal welfare groups. The reaction of these groups to the news that the tests were not even of use must have been furious.

At the time of writing, contraceptive vaccines may work in one of two ways. The first causes the body to release antibodies which cover up the egg and make penetration of it by sperm impossible. The second allows conception to take place, but prevents the message that this triggers from getting to the hormone which would normally stop the shedding of the womb lining. Although the difference is subtle, the second crosses the ever-finer line between contraception and abortion.

The contraception-watcher of 1983 was promptly reminded of the ancient Greek approach to conception, when the *Daily Star* ran a piece under the headline 'Never mind the Pill. Try salad.'[33] The story was that Dr Michael Nassar had used wild cucumber juice as a contraceptive for thirteen years and that it had been effective. This was, you'll remember, a method advised by Soranus. Nassar's theory was that the effect of using the juice was to slow down the sperm (or 'reduce sperm motility' as the health books would have it) from an average of 60 mph to a geriatric 1 mph or less. John Riddle, expert on herbs used as contraceptives, says in his book that what is also known as 'squirting cucumber' works by stopping ovulation in women. Whether one explanation or the other is right, the world will not know until serious research is carried out.

Also under the 'foodstuffs with unexpected contraceptive properties' banner came coffee, as the result of a survey done in America in 1988. This was taken among women who wanted to have babies, and found that those who drank more than one cup per day were half as likely to become pregnant. According to esteemed medical journal the *Lancet*, caffeine was the culprit, which meant that other drinks containing caffeine could have the same effect.[34] Starbucks – the population's solution to the problem of its own success.

Whether or not it was due to caffeine again, serious research at the Harvard Medical School in Boston found that Coke, especially Diet Coke, slowed up sperm. According to an edition of *The Times*,[35] this followed reports that in some developing countries douching with Coke after sex was commonplace. 'At least in the area of spermicidal effect,' confirmed the scientists, '"classic" Coke is it.' Wisely, Coca-Cola did not get involved. 'We do not promote Coca-Cola for medical purposes,' a spokesman said. 'It is a soft drink.'

A new device which was, officially, a form of contraception was also trialled, although it was branded 'bizarre' by the *Observer* newspaper.[36] This was a tiny battery 'the size of a match-head' designed to attach itself to the cervix and emit a low-level electrical field, which sperm don't like. Dr Steven Kaali, medical director of New York contraception and fertility clinic the Women's Medical Pavilion, who was developing the thing, said to the newspaper: 'We know that a low-level electrical current does not do any harm, because pacemakers have been used in patients' hearts for so many years.'

As with so many developments in contraception throughout history, he added: 'We do not know the exact mechanism by which the device works.' He went on to describe three theories, two involving cervical mucus, and the third involving interruption of the electrical charge in the tail of the sperm, which makes it move. Broadly, it threw a spanner in the works.

The solution of Conservative MP Edwina Currie, then junior Health Minister, to the contraception dilemma came from a different angle.[37] She said having a mortgage was the best method. 'It makes people think about how many children they can afford. And this is right,' she said, when she visited a family centre run by the National Children's Home in south London. This is all very well, Edwina, but a fair proportion of the people you were talking about would not have been in a position, financially, to afford the luxury of a mortgage.

Similarly practical advice was given to Prince Charles by Lil Hill, Bristol mother of eleven, when the Prince told her he and Diana were having trouble with William: 'Keep your pyjamas on,' she said, according to the *Mirror* in 1984.[38] Her explanation for her seven sons and four daughters was that she and her husband 'didn't have a TV and went to bed at 9.30 in the winter'. She could also have advised him to take a careful mistress, of course. Incidentally, Prince Charles ordered a toilet roll holder made out of miniature chastity belts from a company in Essex. According to *Time Out* magazine, 'The firm applied for a royal warrant'.[39]

In fact it was not just Lil and Edwina, it was an altogether bossy decade, and music was – more often than not – using sex as its subject matter, in an increasingly overt way. 'Relax', challenged Frankie Goes to Hollywood, earning themselves a radio and television ban in the process, due to the song's unequivocally sexual nature. 'Don't Stand So Close To Me' warned the Police, in a song about that special kind of sex education between teacher and pupil. 'Move Closer' oozed Phyllis Nelson, as the author had her first slow dance, actually more like a swaying hug. 'Beat It' cried Michael Jackson, but no one was scared.

Ironically, when the providers of the decade's love-soundtrack were not dishing out orders, they were being indecisive. Buck's Fizz sang 'Making Your Mind Up' – here the sex was in the taking off of the skirts in the dance, and it obviously worked for the judges of the 1981 Eurovision Song Contest, because the song won. The Clash sang 'Should I Stay Or Should I Go?' – here the sex was in the guitar riff. Others were more direct: 'Let's Get Physical', panted Olivia Newton-John, and although the video pretended it was about working out in a gymnasium, no one was fooled. 'Like A Virgin', teased Madonna, making, once again, that religion/sex link. Here was another aspect of the eighties. Not only was sexuality being more overtly expressed, it was being overtly expressed by women for the first time. Apart from Madonna's contribution there was Page Three glamour model Sam Fox's song 'Touch Me' in 1986 which was – intentionally – cheap in the extreme and, the following year, the more progressive 'Push It' by rappers Salt 'n' Pepa.

Finally, in the Levi jeans advert at the launderette and to the strains of 'Heard It Through the Grapevine', Nick Kamen was giving women everywhere *that* feeling. You know the one, the one which, according to Marvin Gaye, means you need 'Sexual Healing'. Obviously most of them weren't going to get it from Nick, though, so they bought Levi jeans instead. Millions of pairs of Levi jeans.

9

Chemistry Sex

> We need a new religion to save us, or at least a new fashion. Fraternity, the care for others as much for as for oneself, must be our guiding ethic.
>
> Charles Handy – *The Age of Unreason*[1]

The 1990s are perhaps best pigeonholed as the decade on which pigeonholing gave up. Culturally it was a time of action and fast reaction – the pendulum swung violently from one extreme to the other, leaving behind at least some people and their views in either place. 'New man' was soon met by primal-screaming 'Iron John'; 'Old school' anything started running into 'New Age'; multinational Goliath jostled with homegrown David; GM found itself faced with organic; surgically enhanced *Baywatch* babe rubbed deeply tanned shoulders with pale and interesting natural beauty.

At the beginning of the 1990s, Britain was clearing up after hurricanes which had whipped through the south of England. Nelson Mandela was about to be freed and subsequently to be made President of South Africa. Bill Clinton was about to be made President of the USA, before making his feelings on the 'is sperm a sacred substance?' debate known to Monica Lewinsky. And the scientists? They were working flat out to control the huge number of potential Spice Girls fans that were being born every minute.

And hundreds of thousands of people in Britain were raving. Not only this, but a survey carried out by sociologist Andrew Thomson in

1996[2] suggested that they were slightly less likely to practise safe sex when they were on the dance, drug ecstasy. But it was not all bad news, at least for the girls. Men were less likely to climax when on that drug, or almost any other for that matter, and if they did, it would take them longer. There was also likely to be more foreplay, partly because ecstasy is primarily a sensual drug rather than a sexual one and partly because erections were less likely on it. As Shakespeare had said nearly four hundred years earlier of alcohol, in the only funny bit of *Macbeth*'s porter scene ('Ohh Miss, pleeease don't make me play the porter'), it 'provokes the desire but takes away the performance. It makes him stand to and not stand to'. In the meantime there was a chance that the effects of the drug would have worn off for the girl and, realising who she was having sex with, she might have extricated herself and returned to the dance-floor.

Most ravers were twenty-five or under, but some were a part of another phenomenon which had started in the late 1980s but really came to fruition in the 1990s – that of 'middle youth'. This started with the programme *thirtysomething*, which allowed people of over twenty to be cool for the first time. Fine. The problem was that the oldies didn't know when to stop. They got so over-excited that they didn't know when it was time to put their toys down and retire, gracefully, to bed. Or just retire, for that matter. This led to a situation by 2000 where, whether you liked it or not, people in their forties were wearing cargo pants and flying around on skateboards.

Apart from the fact that youngish people were taking drugs, another thing was abundantly clear. In the West, the concept of the functioning nuclear family was dead and buried. Certainly, single parents had been around for some time and the world was starting to get used to that. But self-confidence has only really been reached when one can laugh at oneself, and few laughed longer or harder at anything in the 1990s than they did *The Simpsons*. This was more than just a cartoon about a yellow family which was, at least initially, dysfunctional – it represented a culture accepting itself.

Not that everyone was happy about this cultural change of shape. Among the worried were some of the respondents to the Mass-Observation Archive's 1990 survey on 'Close Relationships'. Overall, they were concerned. Not in a knee-jerk, fire-and-brimstone posturing sort of way (there would have been little point; the respondents remain anonymous, who would they be trying to impress?), but in a relatively considered manner. One woman of eighty-two said:

> There are so many birth control aids available today I am very surprised so many young women and girls get pregnant. I think many do not want to go out daily to a job now the state hands out so much help in money. The pregnancy becomes a passport to housing, furniture and a regular income without any effort on their part. The men get away with paying no maintenance and I hope the government really do intend to catch these errant fathers. When I was young men knew if they made their girlfriends pregnant they would have to be responsible for the offspring one way or the other.[3]

And she was not a part of the old-school hang 'em and flog 'em brigade at all. When asked what advice she would give a young gay man, she said, 'My advice would be to act discreetly; not sleep around and try and stay with one partner.' On advice for a young pregnant girl, she said, 'My advice would be to consider the options very carefully, to consider abortion providing it is done early enough. I would tell the girl to ask her mother's help or a very close relative if she had no mother, someone who would see the young man concerned was made to be responsible.'

Another man, an engineer aged sixty-two, says, of procreation, marriage and the whole lot:

> Somewhere in all this there ought to be lurking a Happy Medium. From the Victorian era to say the 1950s, a pregnancy would be hidden. Disgrace, severity, even suicide were applicable words. Now we have one-parent families by the hundreds of thousands, and plenty of single women who think this is the high pinnacle of achievement. Parenthood is certainly this – but there's a thing called horse-sense too, and, usually, this demands a partner.[4]

This man's views on politics are along the same lines. Having heard that many *Guardian* readers had joined the Mass–Observation Unit's study, he said:

> I just wish to mention that several years ago, Jill Tweedie had a column in that paper. On one occasion she wrote about marriage. 'I ought to know what I'm talking about on the subject of marriage,' she wrote. 'Because I've had three goes at it already'! God. What's the use? Surely this just goes to show that the *Guardian* is in the grip of such people, just as the *Telegraph* is in the hands of the Conservative smoothies. Tory party is all Eton, Civil Service is all Oxbridge, Labour Party overloaded with wild ones . . .

The scientists, wisely, just kept their heads down and focused on hormones rather than ferociously temperate engineers. The main difference between these hormones and the ones before was that they were not taken orally. Oral contraception was no longer trendy because it had been established that whenever a drug has to pass through a person's system (in particular through their liver) there is a chance that its effectiveness will be reduced by such things as stomach upsets. There is also 'wastage', in the process. The upshot of this was that, to allow for 'wastage' higher doses of the hormone had to be taken if oral contraceptives were to be used.

Overall this made the idea of finding other ways of taking hormones a good one. Potential solutions included the injectable contraceptive, the hormone-releasing IUD, the hormone-releasing patch – like those used to help people give up smoking, but designed to let people indulge their cravings rather than overcome them – the vaginal ring, and the hormone implant. This is another way of saying what Soranus had said, thousands of years ago, which was that he thought pessaries to be more dangerous than oral-route drugs. In other words, introducing a drug straight to the place where it was needed would mean its effect would be intensified. Again, if something has to go on a journey there is more of a chance that a part of it will be lost along the way – if the oral-route Pill doesn't get the point across, think of Chinese whispers.

The difference between this time and the time of Pincus and Rock, and Stopes and Sanger before them, was that the progress of contraception was more fiercely governed – or perhaps affected; 'governed' implies a degree of control which is not there – by big business than ever before. Advances were often made, at least this century, if pharmaceuticals companies thought those advances were going to earn them money; obviously the lack of money in herbal remedies, which can't be patented, is a big fat reason for this area not having been explored. By now, there was also a lack of loaded philanthropists and the marketplace was all. Not only that, but the marketplace was now, more than ever, at the mercy of the media.

A more late twentieth/early twenty-first century example of science being at the mercy of, and in this case being held accountable by the media is found in the area of genetics. There is widespread debate over whether or not discoveries about DNA should be shared by scientists for the benefit of mankind. The scientists (or more likely the people that pay their mortgages) want to keep their labs' results to themselves, a bit like children crooking their arms around their work so that those on the adjacent desks cannot copy them – only the grown-ups do it out of greed, while claiming that further development will not be possible without funding, and funding will not be forthcoming unless information is protected. The people think the information belongs in the public domain and it looks like they are getting their way.

It is difficult to imagine this happening to the same extent in the time of Robert Dickinson and his peers, but perhaps this view has a ridiculous rose tint which is best ignored. The other obvious difference is that companies have names with Big Brother overtones – Schering, Unipath, Syntex – and make products with even scarier names – Eugynon, Brevinor, Loestrin 30, Ovysmen and so on. Even when Gregory Pincus was photographed looking crazed and holding a rabbit by the ears, the pioneering end of science was cuddlier than it is now. The face of science may have been that of a mad professor, but at least it *had* a face. Possibly the moment when animal liberation took hold was the moment when individual scientists started to hide their faces. Obviously the theorists didn't count. Evolutionary biologists Richard Dawkins and Steven Jay

Gould can be as cuddly as they wish (which isn't very) and still they make money because accessibility is the name of their game and they don't mess around with monkeys, rabbits or beagles.

But if the Mass-Observation Archive's respondents were right and young people had lost a notion of responsibility relating to birth control at grass-roots level, there was also a sense in which responsibility was being lost at a corporate level. If something without a face does harm to you, how can you blame it? If a pharmaceuticals company produces a contraceptive, or a drug of any kind, which has horrific side-effects and the public using the drug isn't privy to the name of the person who put it on the market or said 'it's ready', there is potential for internal buck-passing of the 'she said it was relatively safe', 'he put it on the market, I'm just doing my job' kind. And those who suffer are, at best, given money and read to from a written statement of apology. Money is not compensation in the true sense. A statement of apology is not the same thing as having a person say sorry.

Of course, there are individuals who contribute to the increasingly litigious society in which we live in, and very occasionally we are tempted to side with the corporation instead. In 2000, Marion Richardson attempted to sue the LRC for £120,000 when she became pregnant following the failure of a condom to perform its function. Some things should surely go under the 'you-pays-your-money-you-takes-your-chances' banner, unless of course a method sets itself up as having a 100 per cent success rate. And that would be a very brave, or stupid, company indeed.

The best example of the media taking over developments in the science of birth control, and one which frames the decade quite neatly, at least in its life in the US and UK, is Norplant. This was a system which involved implanting six 'matchstick like' rods just below the skin of the upper arm. These released progestogen over a period of five years and worked in two ways: for the first three years they stopped ovulation, and they thickened vaginal mucus, making it difficult for sperm to make it into the womb. They took ten minutes to implant and twenty to remove – unless the doctor was inexperienced, when the process took anything up to an hour.

The closest that contraception came to the philanthropist in the 1990s was the charitable organisation, and Norplant had its own: The Population Council of New York. Instigated by this charity, trials of the system were first carried out in 1975, in Brazil, Chile, Denmark, the Dominican Republic, Finland and Jamaica, although research into the hormone had started in the Council's labs in 1966. The response was very positive at this stage, with the vast majority of women (80 to 85 per cent) describing their experience with the drug as 'good' or 'very good'. Three-quarters said they would use it again and that they would tell their friends. The only real problem that it seemed to have was shared with many other drugs involving hormones; it threw women's periods out of whack.

Still, Norplant got its licence – first in Finland in 1983, then in the US in 1990 and finally in the UK in 1993. In the UK, the trouble started two years later, when the press started to run stories about the occasional implant becoming infected. Before this, the only real problems people had with the method, apart from the irregular bleeding, were that it was sometimes a bit fiddly to remove and it didn't look very nice. By the end of 1999, the contraceptive's UK manufacturer, Aventis, had decided, whilst maintaining that it was a good drug, to stop producing it. It was no longer commercially viable because the papers had given it a bad name. In the UK at least, those 3.4 cm rods were not invited to the millennium party.

But it lived on in many other countries. Norplant 2, involving two slightly longer implants which worked for three years not five, caused great excitement in the UK until the year 2000, and has been shown in trials to be effective. For the time being the tiny British baton was passed to companies overseas like Leiras in Finland, which continued to manufacture and sell Norplant. We must be more squeamish about bad press for pharmaceuticals than the Finns. Meanwhile the company Organon continued to develop Implanon. This method used only one rod, but trials in Indonesia and China showed that it was just as effective as the implants which used more.

Hormone-releasing IUDs were also made available in Britain in 1996. The best-known of these was Mirena. A capsule at the bottom of the contraption contained progestogen, and released it in very low doses. These work by thickening mucus, as with Norplant, and by thinning the womb's lining, which makes implantation of the egg less likely to occur. They also have some effect on ovulation – one in four of those who used it stopped ovulating. Again, like Norplant, the method worked over a five-year term, though in the UK they are currently only licensed for three years. Again, they were very effective (0.1 failure per 100 woman years this time), the main snag being that they often initially caused irregular bleeding. In some texts amenorrhoea – in layman's terms, absence of periods – is described as 'common' when the method is used.

The main problem with Mirena was, and remains at the time of writing, practical. The part containing the hormone made the device thicker; this, without going into too much wince-inducing detail, made them harder to fit than normal IUDs, particularly for women who have not yet had children. Experts Guillebaud and Szarewski suggest a local anaesthetic to deal with this.[5] Overall, in the league table of contemporary contraceptive options, the medic's view seemed to be that this method is somewhere near the top.

Of course, we don't have to put hormones in our bodies. Despite the continued growth in popularity of the recreational drug ecstasy – no one is quite sure how many people took it in the 1990s, but in 1995 writer Nicholas Saunders estimated that somewhere between one and five million British people had tried it[6] – many were 'just saying no' to the idea of ingesting chemicals in order to ward off pregnancy. One man surveyed in 1990, who had been the manager of a menswear shop in Sussex, thought we still had a 'good deal to learn' about the Pill: 'The risks outweigh the advantages in my view,' he said. 'For they interfere with a woman's chemistry, a risky choice if it can be avoided.'[7]

And of course it can be avoided, although the alternatives are not without risk. Perhaps the main application of science to non-hormonal methods in the 1990s came in the form of Persona. This was the laboratories' spin on the age-old 'rhythm method' of contraception, which relies on calculating the days in a woman's cycle when she is least – or most, if you are trying to have children – likely to be ovulating and hence when she is least (or most) likely to conceive. We have clearly come a long way since the 1800s when, with disastrous results, the 'safe' period was calculated according to the cycles of dogs. There are now a number of ways of calculating the 'safe' period.

One relatively old-fashioned way of working out the 'safe' period is to take your temperature every day and plot a graph. Broadly speaking, when your temperature rises consistently, ovulation is occurring. Obviously, though, there are reasons for the body's temperature to vary other than hormonal changes, so this method, without a back-up of some sort, is risky. Flu, for example, would give a misleading reading – not that you'd feel up to sex in that case anyway. If the woman trusts herself, this can be supplemented with the 'calendar method'. According to Szarewski and Guillebaud, the calendar method may be worked out as follows:

> First you must keep a diary of your cycles for at least six months. Work out what your longest and shortest cycles are. The earliest you could ovulate would be sixteen days before the end of your shortest cycle (for example if this was twenty-five days long, you could ovulate on day 9). Now deduct another seven days to allow for sperm survival [it's since been suggested that sperm may survive within the fallopian tubes for ten days]. That brings you to day 2. The latest you could ovulate would be twelve days before the end of your longest cycle, so if that was thirty days, you could ovulate on day 18. Now add 48 hours for egg survival, to be on the safe side. That brings you to day 20. Using this method, you can see that you cannot safely have sex from the second day of your period until the twentieth day of your cycle. In effect you will have between five and ten days each month when sex is 'safe'.[8]

For those people who like the idea of the rhythm method but not the 'if it takes two men with three spades six hours to dig a hole nine feet deep, how long does it take to fill it up again?' style problem-solving (and very few people can solve those problems – how sensible of Szarewski and Guillebaud to put the word 'safe' in inverted commas), the only possible solution is Persona.

This method, available since the early 1990s in Britain, was a small computer which did all the above brainwork for you. It measured two important hormones in your urine and on this basis worked out when ovulation was likely to occur. It needed three months to get to know your cycle, and was then able to tell you, by means of red, yellow and green lights, whether or not it thought you were safe to have sex. Early versions included the 'sexometer', reports on which appeared in the newspapers in 1981. This was worn like a necklace and had only a red and a green light. It came to its conclusions on the basis of a reading taken by the computer when the woman put a sensor in her mouth which measured her body temperature, as opposed to her hormones.

Right from the beginning of the 'getting to know you' phase, the person using Persona had to be free of all hormonal methods of birth control, and if even the morning-after pill was used at any stage during its application it was back to square one (i.e. the computer had to familiarise itself with your cycle all over again). The machine could be thrown by anything which introduced additional hormones into the system. This meant that people who were approaching the menopause or who were breastfeeding should not use it. It was also out for women whose menstrual cycle lasts less than twenty-three days or more than thirty-five days. More maths to think about.

The method suffered a serious setback in 1997, when the BBC's *Watchdog Healthcheck* programme, which aired in April, questioned the manufacturers about what seemed to be a high failure rate. The word was already on the street. Anyone who knew anyone who had been in the waiting room of an abortion clinic in the 1990s could have told you that the method was failing, although, to be fair, it could easily have been the operators that were failing rather than the method. Of the 100,000 people who had bought Persona since October 1996, manufacturer Unipath admitted that at least 450 pregnancies had resulted from its use. The company resolved to reduce its claimed success rate from 95 to 94 per cent.

The rhythm method has been the method of choice for Catholics ever since Antoine de Salinis, Bishop of Amiens established with the Penitentiary that it was okay in 1853. For some, though, the rhythm method was not effective enough. Father of the Pill John Rock was not the last to suffer from a serious conflict between the Pill and Catholicism. A Catholic mother of seven told the Mass-Observation Archive of her experience:

> In the early days of our marriage we would not consider the use of any artificial contraceptive – indeed at first none at all, because of our religious beliefs as Catholics. Within 21 months of our wedding we had become the parents of two children. I became alarmed at the ease with which I was conceiving and then resorted to 'safe period' methods – a simple calendar method at first, then, after two more babies, a more 'scientific' method using a thermometer – this entailed regular and precise temperature checking. This method slowed the pregnancies a little and even made a short gap in our family of two and a half years between the fourth and fifth babies. My hopes were raised, but eventually the fifth was succeeded by the sixth and then the seventh – and the first was still under ten years old. My husband was then 50, and I then made the big decision which was, in effect, a choice between the happiness of our marriage and my strict allegiance to the church – I began to use contraceptive pills and continued to do so for 15 years. They brought me a freedom we hadn't experienced since the early days of our marriage. I had no unwanted side-effects, and indeed my health improved once I was free from continual pregnancies.[9]

There were still silly methods cropping up all over the place. The principal and vice-chancellor of Strathclyde University, a person whose position might suggest that he was capable of seriousness, thought that contraceptives should be introduced into cereals to rid the world of its population problem. It was not the first time that someone had connected breakfast with birth control. In 1928, a German doctor called Heinrich Detlen advertised something called 'Anti-Baby Marmalade' which women were to put on their bread in the morning and which was supposed to work as a 'morning-after' contraceptive.[10] Eventually the word of many pregnant and angry women reached the police, who arrested the bad doctor. Tests showed that the paste consisted mainly of peas.

Exactly what prompted the excruciatingly funny *Onion* magazine – which is in the business of spoofing newspapers – to pick up and run with the idea of a 'morning-after' burrito is not obvious, but we should be glad that it did. In a March 1997 edition, there was a 'story' claiming that 'PepsiCo subsidiary Taco Bell launched its controversial "morning-after" burrito, a zesty, Mexican-style entrée that prevents unwanted pregnancies if ingested within 36 hours following inter-course'. It was called a 'ContraceptiMelt' and you could have it on its own or with sour cream and extra cheese. 'In the past, young women literally had to "make a run for the border" to terminate an unwanted pregnancy,' Taco Bell PR director Grant Lesko said. 'But now, women can make that same run for the border at more than 7,300 convenient locations right in their own home towns.' The discovery was 'a safe, effective alternative to traditional forms of birth control that must be administered before intercourse', Lesko continued. 'Plus it's delicious.' 'Parental consent laws in 37 states require that minors who wish to purchase the ContraceptiMelt obtain permission from a parent or legal guardian unless they order a side of Cinnamon Crisps and a large beverage.'

Rumours also started in the nineties that the Chinese were developing a spermicide made from earthworms. They had clearly changed their minds since ancient times about the sacred nature of sperm. Contraceptive devices were also starting to be used in art. Not only did Tracey Emin's Turner Prize offering of 1999 include a used condom beside an unmade bed, but Liz Lee, a Bristol doctor, created artworks in 2000 using her patients' contraceptives and the coil which she herself had worn for twenty years.[11]

There was brief excitement at Sussex University in 1994 about the contraceptive properties of the fruit papaya, when it was established that Sri Lankan women had been using it to control births for gener-ations.[12] It works by disabling progesterone, which is the hormone responsible for making the womb ready for a foetus. There has been no word about the fruit since, perhaps because it is also believed to calm the libido of those who eat it. In one of those bizarre but pointless coincidences, the plant also contains latex.

The big (and redundant) balls prize of the nineties went to one

Andy Bryant, who underwent a vasectomy at the Marie Stopes Clinic in London without anaesthetic. This he achieved, according to the *Daily Mail*, by self-hypnosis.[13] 'I have very specific wording which I will read to myself before going into theatre,' he told the paper. He also had a guru: 'a droopy moustached Antipodean called Mervyn whom he likened to a "boxing trainer"'. During the actual operation, he 'felt a slight twinge when he had not taken into account the nerves stretched right up from his groin to his stomach. But in a cool display of mind over matter he brought his abdomen under control, and with Mervyn whispering "guard against pain", pulled through.' Mr Bryant, who was a hair consultant by trade – and who advised Labour MP Bryan Gould to hang upside down to cure his baldness – 'then did a half-hearted high kick – and walked off without even a limp'.

There were those who were sticking with the condom, including the sixty-seven-year-old manager of a shop in Southampton. 'The condom is the only safe method when you think about the side-effects of some of the other methods in use today,' he said in 1990. 'Fifty years ago it was what kept our army men fit to fight while the USA numbers were reduced from sex-related illness.'[14]

In 1992 'the world's most collectable condom' was auctioned at Christie's and someone paid £3,300 for it. *The Times* described it as 'made of sheep's intestine and tied with a silk ribbon'. According to Christie's, an illustration on it 'depicts a nun, two monks and a bishop. She appears to be choosing between them.' Two years later a more modern variation on the condom theme was being patented in Italy by Lini Missio. This was coated with a material that, if torn or otherwise damaged, set off a microchip which let out a warning sound. It even played a tune, the most popular choice being Beethoven.[15]

Just in time for millennium madness, condoms were invented for vegans. *The Times* again reported, 'The Vegan Society has approved a range of condoms made without animal ingredients or derivatives. Milk protein is used in the production of latex for most condoms, but the German firm Condomi uses cocoa powder instead for the new range.'[16] Hopefully this provided the most reliable breakfast option yet for vegetarians requiring contraception.

And when the Germans weren't developing new kinds of condoms they were stealing them. In fact, according to a survey, it was estimated that one third of all condoms worn by Germans at the end of the 1990s were stolen.[17] This was leading pharmacists all over the country to remove them from their counters. So what brought on this spate of criminality? Was it poverty? Or boredom? No, it was concluded, it was shyness.

The French, too, were still up to no good. Or were they actually being as progressive as ever? They were handing out the morning-after pill to pupils in an attempt to lower the number of teenage pregnancies, which was already much lower than the number in Britain.[18] Still, at least our men were better in bed, or so the *Daily Mail* claimed in an article with the headline 'Move over, Monsieur'.[19] According to a survey, 75 per cent of Britons did not see their own satisfaction as one of the three most important factors that made for good sex, compared with 10 per cent of the French.

The British male was also more involved with the contraception issue that the French. Still, Oliver James, a psychologist, left the door wide open for the French to be better lovers. 'Their attitudes to sex derive from their parents who grew up when Catholicism was very strong and people didn't use contraceptives,' he said. 'They had to use more imagination to gain any pleasure. They view sex almost totally as being about pleasure in much the same way as they view food as being pleasurable and not about nutrition.' So what do the British do? 'In Britain, we tend to regard sex and food more from the biological point of view.' Hmm. Tricky. Which sexual partner to choose?

The Marie Stopes organisation in the UK produced a family planning pack designed to prevent unwanted pregnancies resulting from getting carried away on New Year's Eve 1999.[20] The pack, called R U Ready 4 Y2K, cost £10 and contained a packet of condoms, a 'Passport to Sexual Health' booklet, a leaflet on contraception and a balloon, the inclusion of which must have led to all manner of confusion for drunken couples. The organisation was right to release the pack. Pregnancies were way up at the beginning of 2000. According to the same organisation, the number of abortions being carried out always goes up in the first four months of the year, but figures for the first year of this millennium were 'unprecedented'.

*

Not everyone had a chance to be naughty in the nineties, however. One man from Manchester, who described himself as an 'unemployed alcoholic', had particularly strong views on those two old favourites of the Church, masturbation and celibacy, the latter of which, despite its association with medieval monks, remained alive and well at the end of the twentieth century.

> My last 'relationship' with an alcoholic woman lasted a week (I think) and that was about 2 years ago. Since then I have not had sexual relations with man, woman, nor beast: nor with child, machinery or other inanimate objects. This excludes myself. Nobody is that bloody pure. So, the old five-fingered widow has had to suffice.
>
> All I can say about celibacy, and I speak from experience, is it's unnatural. No one in their right mind, at least no man, would wish to be celibate. For me it is an enforced condition. I cannot find a girlfriend so I'm celibate and it's driving me bonkers (*or is it bonkless?*)[21].

In case you were wondering, he also hated the idea of prostitution, and didn't know why women like men because they are 'bony and hard', adding that he didn't fancy skinny women either.

At least one man, from South Wales, had been abstaining too, although not through any choice of his own and not for *too* long:

> Having just lost my virginity at the grand age of 34, I have only recently learned some of the technical difficulties of sexual intercourse and also of using condoms. Being gentle and understanding with each other has been important to us as we learn. I realise it will take some time to achieve the level of physical pleasure that can be reached when masturbating.[22]

A fifty-seven-year-old woman, on the other hand, found it difficult to imagine that anyone was really celibate, whatever they said: 'Lots of people are celibate on the books but one way or another cohabiting or have a gentleman friend. That's why there were all those jokes about

Roger the lodger.' Certainly her best friend has not held back since her divorce: 'For about 10 years she had say, 4/5 men friends with whom she slept and 2/3 with whom she did not sleep and 4/5 straight female friends. She was brought up strictly in Wales, where the Minister said "It's alright to have sex on a Sunday as long as you don't enjoy it", but she managed to overcome her childhood conditioning remarkably well.'[23]

The Mass–Observation Archive managed to find an enlightened clergyman who, despite not being celibate himself, was prepared to defend celibacy:

Where would we be without sexuality? But, when all passion's spent, there is a degree of liberation. This is what celibacy is all about, I suppose. It is an option in the Church for those who want to devote themselves to a higher end. Not being celibate, I presume that the advantage I enjoy is that I have the same kind of life as the people I serve. I worry just as much as they do about the quality of my children's A levels. Actually I'm not sure I'm all that much better off, because my children are bright and healthy. Did I really understand the plight of the woman with the son with special needs, or John and Sue who had two boys with Muscular Dystrophy? Is there not an element of 'There but for Fortune go I'?

The celibate, on the other hand, is detached and thus able to laugh with those who laugh and cry with those who cry. The Celibate is the true Clown. The victim and the victor. Monks and nuns are, in my experience, very jolly people, though the Anglican kind of nun is, according to Evelyn Waugh, less the jolly soul than the parched maiden lady. But he would say that, wouldn't he?[24]

For some sectors of the Church in America, the pendulum had swung quite far enough in the permissive sexual direction, thank you very much, and it was time to take control again. The most highly publicised incarnation of this sentiment was a campaign known as True Love Waits, which was launched by LifeWay Christian

Resources, 'the world's largest provider of religious products and services', in April 1993. The basic principle here was that there should be a return to abstinence from sex until marriage. The form that this took with True Love Waits was that young people – mainly students and all thirteen years old or over – should sign a card which said:

> Believing that true love waits, I make a commitment to God, myself, my family, my friends, my future mate, and my future children to be sexually abstinent from this day until the day I enter a biblical marriage relationship.

At the time of writing, the campaign's website contained information and pictures of a lot of moderately hip-looking young people. Just one part of it needed fixing. At the beginning of a section called 'What's the word on the street about True Love Waits?' underneath a picture of a very cool guy sporting dreads, a goatee beard and trainers was a letter beginning, 'Hello, My name is Brenda. I accepted Jesus Christ as my Saviour about 2 years ago. I am 16 years old' – I think not.

The site listed a number of reasons for making the above promise. Several of these were reminiscent of a much more fire-and-brimstone era, at least in Britain. It is difficult to imagine the Church in Britain applying such tactics these days – it is far too apologetic about itself. Fairly early on there is mention of the fact that, having made the promise, 'your concern for yourself can allow you to choose to avoid that which leads to guilt, broken relationships, disease, and even death', which starts to sound like a good idea, especially when combined with the next bombshell: 'Sex before marriage always hurts people. You can choose not to hurt others through sexual misbehaviour.' Blimey. What are we waiting for? Phone your friends. Spread the word. Never have sex again. Scare tactics? Surely not.

The website also has advice for the families of those teenagers who need to be frightened away from having sex. According to the National Longitudinal Study of Adolescent Health, if the parents and families of teens make their disapproval about adolescent contraception known, this will protect these teenagers both from early sexual involvement and from pregnancy. What a different place America must be from Britain. In this country, if the parents and families of teens made their disapproval about adolescent contraception known, that teenager would run away from home, cringing as they did so. The same goes for 'parents who give clear messages about delaying intercourse'. Their survey said that this would result in children who were less likely to have early intercourse.

But then, if you read on a little, all becomes clear. Those who are more likely to wait, says the survey, are those for whom 'a higher level of importance is placed on religion and prayer', who 'appear younger than their age mates' and who have 'a higher grade point average'. In other words they are a tiny minority of students and the vast majority do not aspire to being anything like them. Having said that, at the time of writing over a million young people in the United States had signed cards. However, America is a huge country and despite the claim that it has become an international campaign, the site can only come up with two cities in Canada and one in Uganda to support this. So, despite the campaign's infamy as a kind of interesting oddity – Durham Union Society debated the the motion 'This House Believes that True Love Waits' and it was defeated by acclamation, Radiohead wrote a single called 'True Love Waits' – the concept has only really been embraced, as it were, by the US.

What about those who have already sacrificed themselves at the altar of sin, but have since seen the error of their ways and wish to join in the abstention/celibacy fun? Is it too late for them? Will the same rather strict God behind True Love Waits let them in the door? Or did they have their chance and blow it? No – all is not lost. They, it was established at the end of the 1990s, again in America, can become Born-Again Virgins. And in *The Cult of the Born-Again Virgin: How Single Women Can Reclaim Their Sexual Power*, Wendy Keller, who 'married at 19 and divorced at 29' and who has 'dated four zillion Mr. Wrongs and asked five zillion relationship questions', can tell you exactly how.[25]

One of the slightly less predictable things that the book claims it can help you to do is to 'improve your career/finances'. This whole movement starts, at this point, to look like a handbook for those who need to put a positive spin on the phenomenon which is taking over the US, most notably Los Angeles, of young, attractive people not having relationships with each other because they are simply too busy. If you claim you are 'celibate' or 'abstaining', you see, it makes you look, and feel, as if you are taking control rather than missing out.

Author Patrick Dixon is interested in the notion of the pendulum swinging 'from restraint to relaxation'. The Victorians were reacting against the relaxation of the eighteenth century, he says in his book *The Rising Price of Love*, and the same thing happened, with the advent of VD, after the permissiveness of the 1920s which in turn followed the enforced separation of people after the war.[26] He thinks, and he is probably right, that phenomena like True Love Waits might be signalling the beginning of a new, more puritanical phase to follow our increasingly sexualised society, although he is not sure how large a swing it will be. For him, the answer will be found 'by looking at six key areas where the sexual revolution has let us down: the need to feel loved, the abuse of sexual power, sexual illness, emotional cost of breakup and divorce, damage to children and the huge cost of paying for it all'. In fact, while some will indeed react against the sexualisation of the Western world, it is so entrenched that others will not. The future is fragmented.

10

And Finally

Your children are not your children
They are the sons and daughters of Life's longing for itself.
                                    Kahil Gibran *The Prophet*[1]

So where are the silver space suits and machines which propel us to
work at a height which just skims the heads of the pedestrians below?
Where are our holidays to the moon? Where's the sweetie which
makes us think we've eaten a four-course meal? Where's the bloody
male Pill? Despite chapter headings to the contrary – and feelings to
the contrary – about the turning of centuries, progress does not divide
itself up into decades or millennia. Contraception for the twenty-first
century is a mixed bag just as it always has been; only the mix has
changed. However innovative, most methods are variations on already
existing themes, be they mechanical or hormonal. What is changing in
many developed countries is the length of people's sex lives. We are
becoming sexually active much earlier and reproducing much later.
Combine this with both the large number of teenage pregnancies and
the developing world's overpopulation problem and it is clear that
contraception is more relevant now than it has ever been before.

In our haste to invent new devices, we have continued to come up
with ideas which are just bizarre. The bikini condom was a proposed
extension of the Femidom principle.[2] If the Femidom seemed to have
features which might distract the most ardent of lovers, it was nothing
when compared with this. The idea with the bikini condom was that

it would take the form, as the name suggests, of a kind of tight pair of pants containing a pouch which fits inside the woman. British chat show presenter Graham Norton featured a rubber version of this on one of his shows in 2000.[3] He found it on the internet – more proof that, however bizarre your fantasy, somebody somewhere has already had it, only more so, and they have built a website dedicated to it.

Science has also ensured that the labs are conducting absurd experiments on behalf of men and, unbelievably, not just for the entertainment of tabloid newspaper readers. The best of these experiments revolve around men's scrotums. 'Scrotum warmers' came about in response to research which showed that men produce fewer sperm (that is *fewer* sperm not *no* sperm – the result being the not-very-marketable safe*ish* sex) when the weather is hot. They have yet to catch on, even for the man who has everything and who gets cold in winter, or perhaps when swimming in the sea.

Marginally more serious work is still being done on the basis that ultrasonic waves hinder production of sperm in the testes. Rats are rendered permanently infertile after having swum through water containing ultrasound waves (their testes were too small for scrotum warmers, so we don't know what the effect of those would have been). Men appear to lose their fertility for two or three years if they do the same thing. Ultrasound does not pass easily through air, so if the method is ever used, it may well involve the male lover immersing his balls in water before lovemaking. Difficult to imagine both the immersion and the woman wanting to make love subsequently, unless he goes behind a screen or something, or his lover is turned on by seeing her man degraded – which has been known.

A kind of jock strap invented by doctors in Egypt in 1992 worked using the same principle.[4] The Egyptians have a tradition of dreaming up unorthodox birth control methods. They were the ones who thought of using crocodile dung five thousand years ago. According to the London *Evening Standard*, the jock strap device was made of polyester 'that uses the body's heat and static electricity to render the wearer temporarily infertile'. Allegedly 'men are even happy to wear it'. Although 'the sperm counts of 14 volunteers dropped to infertile levels after an average of 140 days of wearing the sling' we do not know how many volunteers it did not work for, or indeed how many couples minded waiting that long before having sex. This was not the only waiting they had to do, either. It took the volunteers' sperm counts 157 days to return to normal. The same principle was at the heart of a new theory in 2000 which suggested that the lowered sperm count of Western men might be due to the fact that they spend so much time sitting down, either in their cars or at their desks. This, it was thought, led to them to get hot crotches and hence to sperm production being reduced.

Ironically, while all this bizarre activity is going on, the other obsession of scientists is to achieve its opposite – to find out why, in Britain and the US at least, the sperm count has become so low in the last few decades. Theories abound from scientists and these translate into advice from newspapers. The *New Scientist* seemed to have a breakthrough at the beginning of 2000. Levels in the US dropped in 1960. The average date of birth of the men used in the survey was 1924 – the same year that iodised salt was introduced. To test the theory, rats were fed on a diet which was low in iodine. According to the magazine, as well as having a higher sperm count 'they ended up with testes twice as big as normal'. So the guy in the 1990s who underwent the vasectomy operation with no anaesthetic had to surrender his big-balls prize to rodents.

Another scientific journal, *Personality and Individual Differences*, claims that sperm levels are dependent on how much partners see each other.[5] Absence, it seems, makes the sperm get stronger. When partners are constantly in each other's company the man produces a mere 389 million sperm per ejaculation. If they see each other just 5 per cent of that time the number increases to 712 million. This, says the journal, is due to 'sperm competition', an idea which was central to the 1996 book *Sperm Wars: Infidelity, Sexual Conflict and other Bedroom Battles*.[6] A woman is not a naturally monogamous creature, according to this theory, but is a creature interested in strong sperm. The more people you have sex with, the more chance you have of finding some strong sperm in amongst all the sperm you encounter. If a man has been away from his partner, his sperm has to strengthen up in order to compete with that of all the men with whom she has probably, if she's followed her nature, been having sex.

The journal goes on to say that one in seven men is not the biological father of a child he believes is his – if you are a swallow the situation is even worse, the figure is one in three. Think of seven pregnant women (famous ones are more fun). The expectant partner of one of those, if this magazine is right, is not the real father. Incredible. Actually, though, if you were 'shooting blanks' and were to take advice from a magazine on how to go about remedying this, you would go for the *New Scientist* over *Personality and Individual Differences*. So scientists sometimes make bras which tell you when you're ovulating, and bikini condoms. But it's better than trying to get pregnant by reading something which might as well be called *Men Are From Mars Monthly*.

A report by the Mass-Observation Unit published in 1945 raises the subject of men not knowing whether they are the father of a child or not. In a discussion on 'Changing Standards of Morality', the author is exploring ideas of monogamy and marriage. These customs, he is saying, are in large part to do with the fact that, prior to the acceptance of birth control, children had always been a likely outcome of sexual union. 'Men have wanted assurance that their wife's child was also their own,' he continues, whilst 'women have needed assurance of the means to support their children'. The last part is a fairly obvious point, but what an interesting thought that men might have stuck with women and expected 'exclusive rights' because if they did not, they couldn't be sure that they were passing on their genes as nature intended.

In fact, another aspect of the same report is still relevant at the beginning of the third millennium AD, which should come as no surprise because it refers to the change of an order which had persisted for millennia:

Society, in fact, is still groping in the dark for new standards, to replace those which were shattered by the advent of birth control. For thousands of years promiscuity had been 'wrong' for the simple economic reason that it results in unwanted children. Maybe it is still wrong – most people, indeed, have some sort of feeling that it is – but so far no one has been able to produce a reason, clear-cut and simple like the old one, as to *why* it is still wrong. The 'loose morals' of the last two decades [the twenties and thirties!] may be regarded, in a sense, as a sort of mass-experiment on this question, an experiment which has so far reached no definite conclusion, though various trends of evidence begin to appear.

Substitute the word 'wrong' with the word 'naughty' or something like it and this is very much the situation today. The new generation does not have such strong feelings of right and wrong as its pre-decessors, but the hardest of hardnut teenage girls thinks it is cool to be promiscuous because it is an act of defiance. In their case it *could* be defiance against their boring old sense-of-right-and-wrong parents. Yet even when the love-children of Ronald Reagan and Margaret Thatcher are promiscuous, they don't feel the same sense of rebellion, but they still think what they're doing is 'naughty' at some level. And they need to. It's no fun otherwise. This is the un-PC argument against soft porn imagery being used openly to sell everything. If it's not covert and private, goes the argument, it's not fun. That's the nature of sex. And there's something in it. Perhaps, just as the world may have come up with Starbucks as a solution to its own population crisis – remember, caffeine reduces potency – it is bombarding itself with so many sexual images that its inhabitants will eventually become desensitised and won't want to have sex with each other any more. Or perhaps, more radically still, saturated by provocative pictures of women in the media, women will start fancying other women more than they do men, and the population crisis will solve itself that way. Not for the first time, all will be revealed.

There being, in contraception as in every other sphere of life, nothing really new under the sun, several methods available today are extensions of those that currently exist. These include Lea's shield, a cervical cap made of silicone that fits on to the cervix by suction. The material it is made from enables it to mould itself to the individual, and it allows fluids out but not in. The Femcap is similar, but it has rims on its sides which are supposed to offer even greater protection from conceiving. Spermicides are also being researched constantly. Primitive (and familiar) as it might sound, a chemical called chlorhexidine prevents the sperm from getting to the egg by making the woman's cervical mucus thick and impenetrable, which is probably how the more contraceptive of the traditional herbs worked, although there is little in the way of scientific evidence to prove this. Another drug which is known to lower blood pressure seems to function as a contraceptive. If a tablet of the chemical is put into the vagina it disables sperm for around twenty-four hours, which is enough time to prevent conception.

Hormone research is here to stay, at least for the near future, and that future will continue to throw up new ways of administering hormones for contraceptive purposes. Injections, pills and implants are now well established. Yet to come are patches which are worn by women and must be changed once a week. These give off hormones in the same way that nicotine-releasing patches used by those who wish to give up smoking give off nicotine, although hopefully with a greater degree of reliability. They are not available yet due to a practical problem. It is difficult to combine oestrogen and progestogen within a patch.

In 1987 the *New Standard* was saying the pad was 'still very much in the pipeline and might not be on the market for another three to five years'.[7] Best make that upwards of thirteen to fifteen years, then. Mr Whitehead, consultant gynaecologist at King's College Hospital, was very confident at the time: 'We will almost certainly produce the first pad of its kind anywhere in the world,' he said. 'The Americans are working on the same project, but we're in front.' The bad news, Mr Whitehead? In July 1999, *Asian Age* proclaimed, 'Trials for female contraceptive patch in US almost complete'.[8] Despite the prediction that the patches would be available in 2000, their arrival was still eagerly awaited at the time of writing.

More appealing than sticking a patch to yourself was ever going to be was a stomach rub which was undergoing trials in America, Chile, Australia and the Dominican Republic in 1997. This was a contraceptive gel containing a hormone which stopped the woman ovulating, and which was to be rubbed over a 10 cm^2 area of the abdomen. Dr Edith Weisberg, who was in charge of the trials in Sydney, told the *Sunday Telegraph*: 'It's a bit more sensuous than taking the Pill every day.'[9] This was fair, but both Dr Weisberg and her method have since gone quiet.

Similar optimism to that witnessed in the *New Standard* over the patch was evident in the *Daily Mail* in 1990. This paper said that 'a revolutionary new contraceptive could be available to British women by the end of the year'.[10] This was the vaginal ring, a soft rubber device about 5.5 cm wide and 1 cm thick. It is hollow, can be left *in situ* for up to three months and 'one size fits all'. It can be removed by the woman whenever she wants and has the advantage of being as close to the place where it is needed as possible. This means that a much lower dose of progestogen, which is what it releases, can be used than is the case with, say, the Pill. If it is removed for three hours or less – long enough for all but the longest of players to make love, for instance – the current thinking is that it will still be effective. Effective, that is, if it is on the market. Which, at the time of writing, it was not. When it does arrive, progestogen will be combined with oestrogen.

According to medical experts Szarewski and Guillebaud, using the vaginal ring is more or less the same as taking the Progestogen Only Pill (POP), without having to actually take the pill.[11] This resemblance extends to its main side-effect which is, like the POP, irregular bleeding, mostly in the first few months of using the method. There is another side-effect at the moment, which caused vaginal rings to be refused a licence in England at the eleventh hour. This is that they produce some reddening of the area around the cervix. Despite this, the users did not notice any discomfort; in fact they liked the method. With some work, it looks as if the vaginal ring is set to be a part of sex in the twenty-first century.

Implants too will continue to be modified. The most obvious way of improving these is to make them biodegradable after their useful life. In this way they would dissolve and no visits to potentially cack-handed doctors would be necessary when your three or five-year term was up. This is more difficult than it sounds, however. Somehow the implant must 'maintain its structural integrity', as the *American Journal of Obstetrics and Gynecology* put it in May 1994, and contain enough hormone that it can be regularly released and effective as a birth control method, but not so much that it continues to release it after it is wanted, thus continuing to act as a contraceptive or to affect the woman in some other way. Experiments are currently under way using what are known as 'copolymers'. Capronor is the furthest advanced of these and, according to the journal, on the 'structural integrity' issue it has one up on Norplant. If a woman should want to remove it in order to conceive, the fact that it does not have 'fibrous sheaths', as Norplant does, means that it can be removed in three minutes instead of twenty-three.

The Pill is not about to disappear either, even though it is not the most direct way for a hormone to prevent conception and despite claims from the press in 1996 that it was about to fall out of favour. For one thing, it is rumoured that it is to be given to both the geese on London's Hampstead Heath and the pigeons in Trafalgar Square, which are reproducing at an alarming rate. In particular, experiments are taking place with a hormone called inhibin which occurs naturally within both men and women and has an effect on the production of both sperm and eggs. It does not seem to carry too many side-effects and could well lead to the first 'unisex' birth control pill. The only thing which is holding this research back is the difficulty involved in producing the hormone in large quantities. It is not, so far, possible to recreate it in the labs. Experience with the Pill and finding a synthetic version of the hormone progesterone suggests, though, that it is probably only a matter of time.

The excitement surrounding this echoes that which was whipped up by the discovery in 1992 of the protein PH30. This protein, according to *The Times*, provided scientists with the link between sperm and egg at the moment of conception.[12] If a vaccine against this protein could be discovered, it was reasoned, the sperm would no longer recognise that it should attach to the egg and conception would not occur. There were already couples unable to conceive because the man's sperm did not recognise the woman's egg. The proposed contraceptive would recreate this situation to the advantage of those who did not want children, and would work for two to three years with few side-effects, it was hoped. The research continues.

Ugly and with a girlfriend or wife on the Pill? Not 'getting it' quite as much as you'd like? On 14 April 2000 the reason for this became clear to *Independent* readers.[13] Women on the Pill are, on average, less amorous, according to research. This, say those who know, should come as no surprise, because the Pill tells your body that you are pregnant, and the libido of a pregnant woman is lower than that of a non-pregnant one. When a sample of half pregnants and half non-pregnants was asked about the attractiveness of various men, the non-pregnants were 30 per cent more 'up for it' (not the *Independent*'s phrase) than the pregnants. So, if your wife or girlfriend is on the Pill and she still wants you, you must be pretty attractive.

The male Pill finally looks set to arrive, and in a survey conducted in Shanghai, Hong Kong, Edinburgh and Cape Town, 66 per cent of men said they would take it, were it available. The delay is not just due to the fact that most doctors are men who are reluctant to put their brothers in such a position of responsibility, or because it does really make sense for women to take the Pill since ultimately they have the most to lose if they have an accidental pregnancy. Nor is it just because a tiny proportion of the amount spent on developing contraceptives for women is spent on contraceptives for men. Science's reason for the male Pill not yet being with us is that the sperm need time to mature. This is more than ironic, when you think how impulsive and adolescent the things can make their owners. Having said that, if one wanted to be competitive, three months – the amount of time sperm require to develop – is relatively young when compared with female ova, which are developed before a female is even born.

At any rate, sperm's development time means that any method which stopped them being produced would only become effective as a contraceptive after three months, which is when they would be making the mile long trip down the tubes which take them to their intended destination, the woman. There is also the danger that some sperm would not be killed outright but would be damaged. If conception were to occur from damaged sperm this could obviously have disastrous effects for the baby. And there are so many sperm to be prevented from coming into the world. Every minute a man produces 100,000. That amounts to 1,000 to 2,000 sperm being produced *every second*.

Not only that, if a method has an effect on the testosterone in the testis as well as on the hormone controlling the production of sperm – and we'll have to believe the scientists when they say it is difficult to block one but not the other – it would be acting on the hormone which makes a man want sex. So the man who was about to be without sperm would no longer want to get in the potential baby-making groove anyway. This loss of libido would not be relevant by the time the sperm had been killed and the man was ready for sex (three months later), but it would mean that his libido would suffer in the condom-clad meantime. And his partner might want sex more than just once, which would mean the process of killing the sperm and the man's ardour would have to be continuous. This has been combatted successfully by a team at Edinburgh University by combining the synthetic steroid, desogesterol, with testosterone itself. In trials this new pill was found to be 100% effective – so it seems that at last we really are close to having a male pill.

However, the avenue was still in need of exploration in 1994, when the *Daily Mail* reported that Kevin and Tracey McQuaide, who, along with thirty-seven other couples in Britain, had taken part in trials involving the injection of testosterone into men, were expecting a baby.[14] According to Dr Frederick Woo, head of the trial, the couple received two counselling sessions and a full information sheet which they had read and understood. They had also signed a full consent form. If what Dr Woo said was true, Kevin and Tracey had obviously failed to grasp the meaning of the word 'trial'. 'It has been a complete disaster for us,' said Mrs McQuaide. 'We were never led to believe there could be a risk of pregnancy.'

Still, research continues to be done into methods which use hormones and rely on men. Not before time for one Mass-Observation Archive respondent, a woman in her late fifties. 'I'm waiting for a male contraceptive,' she says. 'One which a partner could know was being used. People can lie about every aspect of sexual activity.'[15]

Some scientists reckon on stopping sperm production altogether and some are working at preventing the maturation of sperm. One hormone, cyproterone, has been used in prisons to decrease the sex drive of prisoners and has possibilities as a contraceptive. Such chemicals have the advantage that they stop existing sperm, which means that their effectiveness does not have the three-month time lag.

There are also drugs (one is called sulphasalazine, another propranol) which slow down sperm. Others tell the woman's body to produce antibodies which attack fully matured sperm once they reach the woman. Psychologically this is quite odd, if you worry about those sorts of things. You make love while your bodies make war. Some men who have had vasectomies automatically produce antibodies which destroy their own sperm. These antibodies in particular are being focused on by researchers at the moment, because they disable sperm more effectively than any spermicide currently on the market.

The most effective naturally occurring drug in the sperm-reducing stakes is called gossypol. This was at one time used in a cotton-growing area in China, for frying food. It was then discovered that it was permanently sterilising one in ten men (according to good witch-doctor Professor Riddle,[16] several pre-industrial societies have been using it to prevent pregnancies and induce abortion for ages). Although this property of it is not without its uses – especially, dare we say it, in a country which is as overpopulated as China, with its state-imposed one-baby policy and the infanticide which that brought – it also lowered potassium levels in the body. The least harmful consequence of this is that it makes a person feel weak and sleepy. The worst is that they get total muscle paralysis. For the moment this has taken the limelight off gossypol, but a helpful cousin of the drug may yet be discovered or produced.

Back in 1980, the *Sunday People* found the place on the Isle of Wight where the plant was being grown for research purposes by the World Health Organisation (the experiments themselves were going on at Leeds University).[17] One of the key players was the curator of the Botanical Gardens in Ventnor, Mr Roy Dore, who was the model of discretion. 'I can't name the species,' he told the paper. 'We don't want to be swamped by teenagers and others trying it out.'

Also in China, research is being carried out into the side-effects of another plant, the Thunder God vine. For years this has been one of those cure-alls, a bit like termite-mounds in Australia, which are used to counteract conditions from skin problems to arthritis. Recently, though, it has been established that it also causes infertility. Not only that but there do not appear to be any other nasty side-effects, as with gossypol.

A stark reminder of the almost magical ability of some plants to act as contraceptives came in the mid 1940s. In Western Australia, between 1941 and 1944, there was a reduction in the number of lambs born per year of 70 per cent. It was quickly thought to be something to do with a new crop of clover upon which the sheep were feeding. Since then, it has been established that the clover contained 'flavenoids'; these are biologically very similar to an oestrogen which, in mammals, controls mating behaviour. In the wonderful book *Jacobson's Organ: and the Remarkable Nature of Smell*,[18] Lyall Watson explains the extraordinary reason for the occurrence of this phenomenon:

> There is only one thing that clover and sheep have in common. They are partners in a plant-herbivore relationship: one eats the other, and the other does what it can to avoid being eaten too often. The clover produces an oestrogen, a chemical that mimics a key mammalian hormone, and this acts as a contraceptive Pill, reducing grazing by reducing the number of grazers.

Watson goes on to say: 'that a plant can do this is not just amazing, it is rather disturbing', concluding:

> The traditional barriers between animals and plants, or predators and prey, all fall away in a world where even the most potent elixirs are passed around like canapés at a cocktail party. And the fact that some of these key chemicals are volatile puts everything, literally, up in the air.

What has become known as 'Nature's Prozac', St John's wort, a yellow hedgerow plant which, according to legend, was found by John

the Baptist, was in the papers in 2000, the subject of an urgent government health warning. There were, said the *Guardian*, 'fears that it can
stop certain prescription drugs from working'.[19] Drugs listed which
'could all be affected' included those for HIV, epilepsy and asthma, as
well as certain heart drugs and the Pill. Professor Breckenridge, of the
Committee on Safety of Medicines, told of studies published in
international medical journals which said that the herb 'may stop
some medicines working effectively by increasing the breakdown of
certain drugs in the liver'.

Michael McIntyre, of the European Herbal Practitioners
Association, issued a cautionary note about the potential potency of
herbal medicines:

> Herbal practitioners are aware that herbal medicines need to be
> prescribed and taken with care. Just because something is
> 'natural' does not mean that it is 100 per cent safe . . . but people
> who are not on other medicines can take St John's wort safely.

This echoes Riddle throughout *Eve's Herbs*, a book which is mainly
concerned with that ultimate power of certain herbs – to cause
abortion or prevent conception. 'Breakthrough bleeding' is possible
for those who are on the Pill, said the report. What is not mentioned
is the fact that, according to Riddle again, St John's wort was used by
some women as a contraceptive in Herzegovina, according to German
records. Even as early as the sixth century, the plant was being
described by medical writer Paul of Aegina as a 'menstrual regulator'.
It is clearly time to do what Tony Blair's government used to call
'joined-up thinking' with our ancestors, which is really what *Eve's
Herbs* is about. A lot of information has been lost to us, and this is
information that is valuable. Even if we don't want to use herbs for
contraception but prefer to rely on doctors, *Guardian* journalists
would like to get hold of some of the old knowledge, if only to make
their news pieces longer.

In fact, forget the male Pill. The Western world's ever-increasing
interest in natural, herbal remedies could well be lighting the way for
the future of contraception. In the old days, knowledge would be

handed on, in particular, from mother to daughter. That knowledge has been lost to most of us, but it can be found again. What used to be called Generation X does not cook for itself, because its mother didn't teach it to. But celebrity cook Delia Smith knows how to do it and she has passed her knowledge on to the Gen-Xers in two books called *How To Cook*, parts one and two, which have sold in staggering quantities.[20] Obviously when cooking goes wrong you can put it in the bin and start again. When contraception goes wrong you're faced with a small human being. So the methods must be tried and tested to satisfy today's rational mind. And there's the rub. The drug companies will not develop the kinds of contraception which are found in nature because these can't be patented and so there is no real money in it.

Again, where are the rich philanthropists to test the herbs which the old wives, among them John Riddle, say are effective? Or perhaps there could be a series of commando-style raids on laboratories, to find out what is being taken from nature and reproduced more cheaply. And then we could just grow it. Let's put the control back into birth control rather than placing it in the hands of the drug companies. Make yourselves heard, philanthropists.

Or you could just have sex with an android. According to *The Futurist* there were prototypes in Japan of 'sexbots', or robots, which were fitted with human features and made from soft, pliable materials.[21] They incorporated a vibrator and were even capable of 'love talk', apparently, all for those who were after that specific kind of hardwiring – or some such innuendo – best produced by a computer expert. This suggests that Woody Allen was not way off-beam when he invented a machine called the Orgasmatron in his 1973 film *Sleeper*.

Better established is taking advantage of computers or, more specifically, the internet. 'Safe sex' using the internet can take several forms, but the most well established, unless you include straight net porn, are chatlines and virtual stripshows or sex shows. In 1999 a company called Virtual Dreams, which charged *$5.99* per minute to watch and direct a stripper and *$2.99* per minute to tune in on the results of the *$5.99* guy's requests, claimed to be 'grossing *$1 million* per month'.[22] Grossing – you said it. Chatlines are less degrading and mercenary, but if you are new to the world of internet 'chat', beware of people inviting you to go into another 'room' with them, unless the written equivalent of an obscene phonecall is what you're after. One chat 'virgin' made the mistake of mentioning to what seemed like a perfectly pleasant guy that she was still in her dressing gown, i.e. that she had to go because she needed to get up and get a life. Very stupid. Indeed, it has been established that using chatlines is one mode of operation for paedophiles exploiting the internet. They target chat-lines for the young, and pose as young people themselves. Very unpleasant indeed.

Inevitably, cybersex can lead to infidelity – virtually. Many couples have had the 'if you just think it but don't do anything about it it's not infidelity' discussion, or perhaps one half of a would-be couple has tried the 'you've thought about it so you've as good as done it, so you might as well do it' angle. How about the 'you've typed your fantasy/vital statistics/underwear colour out to someone whom you know nothing about and they've responded' dilemma? Apparently a man from New Jersey filed for divorce on the grounds that his wife's messages to a man she didn't know, apart from via email, were adulterous. As the authors of *Next*, a report which tells us where today's trends are taking us, put it, 'the judge didn't agree – this time'.

The Church has gone quiet, and who can blame it when it is slapped down so hard by people like Germaine Greer, for whispering what it has always said? In response to a mere press release issued by The Right Reverend Dr Nazir-Ali, Bishop of Rochester, saying that marriage was all about having children, Greer began her attack thus:

This combination of lame-brainedness, illiteracy and pathetic eagerness to see itself in the news [!] is now characteristic of the Church of England. In a millennial version of martyrdom by media, the bishop got himself sneered at as a bloke in a purple frock who had never done a hand's turn in his life, yet imagined that he had a brief to tell people who neither attended his church nor worshipped his God what to do with their lives.[23]

That'll teach him to be a bishop. Her problems with the press release were many, but one was that he says 'the development of effective contraception has led to the view that women and men have been liberated from the traditional structures of the family'. Actually contraceptives have developed in response to the changing structures of the family, she says, fairly. She also claims that 'when people stop wanting children, they find ways of not having them, regardless of available technology'. In fact, this echoes the report by the Mass-Observation Unit published in 1945, when, post-war, everyone was worried about the declining birth rate. In response to statements very like the bishop's, it says:

> There is ammunition here for the foundation of a movement for the abolition of contraceptives based on the statements of the experts. Remove the cause and you will remove the effect. Remove contraceptives and the birth rate will return to its pre-contraceptive level. Those who say that birth-control is the cause of the declining birth rate are laying themselves open to misuses of their own statements which they would, no doubt, be the last to desire.
>
> But there is a broader query than this. To what extent can the spread of information on the voluntary control of family size be called a 'cause' at all? To what extent is it rather an 'effect' of a demand which if it had not been met in one way, would have been met in another?[24]

Some in Manila in the Philippines hope that contraception, together with education, can be a 'cause' of lowering the birth rate. British journalist Julian Pettifer went to Manila and Baseko, a squatter settlement outside it, for BBC Radio 4.[25] He found that three Filipinos are born every minute and the birth rate has doubled in the last thirty years. The Pro-Life Foundation is very vocal and powerful, and its national co-ordinator, who is a nun, says 'we are against the distribution of contraception in any circumstances', before swiftly going on to lump contraception together with abortion, prostitution and pornography.

The mayor of Manila is the chair of the pro-life movement, and he refuses to see a connection between high birth rates and poverty. He also thinks contraception a 'destructive practice' and sees the West as having a serious problem with the irresponsibility of its young, which is partly to do with the availability of contraception. In other words, his views are not far from those of Germaine Greer's bishop. Meanwhile, in the squatter settlement where there are eighty or ninety children per class at the high school, a Women's Health Foundation clinic is providing people with the Pill, the IUD and condoms, hoping to stop the continuation of the explosion.

Mothers interviewed often expressed regret about the number of children they had, saying that they would like to have fewer and to educate them. Presumably some of these parents are not so different from the mothers interviewed by the Mass-Observation survey in 1945. 'We didn't want four. But that's how it happened. It sort of came about,' said one.[26] If they'd felt like they had a choice they would have had fewer. Contraception provides choice. This is not the same thing as saying it encourages irresponsibility. Quite the opposite. 'When people stop wanting children, they find ways of not having them, regardless of available technology'? Not in the Philippines or in Britain in the mid-1940s they don't.

Greer continues that 'the bishop should consider the fact that responsible parents are the chief users of contraception'. She concludes by expressing her chief worry:

Many husbands walk out on a pregnant wife and many on a wife with a new baby. And many threaten to walk out if a pregnancy should begin and not be terminated. It is not unknown for such a man, who has deprived a woman of the children she longed for, to leave her and become the ecstatic father of the children of a younger woman.

There is hope for the bishop, though. 'If the bishop should choose to lash such men from the pulpit with the invective of a Savonarola [a fanatical fifteenth-century preacher], rather than his limp, parochial PR-speak, I would cheer him on,' she says. Even if he doesn't choose to lash, he made it into the *Telegraph*, so he probably counted his blessings.

Ironically, other nations are trying to encourage people to reproduce because the birth rate has become so low. In some parts of rural southern Italy, priests are reduced to wandering into bars and trying to persuade young men to stop living with mama, get married and have babies, so that the local school does not have to close down and cause the community to be further eroded. In Japan it has reached corporate level, with toy manufacturer Bandai offering employees a 1 million Yen bonus (around £6,500) for having a third child. The company says it is because of the reduction in the birth rate – we know that without children there would be no need for toys.

The newspapers still worry about sex education too, even the grown-up papers. In the *Independent*'s comment pages in 2000, John Walsh wrote that 'despite the carpet bombing of our senses with images of sexual abandonment from all sides – when it comes to grappling with the subject in the nation's classrooms, we have barely got its shirt off'.[27] Contrary to the family planning nurse who thought that sex education should not be taught early in schools, and a number of Mass-Observation respondents, Walsh and James Lawrence, director of the Aids Research and Education Trust, believe that 'Sex education is set up to fail if it is taught too late'. He goes on, 'it needs to be comprehensive and age-appropriate, basically going all the way before young people do'.

People who say it is taught too early need only look for ammunition to a television programme broadcast just three days before Walsh's piece. On *Tonight with Trevor McDonald*, teenage girls who lived in Doncaster, one of the places in Britain where teenage pregnancy is most common, told tales of losing their virginity at twelve. Why did they do it? asked the interviewer. 'Because it looked exciting,' said one. 'Because I'd had sex education and thought I'd try it,' said another. Perhaps she really was intrigued by a teacher, squirming with embarrassment, drawing diagrams on the blackboard. Perhaps, in the same way, she runs home and tries to recreate chemistry experiments in the privacy of her bedroom. Perhaps. Or perhaps she refused to take responsibility for her own actions. Perhaps she couldn't resist blaming the grown-ups, and teachers? Even better. Girls have sex at twelve because they feel pressurised, and not by the force of a limp condom being passed around class, but by their peers, who in turn are influenced by the society around them. This pressure needs to be tackled, and if the parents won't do it, maybe the teachers will have to.

Which teachers? Walsh says of pupils being taught about sex:

What they are not taught is: how to say no to sexual overtures from someone, of either sex; how to discourage an importunate partner with tact or humour, so as not to get labelled a prude or a tease; how to talk about sex without dying of embarrassment; how to establish an understanding with your boy or girlfriend so that, the next time everything goes suddenly quiet and intense, you'll trust each other about what happens next . . .

But these are not issues for a biology class. The Brains Trust was a panel of distinguished experts of various kinds selected by the BBC for a radio programme based on the debating of questions raised by an audience. In 1944 it suggested that 'it is for the sociologist to take a keener interest in sex education'.[28] What is the closest thing a twelve-year-old has to a sociology teacher?

In 2000 she or he had Geri Halliwell, UN Goodwill Ambassador and ex-Spice Girl. She addressed the Model United Nations Millennium Summit in London in August 2000, and explained herself thus: 'You may wonder what I do as Goodwill Ambassador. I work for the United Nations Population Fund, and Marie Stopes. It's my job to raise awareness about the need to improve sexual reproductive health.' A laudable activity, you'll agree, and doubtless what she was trying to say by making her entrance on to the stage at the Brit Awards in 2000 from between an enormous pair of spread female legs. 'That means more than telling people to wear a condom when bonking,' she continued. 'It's about healthcare for everyone around the world.' Beyond that, the speech was a kind of pep talk, reminding young people in Britain how lucky they are to have birth control at all and telling them to lobby their MPs about 'the kind of world you'd like'. It would be too easy to mock it. It probably did more good than harm, although it wasn't clear whether the young people she addressed were being urged to act or just to be aware of their own ability to make a difference.

Whoever takes on the sex education mantle in the schools of the twenty-first century and beyond will have to make 'just saying no' a lot cooler. They could use people like film actress Mary Tyler Moore as role models. She was, apparently, the only woman to star opposite Elvis Presley – in the 1970 film *Change of Habit* – and to say no to his sexual advances. To be her and not another one of Elvis's sexual conquests is cooler than cool. It makes Elvis look like an out-of-control little boy. She rules.

Afterword

Whatever Happened to the Crimson Burst of Anger?

Every great advance in natural knowledge has involved the absolute rejection of authority'.

Thomas Henry Huxley, 1825

Every period in history has had those that it sent on ahead; those figures who were prepared to reject authority, be ridiculed and stand right in the line of fire. The dirty old ancient Greek men and their worship of the male form have almost certainly given strength to the wretched and confused homosexual who is still in the closet. The witches of the Middle Ages and early modern period gave us homoeopathy and, in the least developed of societies, any medicine at all. The reformers of the nineteenth century – Francis Place, J. S. Mill et al – gave rights to human beings and the vote and choices about family size to women, and won spells in prison for their pains. Like those other witches before them, Marie Stopes and Margaret Sanger took birth control away from the medical men and helped to put it back into the hands of the women who needed it, and they too had their brushes with authority. John Rock sacrificed his much-beloved Catholicism not because he wanted to become famous for being the man who created the Pill, but because he was worried about the poor having large families.

It would be easy to think that the twenty-first century is without heroes, apart from the kind that earn vast quantities of money for playing football, or singing songs, or appearing in movies. Perhaps, though, whole movements now do the job that individuals used to. Rock 'n 'roll gave us teenagers. Hippies and punks in their own ways taught those teenagers to challenge convention and think for themselves. Perhaps, unfashionable as the view has become, 'political correctness' went some way towards making people a little more considerate towards each other so as to counter the 1980s 'me' mentality. 'New Age' has probably introduced concepts like Eastern religion and alternative remedies into the mainstream in the same way. 'Eco-warriors' have, with time, made us think more about organics and the world in general.

When Margaret Sanger's *The Woman Rebel* first came out in 1914, a part of its rapturous reception was due to the fact that people had started to feel they lacked a much-needed moral purpose. Letters to that effect came flooding in to the magazine, with new readers saying that they had wanted to be heroic, or that they had wanted to be angry for the sake of humankind, but that before now they had lacked a focus for these feelings. Much of the Western world feels like that now. How do we know? For one thing, the number of people applying to work for Voluntary Service Overseas has rocketed, and those volunteers are not just longhairs any more, they are managers, doctors and lawyers. Thousands of people, most of whom have lost the religion of their parents, are starting to think that 'there must be more to life than this'.

So we failed to see the turning of the wheel or the river of fire on New Year's Eve 1999. Comedian Al Murray was right, a river was never going to catch fire, we should have realised that from the start. We must also realise that contraception will probably continue to be an absurd business. *Daily Mail* readers will continue to rejoice that their children can be removed from sex education classes and newspaper columnists will continue to worry about Lolitas. Girls will continue to become fertile younger, approaching the age at which girls in Africa are fertile. Teenagers will carry on having sex under age, whether the media, the family planning clinics, the parents or the teachers are blamed. And the media, the family planning clinics and so on will continue to pass the sex-education buck to each other unless they all decide that, although it might not strictly be their job to educate young people, it might just be a good idea to do it. The world did not blow up as the noughts appeared. It continues to evolve and there is, occasionally, progress. But don't get too complacent. Just remember all those people dropping their smart jobs and going to Africa and South America and India to help. Something's stirring . . .

Notes

Introduction

1 Sigmund Freud, 1898; quoted in Angus Maclaren, 'Contraception and its Discontents', *Journal of Social History*, 12 (1979).

Chapter 1   Romantic Loves and Going Greek

1 Quentin Crisp, introduction to *The Gay and Lesbian Quotation Book* (Robert Hale, London, 1955).
2 Aristotle, *Politics*; quoted in K.J. Dover, *Greek Homosexuality* (Duckworth, London, 1971).
3 'Peasants, who may as well be called pigs/These are the only men who should resort to women'. Quoted in *The Gay and Lesbian Quotation Book*.
4 Stanley Kubrick's *Spartacus*, 1991 version – the original won four Oscars.
5 Aristotle, *Politics*; quoted in Angus McLaren, *A History of Contraception* (Blackwell, Oxford, 1990).
6 Plutarch, 'Solon' in *Plutarch's Lives*, tr. Bernadette Perrin (Harvard University Press, Cambridge, Mass., 1919); quoted in McLaren, *A History of Contraception*.
7 Mitchell Symons, *The Lists Book* (André Deutsch, London, 1977).
8 Antiphon the Sophist, Kathleen Freeman, *Ancilla to the Pre-Socratic Philosophers* (Harvard University Press, 1984) fragment 49.
9 Ova, ibid
10 Quoted in McLean, *A History of Contraception*.

198

11 Plato, *Timaeus*.

12 Aretaeus, *The Extant Works of Aretaeus the Cappadocian*.

13 *The Hippocratic Treatises*, 'On Generation'; quoted in McLaren, *A History of Contraception*.

14 Matt Ridley, *The Red Queen* (Penguin Books, London, 2000).

15 *Daily Mirror*, 8 February 1999.

16 John Langdon-Davies, *Sex, Sin and Sanctity* (1954).

17 Archilochus of Pharos, from Mary Lefkowitz and Maureen B. Fant, eds., *Women in Greece and Rome* (Samuel Stevens, Toronto, 1977); quoted in McLaren, *A History of Contraception*.

18 The medicinal properties of various plants are detailed in John M. Riddle, *Eve's Herbs* (Harvard University Press, Cambridge, Mass., 1977).

19 Shirley Green, *The Curious History of Contraception* (Ebury Press, London, 1971).

20 Ibid.

21 Pliny, *Natural History*, tr. A. Rackham (Harvard University Press, Cambridge, Mass., 1940).

22 Emiel Eyben, 'Family Planning in Graeco-Roman Antiquity', *Ancient Society*, 11–12 (1980–1). I am indebted to Eyben for the following account of Musonius, contraception and abortion in the ancient world.

23 Ridley, *The Red Queen*.

24 Eyben, 'Family Planning in Graeco-Roman Antiquity'.

25 Dover, *Greek Homosexuality*. The following account owes much to this work.

26 Keith Hopkins, 'Contraception in the Roman Empire', *Comparative Studies in Society and History*, 8 (1965–6).

27 Ridley, *The Red Queen*.

28 Rufus of Ephesus, *Oeuvres de Rusus d'Ephèse*, tr. Charles Daremberg (L'Imprimerie nationale, Paris, 1879), Caelius Aurelianus, *On Acute Diseases and On Chronic Diseases*, tr. I.E. Drabkin (University of Chicago Press, Chicago, 1950); both quoted in McLaren, *A History of Contraception*.

29 Aulus Cornelius Celsus, *De Medicina*, tr. W.G. Spencer (Harvard University Press, Cambridge, Mass., 1935).

30 *Daily Mirror*, 8 February 1999.
31 Lucretius, *De Rerum Natura*; quoted in McLaren, *A History of Contraception*.
32 Paulus Aegineta, *The Seven Books of Paulus Aegineta*, tr. Francis Adams (Sydenham Society, London, 1844–7).
33 Riddle, *Eve's Herbs*.
34 Jeannette Parisot, *Johnny Come Lately: A Short History of the Condom*, tr. Bill McCann (Journeyman, London, 1987).
35 Dr Eric Chevallier, *The Condom: Three Thousand Years of Safe Sex*, tr. Patrick White (Penguin Books, London, 1995).

Chapter 2   Clergymen Behaving Badly
 1 Norman E. Himes, *A Medical History of Contraception* (Williams and Wilkins, Baltimore, 1936).
 2 William H. Robertson, *An Illustrated History of Contraception* (Parthenon, New Jersey, 1990).
 3 Ibid.
 4 Jakob Sprenger and Heinrich Kramer, *Malleus Maleficarum* (*Hammer of Witches*) (1486); quoted in Richard De'ath, *French Letters and English Overcoats* (Robson Books, London, 2000).
 5 Otto Weininger, *Sex and Character* (1903).
 6 Geoffrey Chaucer, *The Canterbury Tales*, tr. David Wright (Oxford University Press, Oxford, 1985).
 7 Celsus, *De Medicina*.
 8 Quoted in Green, *The Curious History of Contraception*.
 9 Green, *The Curious History of Contraception*.
10 Hopkins, '*Contraception in the Roman Empire*'.
11 Avicenna, *Canon of Medicine*; quoted in McLaren, *A History of Contraception*.
12 Riddle, *Eve's Herbs*.
13 Ibid.
14 Green, *The Curious History of Contraception*.
15 St John Chrysostom, *The Homilies of St John Chrysostom* (Parker, Oxford, 1841), Clement of Alexandria, 'The Instructor' in *The Ante-Nicene Fathers*, tr. B.P. Pratten (Eerdmans, Grand Rapids, 1951); both quoted in McLaren, *A History of Contraception*.

16 William of Clonches, from Danielle Jacquart and Claude Thomasset, *Sexuality and Medicine in The Middle Ages*, tr. Matthew Adamson (Polity Press, London, 1988); quoted in McLaren, *A History of Contraception*.

17 Emmanuel Le Roy Ladurie, *Montaillou: The Portrait of Life in a Medieval Village*, tr. Barbara Bray, Scolar Press (Penguin Books, Middlesex, 1980). Much of the following account is drawn from Ladurie's book.

18 Thomas Sanchez, *De Sancto Matrimonio*; quoted in John T. Noonan, *Contraception* (Harvard University Press, Cambridge, Mass., 1966).

19 Quoted in Noonan, *Contraception*.

20 Sanchez, *De Sancto Matrimonio*; quoted in Richard De'ath, *French Letters and English Overcoats* (Robson Books, London, 2000).

21 McLaren, *A History of Contraception*.

22 Georges Duby, *The Knight, the Lady and the Priest*, tr. Barbara Bray (Pantheon, New York, 1983); quoted in McLaren, *A History of Contraception*.

23 'a sad or weeping woman cannot conceive'. Giovanni Sinibaldi, *Geneanthropeia* (1642); quoted in De'ath, *French Letters and English Overcoats*.

24 *The Encyclopedia of Unusual Sexual Practices* (Greenwich Editions, London, 1999).

25 De'ath, *French Letters and English Overcoats*.

26 Quoted in De'ath, *French Letters and English Overcoats*.

Chapter 3 The Condom Conundrum

1 Ogden Nash, 'Inter-Office Memorandum'; *I'm a Sstranger Here Myself* (Little, Brown, Boston, 1938).

2 Quoted in De'ath, *French Letters and English Overcoats*.

3 McLaren, *A History of Contraception*.

4 Quoted in De'ath, *French Letters and English Overcoats*.

5 Ibid.

6 Riddle, *Eve's Herbs*.

7 Quoted in De'ath, *French Letters and English Overcoats*.

8 McLaren, *A History of Contraception*.

9 Noonan, *Contraception*.
10 Green, *The Curious History of Contraception*.
11 McLaren, *A History of Contraception*.
12 Quoted in De'ath, *French Letters and English Overcoats*.
13 Hopkins, '*Contraception in the Roman Empire*'.
14 Riddle, *Eve's Herbs*.
15 Noonan, *Contraception*.
16 Brantôme, '*The Duchess of Portsmouth's Garland*' (1690); quoted in McLaren, *A History of Contraception*.
17 James Reed, *From Private Vice to Public Virtue: The Birth Control Movement and American Society* (Basic Books, New York, 1978).
18 De'ath, *French Letters and English Overcoats*.
19 Quoted in McLaren, *A History of Contraception*.
20 Parisot, *Johnny Come Lately*.
21 McLaren, *A History of Contraception*.
22 Quoted in Parisot, *Johnny Come Lately*.
23 Ibid.
24 Ibid.
25 De'ath, *French Letters and English Overcoats*.
26 Quoted in Chevallier, *The Condom: Three Thousand Years of Safe Sex*.
27 From a collection of handbills kept at the British Museum, London.
28 Quoted in Parisot, *Johnny Come Lately*.
29 Ibid.

Chapter 4   Science is Golden

1 Thomas Malthus, *An Essay on Population* (Johnson, London, 1798).
2 William Godwin, 'Thoughts Occasioned by the Perusal of Dr Parr's Spital Sermon' (1801).
3 Malthus, *An Essay on Population*.
4 Green, *The Curious History of Contraception*.
5 Quoted in J. A. Banks, *Prosperity and Parenthood: A Study of Family Planning among the Victorian Middle Classes* (Routledge and Kegan Paul, London, 1954).
6 Ibid.

7 Quoted in Angus McLaren 'Contraception and Its Discontents', *Journal of Social History*, 12 (1979). Subsequent quotations concerning Freud are also taken from this article.

8 Quoted in De'ath, *French Letters and English Overcoats*.

9 *The Times*, 15 April 1857, *The Economist*, 25 April 1857; quoted in Banks, *Prosperity and Parenthood*.

10 Quoted in Elizabeth Hampsten, *Read This Only To Yourself: The Private Writings of Midwestern Women 1880–1910* (Indiana University Press, Bloomington, 1982).

11 Ibid.

12 Quoted in Reed, *From Private Vice to Public Virtue*.

13 Quoted in Hampsten, *Read This Only To Yourself*.

14 Riddle, *Eve's Herbs*.

15 Himes, *A Medical History of Contraception*.

16 Quoted in Banks, *Prosperity and Parenthood*.

17 Quoted in Banks, *Prosperity and Parenthood*.

18 Charles Knowlton, *Fruits of Philosophy* (Watson, London, 1841).

19 Quoted in Banks, *Prosperity and Parenthood*.

20 Banks *Prosperity and Parenthood*.

21 Alexander Skene, *Education and Culture as related to the Health and Disease of Women* (Detroit, 1889); quoted in Reed, *From Private Vice to Public Virtue*.

22 Banks, *Prosperity and Parenthood*.

23 Alice B. Stockham, MD, *Tokology, A Book for Every Woman* (Sanitary Publishing, Chicago, 1887).

24 Banks, *Prosperity and Parenthood*.

25 Riddle, *Eve's Herbs*.

26 Ibid.

27 Banks, *Prosperity and Parenthood*.

28 Blackmail Chrimes brothers, *British Medical Journal* (14 January 1899); quoted in Banks, *Prosperity and Parenthood*.

29 *Chemist and Druggist*, 10 July 1897; quoted in McLaren, *A History of Contraception*.

30 From a 1949 report by the Royal Commission on Population; quoted in McLaren, *A History of Contraception*.

31 Reed, *From Private View to Public Virtue*.
32 Quoted in Noonan, *Contraception*.
33 Ibid.
34 Edward Clarke, *Sex in Education* (Boston, 1873); quoted in Reed, *From Private Vice to Public Virtue*.

Chapter 5   Handbags at Dawn

 1 Marie Stopes, *Marriage In My Time* (Rich and Cowan, London, 1935).
 2 Reed, *From Private Vice to Public Virtue*.
 3 Ibid.
 4 Ibid.
 5 Letter from Margaret Sanger to Vincent Brome, 6 January 1954; quoted in Reed, *From Private Vice to Public Virtue*.
 6 Françoise Delisle, *Friendship's Odyssey* (London, 1946).
 7 Mass-Observation 1945.
 8 'Wine That Turned To Vinegar' from Marie Stopes, *Man, Other Poems and a Preface* (Heinemann, London, 1914).
 9 *Woman's Hour*, 3 Jan.–14 Jan. 2000, Radio 4.
10 Noonan, *Contraception*.
11 Jane Lewis, *The Politics of Motherhood* (Croom Helm, London, 1980); quoted in McLaren, *A History of Contraception*.
12 Reed, *From Private Vice to Public Virtue*.
13 M–O K1515.
14 M–O C2142.
15 M–O, woman overheard.
16 M–O A1733.
17 John Murray, *Britain and Her Birth Rate* (Mass-Observation, 1945).
18 M–O FR2205.
19 M–O, woman overheard.
20 M–O, woman overheard.
21 M–O, man overheard.
22 There is a fuller account of the life and work of Robert Dickinson Reed, in *From Private Vice to Public Virtue*.
23 Reed, *From Private Vice to Public Virtue*.
24 Ibid.

25 Ibid.
26 Anne Szarewski and John Guillebaud, *Contraception: A User's Handbook* (Oxford University Press, Oxford, 1998).
27 Reed, *From Private View to Public Virtue*.
28 Ibid.

Chapter 6   Bill Papas

1 Graham Greene, *The Comedian* (The Bodley Head, London, 1966).
2 Reed, *From Private Vice to Public Virtue*. The following account of the development of the contraceptive Pill owes much to this work.
3 Quoted in Malcolm Gladwell, 'John Rock's Error', *New Yorker*, 13 March 2000.
4 Gladwell, 'John Rock's Error'.
5 Ibid.
6 John Rock interviewed by Sara Davidson; quoted in Gladwell, 'John Rock's Error'.
7 M-O 1990, A2055.
8 M-O 1990, A1530.
9 *Guardian*, 19 June 1974.
10 *The Times*, 3 June 1968.
11 Ibid.
12 *Daily Mail*, 2 March 1968.
13 M-O 1990, B1224.
14 M-O 1990, A1292.
15 *News of the World*, 11 September 1966.
16 *News of the World*, 9 October 1966)
17 Quoted in *The Encyclopedia of Unusual Sexual Practices*.
18 *Daily Mirror*, 27 October 1964.

Chapter 7   Blame it on the Boogie

1 Germaine Greer, *The Female Eunuch* (Flamingo, London).
2 *Daily Express*, 12 April 1972.
3 *News of the World*, 16 June 1972.
4 *Daily Mirror*, 1 November 1972.

5 Catherine McDermott, *Book of Twentieth Century Design* (The Overlook Press, Woodstock, 1998).
6 *Guardian*, 19 April 1972.
7 *Daily Mail*, 15 May 1978.
8 M–O 1990, B2238.
9 M–O 1990, B2046.
10 M–O 1990,C2398.
11 M–O 1990, A1292.
12 M–O 1990, C1242.
13 Fred Vermorel, *Fashion and Perversity* (Bloomsbury, London, 1977).
14 M–O 1990, B1565.
15 *The Times*, 10 April 1978.
16 *Sunday Telegraph*, 15 April 1978.
17 *Daily Mail*, 27 January 2000.
18 Noonan, *Contraception*.
19 *Male and Female Sterilization* (Contraceptive Education Service, 2000).
20 M–O 1990, B1386.
21 *Daily Mail*, 7 January 1971.
22 *Evening News*, 6 March 1978.
23 M–O 1990, H2415.
24 *The Times*, 10 April 1978.
25 M–O 1990, C1883.
26 *Daily Star*, 6 August 1979.
27 *Northern Daily Mail*, 20 February 1979.
28 *Daily Mail*, 19 July 1979.

Chapter 8   Yuppy Love

1 Mark Twain, 'Pudd 'n head Wilson's New Calendar', *Following the Equator* (Hartford, US, 1897).
2 *The Times*, 12 August 1991.
3 Ibid.
4 M–O 1990, A2212.
5 M–O 1990, A1292.
6 Wendy Dennis, *Hot and Bothered: Men and Women, Sex and Love*

in the 90s (Grafton/HarperCollins, London, 1993).

7 *New Standard*, 6 December 1983.

8 Quoted in *The Gay and Lesbian Quotation Book*.

9 *News of the World*, 22 January 1984.

10 Matthew Rettenmund, *Totally Awesome 80s* (St Martin's Press, New York, 1996).

11 *Daily Mirror*, 11 December 1999.

12 *Independent*, 3 December 1999.

13 *Sun*, 20 December 1985.

14 Bret Easton Ellis, *Less Than Zero* (Simon and Schuster, New York, 1985).

15 *Sunday Express*, 8 September 1991.

16 Ibid.

17 *Daily Mail*, 23 June 1981.

18 M-O 1990, A1645.

19 M-O 1990, B2240.

20 *Daily Mail*, 10 August 1983.

21 *Sunday Mirror*, 17 January 1983.

22 *Daily Express*, 4 December 1980.

23 Evelyn Billings and Ann Westmore, *The Billings Method, Controlling Fertility Without Drugs or Devices* (Allen Lane); quoted in *The Times*, 16 November 1981.

24 M-O 1990, C108.

25 *Daily Mail*, 10 January 1985.

26 *Daily Mail*, 6 March 1981.

27 *Sunday Times*, 13 November 1983.

28 John Guillebaud, *Contraception Today*, third edition (Martin Dunitz, London, 1988).

29 Ibid.

30 *Daily Mail*, 7 July 1987.

31 *Evening News*, 27 August 1987.

32 *Today*, 27 June 1988.

33 *Daily Star*, 8 November 1983.

34 Quoted in *Daily Mail*, 23 December 1988.

35 *The Times*, 23 November 1985.

36 *Observer*, 22 February 1987.

37 *Daily Express*, 1 October 1986.
38 *Daily Mirror*, 27 October 1984.
39 Quoted in De'ath, *French Letters and English Overcoats*.

Chapter 9   Chemistry Sex
  1 Charles Hardy, *The Age of Unreason* (Arrow Books, London, 1995).
  2 Quoted in Nicholas Saunders, *Ecstasy and the Dance Culture*, (1995).
  3 M–O 1990, B2086.
  4 M–O 1990, A2055.
  5 Szarewski and Guillebaud, *Contraception: A User's Handbook*.
  6 Saunders, *Ecstasy and the Dance Culture*.
  7 M–O 1990, E1293.
  8 Szarewski and Guillebaud, *Contraception: A User's Handbook*.
  9 M–O 1990, A2168.
10 De'ath, *French Letters and English Overcoats*.
11 *The Times*, 12 January 2000.
12 *Daily Telegraph*, 18 February 1994.
13 *Daily Mail*, 29 April 1994.
14 M–O 1990, 2234.
15 De'ath, *French Letters and English Overcoats*.
16 Quoted in De'ath, *French Letters and English Overcoats*.
17 *Independent*, 22 January 1998.
18 *Daily Telegraph*, 1 December 1999.
19 *Daily Mail*, 3 August 1992.
20 *Evening Standard*, 11 November 1999.
21 M–O 1990, C2203.
22 M–O 1990, C2177.
23 M–O 1990, A1292.
24 M–O 1990, B2238.
25 Wendy Keller, *The Cult of the Born Again Virgin: How Single Women Can Reclaim Their Sexual Power* (Health Communications, Florida, 1999).
26 Patrick Dixon, *The Rising Price Of Love* (Hodder and Stoughton, London 1995).

Chapter 10   And Finally

1 Kahil Gibran, *The Prophet* (Pan, London, 1991).
2 Szarewski and Guillebaud, *Contraception: A User's Handbook*.
3 *So . . . Graham Norton*, Channel 4, 2000.
4 *Evening Standard*, 7 September 1992.
5 Quoted in *Metro*, 20 March 2000.
6 R. Robin Baker, *Sperm Wars: Infidelity, Sexual Conflict and other Bedroom Battles* (Fourth Estate, London, 1996).
7 *New Standard*, 15 July 1987.
8 *Asian Age*, 24 July 1999.
9 *Sunday Telegraph*, 14 December 1997.
10 *Daily Mail*, 18 January 1990.
11 Szarewski and Guillebaud, *Contraception: A User's Handbook*.
12 *The Times*, 19 March 1992.
13 *Independent*, 14 April 2000.
14 *Daily Mail*, 24 August 1994.
15 M-O 1990, B1220.
16 Riddle, *Eve's Herbs*.
17 *Sunday People*, 20 September 1980.
18 Lyall Watson, *Jacobson's Organ: and the Remarkable Nature of Smell* (Allen Lane, London, 1999).
19 *Guardian*, 2 March 2000.
20 Delia Smith, *How To Cook*, (BBC Books, London, 1999).
21 Quoted in Ira Matathia and Marian Salzman, *Next: A Vision of our Lives in the Future*, (HarperCollins, London, 1999).
22 Ibid.
23 *Daily Telegraph*, 15 March 2000.
24 Murray, *Britain and Her Birth Rate*.
25 *Crossing Continents*, BBC Radio 4.
26 M-O, woman overheard.
27 *Independent*, 17 April 2000.
28 Debate organised by the Society for Sex Education and Guidance, 13 May 1944.

Index